A Conservative Walks Into a Bar

A Conservative Walks Into a Bar
The Politics of Political Humor

Alison Dagnes

palgrave
macmillan

A CONSERVATIVE WALKS INTO A BAR
Copyright © Alison Dagnes, 2012.

First published in 2012 by
PALGRAVE MACMILLAN®
in the United States—a division of St. Martin's Press LLC,
175 Fifth Avenue, New York, NY 10010.

Where this book is distributed in the UK, Europe and the rest of the world,
this is by Palgrave Macmillan, a division of Macmillan Publishers Limited,
registered in England, company number 785998, of Houndmills,
Basingstoke, Hampshire RG21 6XS.

Palgrave Macmillan is the global academic imprint of the above companies
and has companies and representatives throughout the world.

Palgrave® and Macmillan® are registered trademarks in the United States,
the United Kingdom, Europe and other countries.

ISBN: 978–1–137–26283–7 (hardcover)
ISBN: 978–1–137–26284–4 (paperback)

Library of Congress Cataloging-in-Publication Data

Dagnes, Alison.
    A conservative walks into a bar : the politics of political humor / Alison Dagnes.
        p. cm.
    ISBN 978–1–137–26283–7 (alk. paper)—
    ISBN 978–1–137–26284–4 (pbk. : alk. paper)
        1. United States—Politics and government—Humor. 2. Conservatism—
United States—Humor. 3. Liberalism—United States—Humor. 4. Political
satire, American—History and criticism. I. Title.

E183.D24 2012
320.973′0207—dc23   2012011372

A catalogue record of the book is available from the British Library.

Design by Newgen Imaging Systems (P) Ltd., Chennai, India.

First edition: September 2012

10 9 8 7 6 5 4 3 2 1

Printed in the United States of America.

For Pete, Maddy, Caroline, and Gus who always cheered me on.
And for Moni, who always cheered me up.

Contents

Acknowledgments

This book was the end result of three years of research, travel, reviewing, and writing, all of which were independent moving parts that came together as one. Accordingly, each part had its own challenges and for each piece I was assisted by a number of people who deserve my gratitude in print.

My lovely friend Rachel Hamilton opened her home, her heart, and her address book to me, and connected me with half of the people I interviewed. To say this book would not exist without her is not hyperbole, so "thanks" doesn't seem to cut it – but it will have to suffice. This leads me to the essential list of interview subjects who gave me their time and attention, and so in alphabetical order thanks to Doug Abeles, Alex Baze, Lewis Black, Kevin Bleyer, Andy Cobb, Nick DiPaolo, Pete Dominick, Kevin Dorff, Will Durst, Adam Felber, Matthew Filipowicz, Peter Grosz, Keegan-Michael Key, Kelly Leonard, Marc Maron, Michael McCarthy, Elaina Newport, David Razowsky, Ned Rice, Ruth Rudnick, Peter Sagal, Evan Sayet, Allison Silverman, Brian Stack, Jimmy Tingle, and Cenk Uygur. A very special thank you to Tim Slagle who kept the conversation going long after he had to (even though he disagrees with me) and who was kind and smart and funny. Thanks to Angela Black, who transcribed all of these interviews.

My friends and colleagues provided encouragement, commentary, and guidance, and so a big thank you goes to Marin Hagen, Michelle Ephraim, Eleanne Hattis, Jason Surbey, Stephanie Jirard, Jan Smith, Sara Grove, Julia Sandy-Bailey, Curtis Berry, Allison Carey, Chris Kelly, Kara Laskowski, Laurie Stader, Lisa Dubbs, and (especially) Niel Brasher for their support, and to Kevan Yenerall,

Lonce Sandy-Bailey, Cynthia Botteron, Mark Sachleben, Amanda Olejarski, Sharron Harrow, Jody Baumgartner, Michael Parkin, Tyler Williams, and Jerry Mileur for their input and critical reviews. Thanks also to Mary Swanson, Chris Depowski, and Joe Dagnes for being awesome.

Appreciations go to Shippensburg University for my employment and my research funding, and to my students who make my job a total joy. Matthew Kopel at Palgrave Macmillan was beyond terrific and provided guidance, enthusiasm, and assistance. My incredible sister, Monica Gocial, put up with my mercurial behavior directly related to this project and deserves something more valuable than gold, and her husband, Brian Gocial, tolerated me, which merits thanks as well. My parents, Dennis Spokany, Sue Spokany, and Ruth Dagnes, each deserve a hefty bit of appreciation for their love and completely biased pride.

Last but not least, to my sweethearts Maddy and Caroline, thank you for your love and your tremendously big hearts. And to Peter G, thank you for absolutely everything in our world. I think we should design a new clothing line in your honor.

Prologue

Otto von Bismarck is credited with saying, "Laws are like sausages, it is better not to see them being made." While true, politics are an important part of our society, and thanks to C-SPAN, we can watch the sausage-making happen live. Thanks to the rest of the media, we have nonstop winded reports and breathless analysis of all the politicking around the sausage-making, which makes for some pretty vivid descriptions of the meat grinding. Our political system is a big and messy one, and in modern America, it is also extremely divisive. It is, then, quite fortuitous that there is political humor with which to mock and distract us from the agonizing sorrow of modernity.

In 1991, I developed a deep and lasting love for political humor when I was working as a production assistant at C-SPAN. All the sausage-making must have taken its toll because I sought refuge in comedy, and lucky for me, it was a presidential election season: there was much to make fun of. *Saturday Night Live* banged a high mark with Dana Carvey's impressions of George H. W. Bush and Ross Perot. Bill Clinton arrived on the national political scene from, of all places, Arkansas, and comedians had a field day with his "owl-sized" appetites. The year 1991 was also when Dennis Miller left *Saturday Night Live* and hit the road as a successful stand-up comedian, one who covered enough politics to make him a satirical dynamo. His comedy progressed throughout the Clinton era with predictable targets, but Miller also took aim at the hypocrisy of the Republican leadership in Congress and the conservative movement as a whole. He took shots at the left (PETA) and the right (evangelical Christians) and felt more libertarian in his sensibilities, magnanimous in his foils, and I became a die-hard fan. Miller had an HBO show that ran for eight years, produced numerous books and CDs, and was at the top of his game when September 11 happened, and, in his own words, everything changed. He went from indignant Bush critic to fawning supporter in one immense and horrific national tragedy. It was a dramatic switch: before the attacks, immediately following the 2000 election, Miller said the following on his HBO program *Dennis Miller Live*:

> And on Monday, movers went to the Governor's Mansion in Austin, Texas to transfer Bush's belongings to Washington. The move itself took very little time once workers discovered that Bush had nothing upstairs. Now, I don't want to get off on a rant here, but as a comedian, with George W. Bush coming into office, I feel like the owner of a hardware store before a hurricane. I hate to see it coming but I have to admit it's good for business (Miller 2002).

But after September 11, Miller became an outspoken supporter of President George W. Bush and the Bush administration's anti-terrorist policies, and this switch angered many of his fans on the left. He didn't anger me as much as he confused me, but he managed to annoy my friends who turned to me in bewilderment, wondering what I still liked about the guy. Miller was proud of his slide right, and asked in response to critics, "Well, can you blame me?" (Weinraub 2004). When speaking about the September 11 attacks, Miller said:

> Everybody should be in the protection business now. I can't imagine anybody not saying that. Well, I guess on the farthest end of the left they'd say, "That's our fault." And on the middle end they'd say, "Well, there's another way to deal with it other than flat-out protecting ourselves." I just don't believe that. People say we're the ones who make them hate us because of what we do. That's garbage to me. I think they're nuts. And you've got to protect yourself from nuts (Weinraub 2004).

About Bush, Miller said in 2006:

> The beautiful thing about Bush is that you always know where you can find him. That approval rating could go up to 70 or down to zero, and he ain't changing... We're in a war on terror, he knows it, and he's willing to let everybody hate him, but he's going to do what he feels he has to do (Deggans 2006).

He could have been talking about himself – someone willing to lose support because of his convictions. And lose support he did. At the same time that Dennis Miller turned rightward, Jon Stewart took the helm of *The Daily Show* (*TDS*) from former host Craig Kilborn. Stewart's *TDS* became far more political than his predecessor's version, and in the years following the September 11 attacks, as the United States first invaded Afghanistan and then Iraq, *TDS* became the go-to place for comedic analysis of some very serious subjects. Pretty soon, *Rolling Stone* magazine said Stewart's brand of faux-journalism "beats the real thing," the national party committees gave the show press credentials to cover their nominating conventions, and a public opinion poll after the death of Walter Cronkite named Stewart as the most trusted newsman in America. Big-name politicians began to appear on the show, and eventually included one sitting president, which gave the program more authority than ever. To recap: during the first years of the Bush administration, one of the more prominent political satirists lost some of his audience because he became "too conservative," and a thundering mass of antiestablishment satire, led by the wild popularity of *TDS*, made its way into the meme. This odd confluence of events, combined with my steadfast devotion to Dennis Miller, made me look around and wonder, why is there so little conservative satire? It must have been a significant scarcity—I noticed it and I'm fairly liberal.

I glean from interviews that Miller and Stewart are friends, but even so it must have felt weird for Dennis Miller to watch his mantle as one of the nation's leading political satirist fall so greatly. Miller still has a strong career today: although his HBO show was cancelled in 2002, he went on to cohost *Monday Night Football* for two years; he hosted another talk show, this one on CNBC, from 2003 to 2005; and he went to Fox News starting in 2006 as a guest commentator, first on *Hannity & Colmes* and then on *The O'Reilly Factor* where he is currently featured on a weekly segment called "Miller Time." He also presently hosts a three-hour radio program that is syndicated by Westwood One, and he tours frequently as a comedian, performing in largish venues around the country. He remains a popular and well-known entertainer, if perhaps not as popular as he was once was, and can be characterized as the most prominent conservative satirist in America today. But that's not a very big statement because there is a sizable dearth of conservative satirists around. It is thanks to my Miller Fan Club membership that I embarked on this research project to find out why he was so alone.

I set out to answer this question by interviewing a significant number of comedians, satirists, and writers. This, of course, was actually a gambit to do "research" by talking with some very funny people, but along the way I discovered a great deal about humor, ideology, and modern political satire. I learned that political humor in general, and satire specifically, is a tough calling—one that beckons a fairly specific type of person to its ranks. But I also learned that the art of comedy shapes a joke based on audience, market, occasion, and context. I learned that conservatives believe in liberal bias and liberals don't, that the satirist is separate from his (or her) material, and that none of these answers are complete or easy to reconcile. Modern political humor is a rich and important field, one that provides some of the most forceful and incisive commentary around today. But in our increasingly particularized political media system, there are efforts now to denounce the merits of political satire because conservatives say it is biased. So is it biased? Yes. Is this a problem? No. There are certainly more liberals in the trenches of political humor than there are conservatives, and this book addresses that. Political ideology does inform the material produced, and so there is an ensuing imbalance in the humor, but it is far outweighed by the fact that the driving force of modern satire is antiestablishmentarianism, and there is a mighty big difference between comedy and activism. Ideology clearly plays a role here because liberalism serves as a better foundation for satire than conservatism does, simply by virtue of its philosophy. Put another way: conservatives want to maintain the status quo and liberals want to change it. Satire aims at questioning the power structure—so why would conservatives want to do that? The short answer is, they don't. But then why would conservatives complain about liberals dominating the satire industry? Because modern political humor has become a powerhouse of cultural influence and Jon Stewart, Stephen Colbert, and their brethren wield an immense amount of sway among voters, especially young ones. When Fox News calls Jon Stewart an activist, it is specifically to discredit his political commentary, at least among Fox's viewers. And since

Stewart spends a fair amount of time denouncing Fox News, all of this makes sense. But conservatives can relax, because for all of Jon Stewart's power, in the end he is an entertainer first and a liberal second. Furthermore, his liberalness makes him question all authority figures, and not just those on the right. The point of satire is to differentiate between what is and what should be, something those at *The Daily Show* and other political satirists do quite nicely, regardless of the politics involved.

I will admit that I was desperate to talk to Dennis Miller himself, and I threw my academic credentials at him, bundled in numerous interview requests. If my husband was quietly concerned about potentially erratic behavior on my part when I met the inspiration for my research, he needn't have worried: Miller rejected my every advance. At first he simply ignored me, but when confronted by the friend-of-a-friend-of-a-brother-of-a-friend with my request in hand, he was pretty adamant about it. So while Dennis Miller never spoke with me (although it certainly was not for lack of trying on my part), many other comedians and satirists did. I owe these men and women a tremendous amount of gratitude for their time and their insight, for without them I would still be guessing the answer to this question: who brings the funny and what does this funny look like?

I am not an expert in comedy. I am a political scientist who is interested in the way political messages are communicated and received. And so this book examines the politics of political humor so that we may better understand the role and consequence of modern political comedy and satire in America today.

CHAPTER 1

Who Brings the Funny?

Why are there so few conservative political humorists? I know what you're thinking: Dennis Miller. P. J. O'Rourke.

It's a good start, but chances are you can't think of too many more. If you get to the "Blue Collar Comedy Tour," you've gone too far, mostly because being blue collar does not necessitate political conservatism, and although these comedians may touch on political issues briefly, their predominant material is not necessarily political. If you get to Stephen Colbert, you're way off course, since Colbert is not *actually* a conservative, although he plays one on TV. And maybe, if you are a comedy nerd, you may get to Nick DiPaolo, who is conservative and who is a comedian but who is also understandably irritated that he is not as well-known as he could be. The bottom line: the average political comedy fan is hard pressed to come up with many more conservative political humorists—because there aren't many.

If you ask the conservative humorists out there why there are so few of them, they will say that there are biases in the entertainment industry that prevent them from succeeding. If you ask liberal satirists, they will think really hard and say, "That's a good question. I never thought of that." And once you raise the subject, other questions quickly follow from all sides: just because there are so few conservative satirists, does this equate to the material being as liberal as the satirists themselves? Is there a bias within the field of satire that stops conservatives from entering the profession? Is there a market for conservative satire—and if not, why not? Does there have to be "conservative" satire or can conservatives enjoy satire that comes from the left with equal appreciation? The big question, is modern political humor liberally biased?

Before readers react to these questions, let me clarify a few points. First, political comedy is supposed to have a viewpoint, so calling it "biased" is sort of like calling the op-ed page of a newspaper "too opinionated." Second, the rage against *The Daily Show* comes primarily from conservative media voices, such as those heard on Fox News, so they are not exactly impartial themselves. And finally, the number of straight-up political comedians or political humor programs is extremely low—it is, as comedian Marc Maron said, "a fairly specialized form of comedy for a fairly specialized audience" (Maron 2011c). In other words, all put together, who cares? Well, I do. Political comedy, humor, satire, what have you, has an incredible amount of influence in America as it shed light on the troubles found in politicians and political events. The late Christopher Hitchens wrote in the October 2009 *The Atlantic* that while humor may not be the single most persuasive feature of American politics, it is high up on the list:

> If any one thing crucially undid the candidacy of Senator John McCain for the presidency, it was his nomination of Sarah Palin to be his running mate. And if any one thing undid Governor Palin as a person who could even be considered for the vice presidency, it was the merciless guying of her manner and personality by Tina Fey (Hitchens 2009).

And, by the way, this was from an article he wrote titled "Cheap Laughs: The Smug Satire of Liberal Humorists Debases our Comedy—and Our National Conversation." And Hitchens didn't work for Fox News.

Political satire has always played an important role in American politics, bringing an element of humor into political and social criticism. What began during the American Revolution as stabs against the brutal injustice of the British monarchy has today flourished into a booming industry. Television satirists such as Jon Stewart and his faux-pundit counterpart Stephen Colbert are widely viewed as the staples of the art, but modern American satire expands well beyond late night television. It expands to print media in the form of political cartoons, political humor columns, and satirical books; to the theater through satirical plays and sketch comedy; and to the Internet by means of viral videos, satirical websites, faux-newsletters, and flash animation. Satire remains an important part of our political landscape for politicians and for the public, and today there is plenty of it to go around. Politicians campaigning for elected office now use the established satirical programming available to prove their own good humor and electability. Americans today—especially younger Americans—are turning to satirical news outlets not only to escape from the real world but also to learn about it. Political satire plays an increasingly essential role in American politics as our desire for entertainment continues to grow, and as our media system expands to deliver varying forms of it.

People increasingly seek out political humor because the news today is bad. It is bad in the sense that we live in difficult times with war, economic hardship, and an angry, polarized political climate. In times of political dissatisfaction, humor is a powerful salve; this helps to explain the burgeoning satire environment we have today. But the news is also bad in the sense that, compared to past journalism, the quality of the news we receive today is dreadful. Punditry has blurred the line between fact and opinion so thoroughly as to be pointless, and an increasing reliance on soft news and info-tainment has left many Americans exasperated with the lack of real information they receive. Into this yawning quality gap falls political humor—smart, funny, and oftentimes very trenchant. So many people have credited *The Daily Show* with better news analysis than the mainstream media that it has become hackneyed to say it. Media entities dedicated solely to political satire have blossomed to effectively spread this brand of political humor. The *Doonesbury* cartoon was moved to the editorial pages because of its force, NPR has two political humor radio shows, satirists such as Will Durst and Andy Borowitz send out rapid-fire satirical "reports" to respond to current events, and *The Onion*, which began as a college newspaper in 1988, has become a trendy website with its own "news" network, which broadcasts on cable TV. In a *Rolling Stone* interview, former MSNBC pundit Keith Olbermann made the distinction between comedians and everyone else in politics: "Comedians are the only ones paid to tell the truth in public discourse. Everybody else—politicians, news broadcasters, religious figures—we're all paid to be oracles, when in fact we are like a good public-relations man" (Binelli 2011). And political comedians are telling this truth quite a bit in twenty-first-century America—modern jesters speaking truth to the kings.

The fact that Jon Stewart, Will Durst, Lewis Black, Stephen Colbert, and their brethren take comedic shots at politicians and newsmakers across the ideological spectrum has not stopped conservative critics from calling it "bias." These critics argue that modern political comedians take greater pleasure in mocking those on the right, and argue that these liberal humorists take it easy on Democrats. To address this accusation, Fox News took on Jon Stewart and called him a liberal activist, a charge Stewart flatly denied:

> Here's the difference between you and I—I'm a comedian first. My comedy is informed by an ideological background. There's no question about that. But the thing that you will never understand, and the thing that in some respect conservative activists will never understand, is that Hollywood, yeah, they're liberal. But that's not their primary motivating force. I'm not an activist. I'm a comedian (DiegoUK 2011).

Despite his protestations against influence, *TDS* is influential and popular, and so its critics heap denunciation on the show and its satirical colleagues alleging a number of crimes: that they unfairly influence their audience against the political right; that satire casts such a negative pall on the entire political system that it breeds cynicism; that these jokes turn serious policy matters into a farce. All of this attention is paid to satire and satirists because of its popularity and the possibility of its political influence, and so, if satire is persuasive, the dearth of conservative satirists raises eyebrows and questions. This book provides some analysis. I looked at modern political humor to gauge the bias, studying the content of satirical shows, columns, and drawings. I examined the guest lists of programs and explored other data on the target of political jokes, and surveyed the long and impressive history of American political satire from the

Founding until today. I analyzed the satirists, their skill sets, political ideology, liberalism, conservatism, and the goals of the entertainment industry. And using dozens of hours of personal interviews with political satirists, comedians, actors, and writers, in conjunction with the rest of the research, this book makes the case that there is, indeed, a liberal bias in political satire *but* this bias is nontoxic because the point of political humor is to amuse and question—its purpose is not to solve anything. And furthermore, one important quality of liberalism is to question everything, so everyone in power is fair game.

The majority of political comedians and satirists are liberal—and in interviews, they conceded this point. In fact, when asked to name conservative satirists beyond Miller and O'Rourke, practically everyone named the same person (Nick DiPaolo), and alarmingly few others were identified.[i] But this imbalance tends to make sense when satire is viewed not as a political vehicle or a method of advocacy but as an art form instead. As a result, the dramatic art of satire attracts those more interested in an unconventional occupation than someone looking for a traditional career path, and accordingly, there are more liberal satirists in the business. There are some very understandable reasons that the majority of satirists are liberal, most of which have to do with the nature of the performing arts, the kinds of people who want to perform, and of the characteristics of the job.

Satire, away from the art form and its performers, tends toward the liberal because this type of criticism is rooted in an antiestablishmentarianism that is inherently freethinking. Conversely, the nature of conservatism does not meet the conditions necessary for political satire to flourish: conservatism is harmonized and slow to criticize people in power, and it originates from a place that repudiates humor because it is absolute. The same phenomenon goes for broader political humor that mocks not only the establishment and its leaders but also social institutions that conservatives hold dear. Put another way—the philosophy of conservatism is incompatible with political

---

[i] This made it all the more cooler and remarkable when my office phone rang and I heard on the other end, "This is Nick DiPaolo—I heard you're looking for me?"

humor but liberalism suits it quite nicely. Conservatism supports institutions and satire aims to knock these institutions down a peg. This doesn't necessarily mean there is bias afoot, but it does mean there is going to be more left-leaning material than right. The very nature of satire mandates challenges to the power structure, targets across the board, and an ability to take a nuanced or relativist examination of an issue in order to make the joke, and this falls squarely into the tool belt of liberalism. Most political comedians argue forcefully that their primary job is to be funny, and they talk about speaking truth to power—no matter who that power is; good satire takes no prisoners, even if the satirists generally lean in one ideological direction. This is another explanation for the dominance of leftist political humor today, and is one possible reason for the scarcity of conservative satire. Take, for example, the *Half Hour News Hour* on Fox News Channel. It was supposed to be the conservative answer to *The Daily Show*, but it was pulled after 15 episodes due to poor ratings. The failure of the *Half Hour News Hour* generated a wealth of questions about the essence of political satire, the biggest being, why couldn't a conservative network with a conservative viewing audience make a conservative satire show work? One possible answer to this question is found in the difference between the political philosophies that make conservative incompatible with the art form. It's not that conservatives aren't funny—many are hilarious; it's more that conservatism itself will not support satirical humor the way liberalism will. Also, comedy does not work on a news channel, but this will be addressed later on in Chapter 5.

Perhaps as important as the nature of satire is the nature of the entertainment industry. While there might be liberal biases at play in the business (and the conservatives whom I interviewed steadfastly maintained that these biases exist), by far the biggest bias is an economic one: the financial imperatives of the industry mandate that the most eyes and ears have to be attracted to humor in order for it to be successful—and ideological screed will not achieve these financial goals. It is, in the end, simply more important to be entertaining than it is to be right, which leads to humor—even political humor—that is easily accessible to the most people. Accordingly, there are biases at play in political humor, but these biases are focused on the need to entertain, versus the need to preach. Ratings win every time.

Accusations of political comedy's liberal bias are, on their own, generally unimportant, but broader condemnations of modern satire writ large produces harmful consequences. By holding comedians to the same standards as journalists, critics degrade the power and responsibility of the real news media. None of the modern political humor produced today aims to achieve the information-gathering mission of journalism—it aims to poke holes in the power structures. Conversely, it is not the journalist's job to poke holes but rather to report the news. Conflating these two jobs further denigrates the already deteriorating American news system. This is not to discount the analytical criticism that satire can provide, because sometimes humor can shed the brightest light on injustice or wrongdoing, but ascribing false duties to comedy further erodes the distinction between entertainment and information. That said, the duty of the satirist is to distinguish what is from what should be, and oftentimes this is a very significant contribution to a broader discussion. Dismissing satirical criticism as exclusionary discounts some of the sharpest commentary available today. Listening to criticism, even if it may disagree with your viewpoint, is a hallmark of the democratic process, and without debate we are sunk. It is easy to see that the wholesale rejection of this type of commentary can contribute to the continuing and growing partisan divisions in our modern media system. Those calling it partisan are repeating the same kind of bias claims that have been made in the past against the news media, which have now been effectively split between liberal and conservative outlets. As a result, we are trending toward a similar divide in our entertainment. This is the most detrimental effect of the wholesale rejection of modern political humor. If we become a nation so divided that we cannot even laugh together, the future of the republic is bleak.

And so this book investigates humor, politics, ideology, people, and punch lines in order to explain why there are so few conservative political satirists today and the effect this scarcity has on humor and American politics. The rest of this chapter explores the ideas and definitions surrounding satire and political humor and also explores its breadth and limits. The next chapter features the experiments, research, and data that assess the ideological bias in modern satire, and Chapter 3 reviews the history of political satire in America. After that, the book explores satirists and comedians in Chapter 4, and the nature of satire, conservatism, and liberalism in Chapter 5. All of these components combine to make modern political satire a largely liberal medium. This book will show why this is not necessarily a prejudicial thing, why political satire deserves to be a vital component of modern political criticism, and why our movement toward ideologically specific media may be dangerous to our democracy.

Humor and American Politics

Laughter is universal. It extends beyond borders and species (British scientists did a study proving animals laugh, too), and everyone likes a good chortle now and then. Some people like to laugh more than others, and some people laugh more easily than others, but in the main, laughing and humor are viewed as positive and desirable things. Types of humor vary wildly. There's self-deprecating humor (my mother wears combat boots to church), cheeky humor (your mother wears combat boots to church), and offensive humor (Jewish mothers wear combat boots to church). Freud distinguished between the healthy, defense-mechanism type of humor and wit, which he deemed aggressive (Freud 1928). There are jokes that go way too far and become socially violating, and material that is so tame as to be universally appealing, if not bland. There have been scholarly studies of humor, including one from Norwegian psychologist Sven Svebak that actually measures one's sense of humor. Called (unfunnily) the Sense of Humor Questionnaire (SHQ), the survey judges three different criteria in its assessment: (1) the ability to identify something funny in a variety of situations; (2) the appreciation of humor; and (3) the capacity to convey humor (Svebak 1996). The problem with using such a measurement is that, like taste, smell, and sight, humor is a sense—and different people find different things funny. Put another way, what I think is funny may not be funny to you. This is one of the challenges of comedy—trying to bring the funny to a wide enough audience. Determining what is funny is a tricky, complicated, and intricate art, and funny changes from person to person and from moment to moment.

Since laughing is a natural joy, politicians have used humor to attract supporters, and citizens have used it to attack their leaders for as long as there has been government. Political humor has a range of targets: politicians, institutions, social movements, groups, leaders, followers, issues. Humor can come from partisan sides trying to make a political point in a more agreeable way, or from individual politicians gently mocking themselves to show good grace and humor. It can come from citizens lampooning politicians or groups, or it can come from professionals mocking the political establishment. Amidst all of this hilarity, there are political points being made, which give the jokes a kind of power. Mark Twain once said, "Against the assault of laughter nothing can stand," and Twain knew his funny. Writes one scholar on political humor:

> One's understanding of political jokes obviously depends on one's understanding of politics. At one level, politics is always a struggle for power. Along with persuasion and lies, advice and flattery, tokens of esteem and bribery, banishment and violence, obedience and treachery the joke belongs to the rich treasury of the instruments of politics. We often hear that the political joke is an offensive weapon with which an aggressive, politically engaged person makes the arrangements or precautions of an opponent seem ridiculous. But even when political jokes serve defensive purposes, they are nonetheless weapons (Speier 1998).

These weapons are especially powerful in an era when the media are so ubiquitous and influential. Humor spreads quickly and efficiently around the electorate. Occasionally, the media reports of humor are taken as fact even when there was no fact alleged. Examples abound, but two will suffice: I always thought that vice president Dan Quayle said that he would not travel to Latin American because he did not speak Latin, but he never actually said that. It was a joke told at Quayle's expense, reported as fact by the media, and accepted as truth by the general public. The same thing happened to Sarah Palin when it was reported that she said, "I can see Russia from my front porch," which she never actually said. Humor can be so powerful that sometimes the national narrative takes on a life of its own. And speaking of Sarah Palin, these jokes-as-weapons achieve even more influence in an era where the only national consensus is disagreement, and right now we are especially divided. Palin is a lightning rod as a political figure, so it makes sense that she would attract the heat of political humor as well. Although historians contend our partisanship is nothing new, we are in a political climate where we take sides without compromise and promise to wage war against one another. There is a different kind of scale that measures one's political ideology, ranging from liberal to conservative to libertarian and we are, as a nation, spread out along it. In modern American politics, there are groups and coalitions that make their political hay from stirring the pot, wreaking havoc on the very idea of consensus because there is too much to gain from discord. But in the end, politicians have to win the votes of just more than half of their constituents, and so it is in their best interest to try and reach some sort of harmony. This means leaving behind the nastiness for enough time to show moderate agreement. One of the challenges of American politics is trying to bring the country together in an increasingly polarized world.

So now picture yourself as a political comedian. You have to bring the funny to the most people in a climate that splits us. Tough job, right?

Political humor has to be funny about a specific topic that has the tendency to divide people, and that task is difficult enough on its own. But if you add to this the mission of making a cogent political argument within the joke then the job seems nearly impossible. This impossible job is the one of the satirist: someone who uses humor or parody or comedy to make a political point; someone who distinguishes what is from what should be. This is a complicated art, too, and it is one that serves an important function in modern society. By bringing humor into a difficult situation, satire allows us to examine tough issues and concepts in a more palatable way. Many of those I interviewed made the point that humor was an effective way to make an argument without hammering people over the head with it. Said one television writer, satire is a backdoor way of arguing, "I think that satire, when people are laughing, it is a back door into consciousness." Along these lines, comedian Andy Borowitz defined satire in an interview with Paul Provenza: "It points you toward the truth in an oblique way, rather than making you want to throw yourself out a window" (Provenza2010). *Conan* writer Brian Stack agreed, noting what the power of humor is: "If you can find a way to make someone laugh and make them say: 'Hey that's true, I never thought about it that way before'" (Stack 2010). Since there is a great deal wrong in America today, the public has found that it is far easier to ingest its news with a sprinkling of satire. Or, more accurately, with a heaping handful of it. In July 2009, *Time Magazine* conducted a poll asking its readers who, in the post-Cronkite era, was the most trusted newsperson in America. The winner was Jon Stewart. The online poll was unscientific but expansive (the polling sample was 9,410), and quite decisive: Stewart, the host of Comedy Central's fake news program *The Daily Show,* was the clear favorite with 44 percent approval ratings, beating NBC News Anchor Brian Williams, who came in second with 29 percent. The obvious significance of this poll is that a comedian was now viewed as a journalist, and one who is more reliable and truthful than those who are trained members of the press. Other evidence supports the contention that Stewart is important in American politics: a 2007 Pew Research study found that among young voters, 23 percent of those polled stated that they were more likely to vote for a candidate if Stewart endorsed him or her (Pew Research Center 2007). But Stewart is far from alone, and the vast array of political satire reflects its popularity today.

One effect of satire's increasing importance, as stated by two experts in the field, is that "politics has undoubtedly broken out of the shells of respect, deference, and distance from people's daily lives in which it had been formerly enclosed" (Blumer and Gurevitch 2000, 163). As satirists criticize those in power positions, they help illuminate the weaknesses of our democracy and those elected to office in ways that are both amusing and enjoyable for the viewer. They also are providing some of the most incisive social criticism that exists today. As our news media soften considerably in their changing work environment, satirists (whether they like it or not) are filling some of the watchdog functions that journalists used to carry out. This makes for a very delicate balancing act for satirists who at one time claim, "I am just trying to be funny," and who then go on to hope that they can make a difference in the world. An example is from Stewart himself, who was interviewed in *New York* magazine and said:

> We're not provocateurs, we're not activists, we are reacting to our own catharsis. There is a line into demagoguery, and we try very hard to express ourselves but will not move into "So follow me! And I will lead you to the land of answers, my people!" You can fall in love with your own idea of common sense. Maybe the nice thing about being a comedian is never having a full belief in yourself to know the answer. So you can say all this stuff, but underneath, you're going "But of course, I'm fucking idiotic." It's why we don't lead a lot of marches (Smith 2010).

But of course Stewart and Colbert *did* lead a march, and a successful one at that. Drawing more than two hundred thousand people to the Washington, DC, Mall, the comedians held a "Rally to Restore Sanity And/Or Fear" four days before the 2010 midterm elections. It came two months on the heels of former Fox News pundit Glenn Beck's "Rally to Restore Honor" and drew more than twice as many attendees. Beck and other conservatives used the march to levy the criticism that the satirists provided a liberal counterpoint to the conservative movement, something that was widely denied by both Stewart and Colbert.

The art of comedy is distinct from other art forms because it can be so socially violating. Discourse in polite society mandates dialogue, respect, civility, and decorum. Comedy is unilateral, and not only permits obscenity, aggression, and mockery, but also encourages it (Purdie 1993). As a result, political satire is a unique form that combines social commentary with entertainment, and anger with laughter. The general definition of "satire" states that satirists use humor to criticize the political establishment, but this definition is incomplete. Satire is often conflated with ideas of humor, laughter, and comedy, but it truly stands alone as a source of political argumentation. Modern political satire takes many different forms and differs from other forms of political humor, but in today's highly mediated environment, political humorists use all kinds of comedy in their material. Definitions are in order.

Parody, Metaphor, Humor, & Satire

In his book that examines satire and humor, British scholar Simon Critchley maintains that we laugh for three fundamental reasons: from feelings of superiority over others; as a release of pent up energy; and as a result of an incongruity between what we know or expect and what actually takes place (Critchley 2002). It is easy to see how politics can garner these types of laughs: we laugh at politicians who nosedive or collapse because we feel better than them; we laugh at the political difficulties facing our nation as a release from our anxiety; and we laugh at a political joke that sheds light on the differences between what is, and what should be. These laughs come from a wide variety of comedic forms, including parody, metaphor, general political humor, and satire. These are very distinctive comedic forms, and volumes have been written on each type of humor, but despite these differences, this book examines satire and political humor together as one.

True satire stands alone as a form of social and political criticism, and general political humor pokes broad fun at politics. Satire is the weapon of the satirist, but political humor can come from a variety of sources: nonpolitical comedians will dabble in the political to mock familiar people or events, and noncomedic actors may use political humor in their work. Politicians themselves use humor to help prove their own good nature, showing self-deprecation and joviality, and to make fun of their opponents. General political humor is widespread in modern America, but satire is an outside observation that distinguishes right from wrong, and the existing from the possible. Since the two are so distinctive, it would seem logical to keep them separate and address satire specifically, but this would be impossible because in modern America, the two are inextricably combined. Modern comedic forms are so blended that to gauge the importance of satire one must take a fairly expansive view of the art form. And so in this work, I examine parody, metaphor, humor, and satire together, acknowledging that this takes a wide-ranging view and definition of satire, but does so on purpose.

Parody

Many political humorists use parody to mock politicians, and this is seen especially in sketch comedy, both on the stage and on shows such as *Saturday Night Live* (*SNL*). Parody is an artistic interpretation where an actor imitates the characteristic style of another person. Communications scholar Robert Hariman argues:

> Parodic techniques involve various combinations of imitation and alteration: direct quotation, alternation of words, textual rearrangement, substitution of subjects or characters, shifts in diction, shifts in class, shifts in magnitude, etc...When the weight of authority is converted into an image, resistance and other kinds of response become more available to more people (Hariman 2008).

Most parody is done for comedic effect or ridicule, and although imitation is said to be the highest form of flattery, this is not necessarily the case in parody. Some parody practitioners argue that their mockery is in good fun, and in an article about *SNL*, the show's creator, Lorne Michaels, maintained that his show lacks the cruelty of other political humorists. After the 2000 presidential elections, for which *Saturday Night Live* skits helped to define the candidates and placed the malapropism "strategery" into the meme, Michaels said, "*SNL*'s spoofs tend to be more affectionate and goofy than mean" (Smith and Voth 2002). Certainly, parody can be used to gently mock the personal characteristics of someone without too much aggression involved. One example of this was seen in one skit on *SNL* when plus-sized (male) actor John Goodman played Monica Lewinsky's (female) confidant Linda Tripp. The parody primarily made fun of Tripp's appearance, and although it went on to weakly strike Tripp for her part in the Lewinsky scandal, it shed no real light on either the scandal or the woman involved, nor did it criticize the politics of the situation. Although most often parody is used to poke fun at personal characteristics, parody also can be used to make a sharper satirical argument. For example, actor Will Ferrell's caricature of former president George W. Bush (seen both on *Saturday Night Live* and on Broadway in Ferrell's show *You're Welcome America*) exaggerated Bush's ineloquence, and this caricature made a stinging contention that he was incapable of leading effectively. This parody had a strong and lasting effect, as Ferrell's parody began during the 2000 presidential campaign and lasted throughout Bush's eight years in office. Scholars Chris Smith and Ben Voth studied the *SNL* 2000 presidential debate skits featuring Ferrell's parody of Bush. They argued, "Voters seeking to understand the substance of ideas in the debate may have found the parodies of the debate to be a useful organizing tool for their inherent complexities," which means people were watching Ferrell for cues about Bush (Smith and Voth 2002). Although Ferrell's initial parody may have been, as Michael argued, created out of affection, the decade-long constancy of Ferrell's "Bush-as-stupid" parody helped to solidify this image in the minds of the American public, the result of which was far from affectionate.

Parody is also seen on the stage when theater troops such as The Capitol Steps change the words to popular songs to make a political point. Song parody, as in personal parody, requires an audience's knowledge of the subject, and in the case of musical parody, it requires familiarity with a song as well. Past Steps albums have been titled "Barackin' Around the Christmas Tree," "O Christmas Bush," and "I'm So Indicted," all of which demand both song recognition and political knowledge. This need for audience awareness stretches across all forms of comedy, since the only way an audience will appreciate humor is if they comprehend what the humorist is actually talking about. It is especially important in parody. According to Steps cofounder Elaina Newport, the audience has to have enough understanding for a joke to land successfully: "So you can do a George Bush malapropisms joke or an Al Gore being stiff joke, but you couldn't do an Al Gore malapropism joke...you have to go with what the audience already perceives." Newport went on: "I dread primary season because, you know, if [the candidates] don't have a clear cut persona they are really hard. People don't really know at least one thing about them" (Newport 2010). *SNL*'s Alex Baze agreed:

I always say if they have to have a lot to hang your hat on, which to me means what does the average American or the average audience member know about them, and then that is kind of up to the media at large. How much do they love this politician and love talking about them? Sarah Palin is a perfect example. Not much as a politician . . . as soon as she got picked we learned everything about her family, her background, pictures of her from college. You know, the media loves her because she is a pretty girl or says pretty good things and so there is lots of stuff to hang your hat on (Baze 2010).

One can fairly point to the weaknesses of the mainstream media with their soft news coverage of politics as fodder for these parody portrayals. When real news organizations pay more attention to the lifestyle elements of a candidate than the policy preferences, it becomes the dominant narrative that describes a politician. *SNL*'s Doug Abeles agreed, and maintained that political people become "reduced to, in the most simplistic way, a one dimensional characteristic. You know, Bush is a dummy, Al Gore is dull . . . it becomes [a] template . . . Al Gore is a dullard so if there is a story about Al Gore in the news, sort of regardless of what it is, that's going to be the angle that you are going with." This may not be fair, argues Abeles, but it persists: "It is very immature in a way, you know. There is that aspect of grade school bullying, of sticking somebody with a characterization that may or may not be fair but for better or worse once that characterization takes hold, it is very hard to undo it" (Abeles 2010).

This leads to a central concern when crafting any kind political humor: the need for audience understanding. This need reinforces sometimes tired or clichéd jokes that comedians sometimes fall back on, but going deeper is difficult to do. Pete Dominick is the host of *Stand Up with Pete Dominick* on Sirius/XM radio, and he says that, unfortunately, most comedians shy away from political material because the audiences do not grasp it. He used the example of former South Carolina governor Mark Sanford, who was caught in a political sex scandal in 2009:

Most comedians don't know that much about Mark Sanford and I should say, actually most audiences don't. So, if I am doing a Mark Sanford joke I have to introduce to my audience who Mark Sanford is, even at the height of it, sadly. But, if I want to do a Lindsay Lohan joke, everybody knows what is going on with her life, so you don't have to (Dominick 2010).

Comedian Marc Maron takes this a bit further and argues that most audiences find politics utterly mind-numbing, which makes it difficult to use as material:

> The one thing I do know is that 90% of the time if you're going to talk about politics the audience's eyes [are] going to glaze over and not know how to take it in because they don't fucking think about it (Maron 2011c).

Since much (most) of the American public finds politics incomprehensible at best and distasteful at worst, the vast majority of comedians spread their material across a wider variety of subjects than simply the political. The parody examples used here help to illustrate this point: The Capitol Steps is based in Washington and plays to a highly politicized audience—the show can keep its material distinctly focused on politics because the inside-the-Beltway audience understands it and expects it. Conversely, *SNL* is a national variety show that plays on TV to a larger and more wide-ranging audience, and so it keeps its political material (even though this is some of the show's funniest material) to a minimum in order to keep the show accessible. *SNL*'s audience expects comedy with a broader range, which drives the depth to which the political jokes can reach.

Metaphor

Metaphor is another mode used in political humor, which asks an audience to compare two unlike images and laugh at the comparison. Often seen in political cartoons, visual metaphor requires the reader to understand both images of a comparison, and consequently, the images used must be easily understood. Symbols work nicely to draw metaphoric comparisons, such as the bald eagle or Uncle Sam to symbolize America, or donkeys and elephants to symbolize our two major political parties. Using a specific symbol to represent a politician can be a stinging indictment on its own. For example, *Doonesbury* cartoonist Gary Trudeau symbolized vice president Dan Quayle as a feather, president Bill Clinton as waffle, and former House Speaker Newt Gingrich as bomb, and all of these metaphors were enough to convey Trudeau's opinion of the politicians. Since the images in metaphor may mean different things to different people, the use of metaphor in political humor is sometimes a delicate dance between cartoonist and reader, and occasionally signals get crossed. This happened during President Obama's early days in office when a political cartoon in the *New York Post* made fun of the president's economic stimulus plan with a depiction of a monkey shot dead by two policemen. To add context to this cartoon, it ran immediately on the heels of a Connecticut chimpanzee brutally attacking its owner. This may have led the artist to believe that chimps were on the minds of the American public, but the cartoon was excoriated in the press. An analysis of the cartoon from the *Huffington Post* argued: "The drawing, from famed cartoonist Sean Delonas, is rife with violent imagery and racial undertones. In it, two befuddled-looking police officers holding guns look over the dead and bleeding chimpanzee that attacked a woman in Stamford, Connecticut. 'They'll have to find someone else to write the next stimulus bill,' reads the caption" (Stein 2009). One possible joke that Delonas was trying to make alluded to the old saw about putting 20 monkeys in a room with typewriters who produce Shakespeare. Or, he could have been arguing that the stimulus bill was so dumb it could have been written by an animal. However, because of the historically racist connotations connecting African Americans with monkeys, the cartoon was viewed by many as racist, and consequently the metaphor failed because of the image interpretation. Major political figures, to include civil rights leader Reverend Al Sharpton, responded to the cartoon and called for action against the cartoonist. The *New York Post* released a statement responding to the uproar, defending their cartoonist, and condemning Sharpton in particular:

> The cartoon is a clear parody of a current news event, to wit the shooting of a violent chimpanzee in Connecticut. It broadly mocks Washington's efforts to revive the economy. Again, Al Sharpton reveals himself as nothing more than a publicity opportunist (Pitney 2009).

The fight over Al Sharpton notwithstanding, the argument of the cartoon was lost in the battle over it. While the *New York Post* tried to stem the criticism, the cartoon ultimately flopped since it did not criticize its intended target, but instead leveled criticism against the artist.

Verbal metaphor is often used in political humor—Dennis Miller being one of the most prominent comedians who uses highbrow metaphors in his material—but the key to successful metaphoric use is the audience's comprehension of what the metaphor connects. For example, Dennis Miller once said: "Elected office holds more perks than Elvis' nightstand," which mandated that his audience understood Elvis (and his drug habits) as much as they understood elected officials (and their benefits). In his article "Richard Nixon as Pinocchio, Richard II and Santa Claus," scholar Bernard Grofman argues that in order for a metaphor to work, it must be easily accessible to the audience (Grofman 1989). In his research, Grofman compares a metaphor to a wardrobe where "we try out the clothes in the wardrobe on the principle subject to see which ones fit" (Grofman 1989). After all, a comparison joke will fail if the audience does not understand the comparison, and so finding the most apt comparison (the one that "fits" the best) is crucial for a joke to succeed. In 2006, Stephen Colbert gave the keynote speech to the White House Correspondent's Dinner in Washington. Sometimes called the "prom" by Washington insiders, this is a very clubby, elbow-rubbing event where the press and policy makers enjoy a lavish black-tie dinner and joke about one another in a good-natured way. Colbert was speaking to members of the press and the Bush administration when he said the following:

> Everybody asks for personnel changes. So the White House has personnel changes. Then you write, "Oooh, they're just rearranging the deck chairs on the Titanic." First of all, that is a terrible metaphor. This administration is not sinking. This administration is soaring. If anything, they are rearranging the deck chairs on the Hindenburg (Colbert 2006).

The use of the sinking of the *Titanic* and the Hindenburg crash were easily accessible metaphors which Colbert used to criticize both the administration *and* the press that covered it. It was a two-fer. Of course, it also skewered everyone in the room, which made for an uncomfortable audience response. But that is the price of political humor in general, especially political satire.

Humor & Satire

So what is satire? According to scholar George Test, the ingredients are aggression, play, laughter, and judgment (Test 2008). Satire, according to Test, must both attack and judge and to this end, it must be rooted in the negative. But what distinguishes satire from straight political commentary is the laughter and play that temper it. Some argue that satire does not have to be funny, which may be the end-state of the joke, but one important characteristic is an attempt at humor. Another common understanding of satire makes the case that it must distinguish between what is and what should be, and to accomplish this goal, satire must be somewhat comparative. When satire sheds light on a perceived injustice, it also references the justice that should be found instead. While specific satirical arguments vary based on topic and circumstance, the general satirical argument speaks to the question, "Can't we do better than this?" Two examples of this from different ideological perspectives help to illustrate this question: first, businessman Donald Trump is credited with the following assessment of the 2010 Obama Healthcare Plan, although it has never been directly sourced to him:

> Let me get this straight... We're going to be "gifted" with a health care plan we are forced to purchase and fined if we don't, which purportedly covers at least ten million more people, without adding a single new doctor, but provides for 16,000 new IRS agents, written by a committee whose chairman says he doesn't understand it, passed by a Congress that didn't read it but exempted themselves from it, and signed by a President who smokes, with funding administered by a treasury chief who didn't pay his taxes, for which we'll be taxed for four years before any benefits take effect, by a government which has already bankrupted Social Security and Medicare, all to be overseen by a surgeon general who is obese, and financed by a country that's broke! What the hell could possibly go wrong? (Obamacare Explained by Trump 2011).

Here, Trump criticizes the health care plan by pointing out the hypocrisy of the political leaders involved: a smoking president, a tax-evading tax chief, and an overweight surgeon general. The writing also takes on the force of government that mandates insurance (purposively) against the will of the public. And Trump takes a sarcastic turn at the end, asking rhetorically, "what could possibly go wrong?" when the run up to the punch line already answered this.

Satire can use sarcasm or invented events to prove a point, as seen in this faux-article from *The Onion* about US foreign policy:

> State Department diplomat Nelson Milstrand, who appeared on CNN last week and offered an informed, thoughtful analysis implying that Israel could perhaps exercise more restraint toward Palestinian moderates in disputed territories, was asked to resign Tuesday. "The United States deeply regrets any harm Mr. Milstrand's careful, even-tempered, and factually accurate remarks may have caused our democratic partner in the Middle East," Secretary of State Hillary Clinton said in an unequivocal condemnation of the veteran foreign-service officer's perfectly reasonable statements. "U.S. policy toward Israel continues to be one of unconditional support and fawning sycophancy." Milstrand, 63, will reportedly appear at an AIPAC conference to offer a full apology as soon as his trial concludes and his divorce is finalized (*The Onion* 2011b).

In this case, *The Onion* takes on diplomacy and argues that the stand of the United States toward Israel is obsequious and AIPAC wields a disproportionate amount of power in Washington, and hints toward an irrational Middle East foreign policy on the part of the United States. The article itself is false, but the tact it takes makes an argument through satire. Using the opposite of the author's argument is one property of satire, a form *The Onion* uses often.

This helps to highlight the inherent and important difference between political satire and more general political humor: humor is geared at making the audience laugh at others, and to this end can focus primarily on physical features or obvious personality characteristics. Political satire is designed to make the audience laugh at another object but also laugh at itself at the same time, and in this manner satire forces an audience to realize a larger set of systemic faults (Baumgartner and Morris 2008). The two examples above do this: the first showing how the policy-making process (and the politics surrounding it) is inherently flawed; the second by arguing that US foreign policy is erroneous. For the reasons already mentioned, modern American political humor focuses on politicians already in the spotlight, which means that much attention goes toward widely recognizable subjects such as the president, well-known political candidates, and politicians in the news for various scandals or indiscretions. Thus, political humor focuses on the most obvious shortcomings of politicians and the political system. For example, when a politician is caught in a sex scandal, comedians make funny—if sometimes obvious—jokes about the scandal. Using a broad brush, this type of political humor is easily accessible, understood, and accepted by an audience since it fits in with the existing narrative that all politicians are scumbags. Political humor that addresses the American political system concentrates on expansive conceptions of inefficiency or perceived corruption. These sweeping generalizations allow an audience to laugh at the target of the humor without any self-examination, and the audience walks away from the joke feeling superior to the target of the humor.

Satire generally does not mock a specific personality flaw or personal characteristic of a single actor, but rather ridicules the larger dilemma that occurs from such failing. When a politician crashes, satirical humor incorporates the larger political environment, media reaction, and public opinion data to make an argument that extends beyond the specific target of the joke. In other words, satire uses humor to indict an entire system within its indictment of an individual actor. The above examples help show this. In the first, Trump indicts the political system in his condemnation of the healthcare plan, and in the second, *The Onion* assails the political system for its fawning treatment of Israel. This makes satire more cutting than general humor, and it drives the creation of a different type of joke. When people argue that satire does not need to be funny, they point toward this piercing critical quality as the primary difference between satire and general humor, and go on to argue that humor is benevolent while satire is dangerous. One important quality of the satirist is that he rarely cares if he offends. Satirist Paul Provenza wrote about his colleagues: "They don't always care about being polite... They don't care about offending you... They don't care if you disagree" (Provenza 2010). This antagonism is what gives satire its critical edge. Robin Williams once said that "comedy is acting out optimism," but taken one step further, it can be argued that satire is acting out anger. There is a hostility to the form that is necessary when criticizing the established norms and taking on the political system. This has several consequences. First, the anger that a satirist feels is going to drive the crafting of the material. When asked if they could write about things that made them mad, the satirists I interviewed were split in their responses. *Wait, Wait*'s Peter Sagal said that if something made him especially angry, he would shy away from making a joke about it, opting instead to go for a run to exorcise his rage (Sagal 2010). Conversely, The Second City's founder, Bernie Sahlins, said that anger was crucial for him to make a point. Both approaches work, but even if a satirist avoids the most difficult of subjects, he brings a point of view with him to his work as he makes an argument. This means a second consequence is that, inevitably, a satirist will anger some people, and this fact didn't bother anyone I spoke with. *Conan* writer Brian Stack told me about the viewers who were enraged enough to write letters of complaint: "I think if you are not receiving any letters, then you have no point of view at all . . . I think it is an inevitable result in having a point of view that someone out there is going to take issue with it and be offended and, otherwise, why even do it?" (Stack 2010).

For the purposes of this book, I define "satire" to be the comic use of a disagreement, a line of reasoning, or of an opposite point of view in order to make a political statement. This distinction between humor and satire mandates that most comedians do not rely solely on satire, which can be a very off-putting form of humor. The anger of comedians such as Lenny Bruce can be ground breaking but rarely is it commercially successful. This is the reason that political comedy solely originating from a place of anger is hardly ever profitable; in order to gain the largest audience (arguably the motivating factor for most entertainers), the material has to be generally appealing. So, although a twinge of anger is not only acceptable but necessary in satire, it cannot be too offensive. The financial imperatives of the entertainment industry drive the train more, it seems, than ideological persuasion.

Consequently, there are very few purely satirical outlets in popular culture today. Most pure satire is blended in with other forms of political humor because satire is a fairly specific thing. Explained *SNL*'s Alex Baze: "I take a very strict literary definition of satire which basically means that you are taking on the point of view of the person you disagree with in order to demonstrate how ridiculous that point of view is" (Baze 2010). *Conan*'s Brian Stack concurred: "I think a lot of times the satirist . . . takes on the point of view of the person that he is satirizing, but goes all the way with it . . . [For example] if he's going to satirize a racist he might as well be a racist in the song. The risk, I think, is how people misinterpret it, but it is such a brave way to add something satirically" (Stack 2010). Using this strict definition, the only exclusively satirical media today is *The Colbert Report*, where Stephen Colbert has created a faux-persona in "Stephen Colbert," a pitch-perfect imitation of conservative punditry a la Bill O'Reilly. Colbert uses this character to argue (loudly and wrongly) the exact opposite of the point he is really making in order to show the faulty logic of his character's point of view. Here, Colbert is not attacking O'Reilly as a person, but rather making a bigger point by mocking O'Reilly's viewpoints and the construction of his show. Many political comedians use satire in their repertoire because it is an effective way of making a political joke, but beyond Colbert no one uses it as a singular style. Comedian Will Durst wrote a column called "Pity the Poor Rich" in which he used satire to draw class lines and argue against tax breaks for the wealthy:

> Isn't it time we stopped demonizing the wealthy simply because they have a couple more bucks? . . . People settle down. The rich are just like the rest of us, only with access to a better class of orthodontists. They put their Egyptian silk trousers on one leg at a time, same as you and me . . . The main problem with being rich is never having enough money. And while liberals gripe and snipe that the rich and their corporations are sitting on trillions (no, really, trillions) of dollars waiting for the "correct political climate" to rehire workers, the fact that they employ thousands and thousands of lawyers to ferret out loopholes to keep from paying taxes goes criminally unreported. It's all about jobs (Durst 2011).

By assuming satirical support for them, Durst levels sharp criticism against the wealthy. And this is a good example of true satire; it not only explains satire but also makes it easy to see that satire is not used all the time. Comedian Andy Borowitz, author of the satiric newsletter *The Borowitz Report*, took aim at media titan Rupert Murdoch, using satire to criticize News Corp's unethical journalistic practices. When the news organizations under Murdoch's control were caught hacking into private email and cell phone accounts, Borowitz assumed Murdoch's personality and sent out "A Letter from Rupert Murdoch":

> Now, I'm sure many of you are wondering how could I, Rupert Murdoch, one of the most powerful men in the world, have no idea what is going on? The answer, my friends, is simple: I get all of my information from my own newspapers. If you relied on *News of the World, The Sun,* and *The New York Post* for your information, I can assure you that you wouldn't have a clue what was going on either... The only TV I watch is the *Fox News Channel.* So not only do I not know what is going on around me, I know nothing about the theory of evolution, global warming, or President Obama's birthplace (Borowitz 2011).

Using the opposite of what you believe to make an argument is difficult and exhausting. *Colbert* former executive producer Allison Silverman said writing for *Colbert* was like "driving in reverse on a freeway," which is a tricky task indeed (Silverman 2010). The Durst and Borowitz examples are satirical in that they take an opposing view to prove their point, but neither Durst nor Borowitz use this form exclusively. In their work, as in most other political comedy, these writers use metaphor, sarcasm, and straight political humor in conjunction with satire. And yet I consider Durst and Borowitz—and Stewart, Lewis Black, Peter Sagal, and others—to be satirists. They use this form enough to qualify, even as they use it in combination with other forms of humor. Since this book is more expansive in its inquiry, and since there are so few pure satirists today, I use the terms "satire" and "political humor" together to explain the general trends in modern political comedy. Satirical argument must be a primary purpose of the material, but it need not be the sole mechanism in which criticism is found. Thus, we can define *Wait, Wait...Don't Tell Me!* as a radio show that has a satirical bend, even if much of the material is not pure satire. The same thing goes for examining the historical work of Benjamin Franklin or the cartoons of Herblock: we can examine satire within this broader definition and in doing so shed more light on the topic.

In broadcast and print, satire plays an increasingly important role in our political understanding, so much so it's becoming difficult to get away from it. Author Lee Siegel makes the argument in his book *Are You Serious?How to be True and Get Real in the Age of Silly* that while we are living in a serious age, we sometimes have a hard time being sober about important matters. Siegel argues that this is nothing new, and the historic importance of satire (see Chapter 3) proves this to be true. But we are getting more of the silly today thanks to an infinite media system that has permeated every single facet of our lives through the complex tangle of news, entertainment, and socialization that dominates our modern society. As political media scholar Shanto Iyengar and Mark Peters wrote in 1982: "Media provide compelling descriptions of a public world that people cannot directly experience" (Iyengar and Peters 1982), which today includes entertaining media and a boatload of satiric material. To help distinguish the satirical from the silly, communication scholar Lance Holbert created a "Typology for the Study of Entertainment Television and Politics" which helps distinguish the varying types of political satire seen on modern TV today, and even though my work extends beyond television to other satirical forms, there are some significant points that apply. Holbert makes the distinction between primary and secondary satire in TV programming, which is an important separation to make: all satire is not created equal. Primary satirical material is found on *The Daily Show, Colbert Report, The Borowitz Report*, in political cartoons, and so on; that is, it's found when satire is the principal purpose of the material. Conversely, secondary satire is found when it is less important and less central to the real purpose of the material. For example, *The Simpsons* and *South Park* can be very political shows, but that is not their main function. To establish this primary versus secondary characterization, Holbert asked two questions:

- To what degree can viewers expect politics or inherently political issues to be raised during the course of a specific piece of media content?
- What combination of explicit versus implicit political messages is being provided in a specific piece of entertainment content? (Hobert 2005).

These two questions allowed Holbert to sort satire into several categories, including "Traditional Satire" and "Satiric Situation Comedies." The problem with Holbert's typology is that it takes an extremely narrow definition of "politics," which is more generally described as the process by which "who gets what, when, how and why." If using this more broad definition of politics, then shows such as *South Park* are largely political because they are about the play of power. This point was reaffirmed in a discussion I had with comedian Marc Maron, who argued that Larry the Cable Guy was political because he made jokes about immigration. While true, I would argue that despite the appearance of political material in Larry the Cable Guy's shtick, he is not what we can call a "political comedian" because of Holbert's (albeit slightly flawed) typology. Most of Larry the Cable Guy's audience do not see his shows expecting political material, and his political material is more often implicit within his routine. Holbert's categories are important because, if one takes an expansive or all-encompassing view of satire in pop culture, then suddenly all popular culture becomes political when it deals with matters of power. Forget Larry the Cable Guy—suddenly *Two and a Half Men* becomes political humor because of its approach to power, gender, and modern society. So in order to narrow down the range of subjects and case studies to a more manageable number, I use primarily satiric material in this study, even if this satire is blended with other forms of political humor. This means that for the purposes of this book, I examine material that answers Holbert's first question with, "An audience will expect political issues within the piece," and the second question, "The political messages are predominantly explicit." As a result, most of the humor referenced here includes (but is certainly not limited to) the following programs, productions, and writings:

The Daily Show with Jon Stewart
The Colbert Report
Wait, Wait...Don't Tell Me!
The Second City
The Capitol Steps
The Borowitz Report
Will Durst's syndicated column
The Onion
late night comedy monologues
pretty much all political cartoonists

Of course, this list is somewhat incomplete, and I will use examples from other formats where relevant, but these are the political humor outlets that best define the medium.

Intellectual Cover & Legal Protection

Satirists and political comedians flourish with a great amount of latitude because they have two intellectual covers: first, they get to say, "Hey! I'm only a comedian. I don't make the policies, I make fun of them." This allows potentially influential people to dodge the responsibility of their influence behind the cover of comedy. Most of those whom I interviewed made the argument that their main job was to entertain, and this contention was supported by *Daily Show* writer Kevin Bleyer, who said:

> We can't steal an obligation to report the news in a way that the nightly news should because the moment we do that we are actually dishonoring our obligation to A) be funny, to entertain; and B) the moment we start to do that I think people who listen to us for the comedy version of the news, if I can put it in that way, would be disappointed (Bleyer 2010).

This defense makes sense, given the mission of the comedian. And Bleyer's argument leads to another good point, which is that if modern satire were influential then the public policies would be different. As satirists and political humorists rail against the establishment in the position of the underdog, they not only shed light on the wrongdoings of government, but they also often argue for a different political outcome. A quick glimpse at modern America proves that they have not made much headway. Said Peter Sagal:

> The people who make jokes are not the guys who make policies. They are not the guys who launch the wars or not launch the wars. And maybe you could find examples of people about whom the jokes become too ridiculous, therefore, they can't proceed with public life, but I can't think of one. I mean, the jokes didn't bring down Elliott Spitzer. We made a lot of jokes about it, but what brought down Elliott Spitzer was that he was a prosecutor acting above the law, you know, the jokes didn't bring down John Edwards. The jokes certainly haven't brought down Sarah Palin (Sagal 2010).

This is one extremely important point: it is a political comedian's job to shine light on a political problem, but it is not their job to go any further than that, by proposing solutions or advocating sides. Another important point is the distinction between satire and journalism. They have two very different purposes, and combining the two is problematic.[ii] The fact that the American public has lost faith in the fourth estate and turns to satirical programming for analysis does not shift the burden of news gathering onto comedians. As a result, this intellectual cover of "I am only joking" works on several fronts.

The second shield satirists utilize comes with the legal protections provided by the First Amendment's freedom of speech. Our Founding Fathers felt strongly about this one, because of the severe restrictions on speech that the royal throne imposed prior to the Revolutionary War. Put another way: the framers fought hard to speak their mind and by God they made sure the rest of us would have the same freedom. Writes Constitutional Law expert Rodney Smolla:

> An obvious starting point is the direct link between freedom of speech and vibrant democracy. Free speech is an indispensable tool of self-governance in a democratic society. Concurring

---

[ii] This will be addressed in greater detail in Chapter 6.

in *Whitney v. California* (1927), Justice Louis Brandeis wrote that 'freedom to think as you will and to speak as you think are means indispensable to the discovery and spread of political truth' (Smolla n.d.).

This means that if a satirist wants to make fun of the president, he or she can do so without the fear of being imprisoned or audited by the IRS (whichever is worse) in retribution.

While we do not have unfettered free speech,[1] it seems that satirists are comfortably protected by much of the First Amendment guarantees afforded to others expressing political opinion. For instance, satirists who criticize the political establishment are hemmed in by the same kinds of libel and slander laws that restrict expression to prevent defamation. These libel laws are, generally speaking, pretty good things: they prevent your neighbor from spreading lies about you that would ruin your career or tear your reputation to shreds. However, the very job of a political humorist means that comedians and satirists get a bit more libel and slander slack than your average Joe. The courts established a test in the case *New York Times v. Sullivan* [376 U.S. 254, 270 (1964)] that said public figures could only recover damages if "actual malice" was incurred, meaning that the speech was intentionally false. Satire fails this "actual malice" test, according to legal scholar Leslie Treiger:

> Because satire works through distortion of the familiar—while at the same time pretending to depict reality—in order to level criticism, it fails to gain protection under any of the three prongs of this standard. First, because it works through distortion, satiric material easily can be identified as falsity or, at best, exaggeration. Moreover, by definition satire often, on its face, has the appearance of fact. Second, satirical material is critical of its subject's character or actions, and hence may be defamatory. Finally, the satirist always writes with actual malice," since she intends the falsity or exaggeration of her statement (Treiger 1989).

Treiger identified the problems with libel laws and satire, as exemplified in a case brought against *Hustler* magazine. In the 1980s, the Reverend Jerry Falwell filed suit against the magazine after it ran an ad parody portraying Falwell having sex with his mother in an outhouse. The Supreme Court, in *Hustler Magazine v. Falwell* [485 U.S. 46 (1988)], determined that the type of satire in the ad parody was protected: "The sort of expression in [the *Hustler*] case does not seem to us to be governed by any exception" to First Amendment protection. There are other protections for satire that apply. In 1974, the court ruled in *Gertz v. Robert Welch, Inc.* that opinions are protected speech: "Under the First Amendment there is no such thing as a false idea. However pernicious an opinion may seem, we depend for its correction not on the conscience of judges and juries but on the competition of other ideas" (Gertz v. Robert Welch 1974). This ruling gives satirists wide berth in which to express their opinions, adding to their freedom. Additionally, in *Campbell v. Acuff-Rose Music* [510 U.S. 569 (1994)], the court ruled that song parody was considered "fair use" and was not a copyright infringement, which left the door wide open for The Capitol Steps political cabaret show, and for the song parodies that other political satirists employ. Put together, this means that political comedians can use their talents to freely mock the political establishment thanks to the practical and legal protections that can defend the satirist from being taken too seriously or from being retaliated against by angry audiences, the courts, or politicians who feel wronged. This, of course, does not stop the extremists who find some of this humor so distasteful as to be worthy of death threats, but in the main, American political humorists are provided with enough shelter to safely do their job effectively.[2] A far bigger threat to satirists is financial viability. It's a big media system out there and getting known now, despite the abundance of available avenues, is just as hard as it once was because an artist has to be read or heard above the din over everyone else. This means most political comedians—even the most strictly satirical ones—have to temper their material in order to be commercially viable. This can be done in two ways: if the material is strictly political, like that of The Capitol Steps, then it must appeal to a wide range of opinions in order to make money. Put another way, if the Steps only hit the GOP, it would lose half of its audience, which is a specific niche audience to begin with.

On the other hand, if a comedian wants to appeal more generally, and use politics in conjunction with other material, then he has to make those political jokes accessible to a nonpolitical audience. Either way, there is very little ideologically driven political satire out there. At the same time that political humor can be widely targeting, however, the vast media system allows anyone with a computer the ability to create their own comedy and broadcast it to the world. So if a humorist wanted to craft an ideologically specific satire program, there's really nothing stopping him or her from doing so. As a result, the fact that there are so few conservative satirists is interesting, and this imbalance raises the charge of bias.

Bias and Its Effects

Allegations of bias make sense in today's political climate, and we see a great deal of biased media in modern society. Bias is different in varying forms, and in the early twenty-first century, we are saturated with partisan and biased news media outlets. Fox News, CNN, CNBC, and MSNBC all prominently feature pundits who have specific ideological slants that make them (and their networks) appealing to one select group of viewers. This slant is spreading to the entertainment media as well, as seen in The Right Network's 2010 launch, an effort to combat what conservatives say is a liberal bias in entertainment programming. It used to be, in the older media system, that there was a race for the middle. The wider the audience, the more money made in terms of ratings shares and advertising dollars, and to a degree this remains the case. But the media have become so vast and fragmented that a broad appeal is difficult to pull off. What we have today is niche programming—niche news in partisan flavors and niche entertainment for varying interests, and within this highly disjointed media system comes new math. It is no longer advantageous to reach for a wide audience sporadically, but instead to maintain control of a smaller, more focused audience all the time. As a result, it is within the best interest of the media outlets to cast aspersions on their competition and keep tight control of their audience.

According to author David von Drehle, this specialized media system is not new, and in fact the "golden era" of journalism, where authority figures disseminated news from on-high, was quite the anomaly:

> I think 20, 30, 50 years from now, when we look at media history, we're going to look at the late 20th century as the aberration. It was created artificially by the scarcity of broadcast -frequency. The people who had that broadcast frequency created enormous monopolies, and with monopoly they had to speak broadly to huge audiences. What kind of journalism does that create? That creates a journalism of the middle. Now we're just back to the way it was before, when anybody with some verve could start up a publication and get it out there, and if it spoke to people, it would grow. Papers would take off, become hugely popular, and vanish almost overnight back in those days. And what does that kind of environment create? It creates point of view, it creates voice, it creates partisanship (Von Drehel 2011).

Von Drehle makes a good point that, since the founding we have been a nation with partisan divides and an abundance of voices. But we have moved beyond partisanship today to hyper-polarization, and this split is magnified in the media, which has become a highly monetized industry with significant financial imperatives.[iii] Given the popularity of *The Daily Show* and *Colbert Report*, it should not be surprising that conservative media outlets trash-talk the competition. Additionally, perhaps satirical entertainment is simply following the established fragmentation of the larger American media system. Put another way: we can now pick our flavor of news. Why shouldn't we be able to do the same thing with our humor? According to VonDrehle's argument, we are moving in that direction.

In a partisan media environment, it makes sense that political entertainers are called "biased" but how legitimate is the accusation, and should these accusations matter? In other words, if it is just a joke, then who cares if it's slanted? One reason for the indictment is that modern satire is not only incredibly popular but also deemed to be extremely influential. There is scholarship

---

[iii] Translation: They want money.

that examines how we watch and read satirical material, and it has determined that satire, in our modern media age, affects the way we think about politics and politicians. Academics have dived head first into modern political humor to see how it affects such poli-sci-riffic things like political communication and voting behavior. Not surprisingly, much of the research has focused on Stewart and Colbert because of their popularity, especially among younger viewers. But the scholarship extends beyond this to examine the impact of political entertainment on the voting public. One of the first and most cited publications comes from Jody Baumgartner and Jonathan Morris who examined *The Daily Show*. They concluded that the snark of *The Daily Show* could contribute to greater political participation, but at the same time, this could just as easily backfire since satire exposure increased cynicism, especially among younger viewers. Their findings neatly summarized one important criticism of satirical shows, especially *The Daily Show*: that they increased distrust. Andrew Pease and Paul Brewer made a similar point, writing that when politicians go on popular shows in order to sell themselves to the public, the public becomes increasingly cynical about the political process. Adding a touch of snark themselves, communications scholars Roderick Hart and Johanna Hartelius wrote an article for the Critical Studies in Media Communication in which they—literally—"accuse Jon Stewart of political heresy":

> Our specific charge is that Mr. Stewart has engaged in unbridled political cynicism. And it is no coincidence that "sin" and "cynicism" have an assonant quality...Mr. Stewart cleverly claims to advance the tenets of democracy during his nightly assignations while in truth leading the Children of Democracy astray. He plants in them a false knowledge, a trendy awareness that turns them into bawdy villains and wastrels...We think that Jon Stewart is both a heathen and a publican (Hart and Hartelius 2007).

Tough crowd! When asked about the importance of these satire shows and the messages they send, often writers and producers of this media scoff at a notion of their own significance or impact, arguing that their shows are purely entertainment. In what may be my favorite interview moment of this project, I told comedian Lewis Black that academics found satire shows to affect political behavior, especially breeding cynicism. Black responded:

> Well, first tell those academics to fuck themselves... Really, tell them it is bullshit... satire doesn't have that effect. If satire was really that important as a way to get things done, then, you know, more shit would be getting [done]... It also doesn't fucking create a malaise. All it allows is laughter which is insulation from what you are caught up in... I get at least one letter, two letters, three letters a month that somebody had cancer and they're father was sick... da, da, da, da, and the only thing his father liked to do he really liked to watch me because he would laugh (Black 2010).

One contention, especially from the television writers, is that a political audience is self-selecting by virtue of the content. Accordingly, material cannot have any influence at all if the audience is not informed to begin with. They state that programming such as *The Daily Show* and satiric "news" from *The Onion* cannot be grasped unless a viewer or reader has an existing understanding of the news to begin with, and this logic makes sense: certainly, a joke about President Obama is not as funny unless you know who he is. And on this point, the scholarship agrees. In fact, some scholars make the argument that when someone brings a bit of understanding to satire, they gain an even better understanding after the jokes have landed. Two researchers, Lauren Feldman and Dannagal Young, argued that attention to satirical programming actually increases awareness of politics. Michael Parkin (2010) made a similar point in an article that examined the 2004 elections, and found that making information more appealing and entertaining helped to supplement the existing political knowledge of a person who got their information from traditional news sources. In other words, entertaining media can assist in one's learning about the world in a way that is fun and occasionally educational. One for satire's "win" column! Also along these lines, political cartoons in print media help to reinforce political knowledge. Author Emmett Buell argued that political cartoons, in their exaggeration and embellishment, spoke loudly enough in the 1988 presidential campaign to educate the public, a theory supported by other scholars in more recent years. Lindsay Neuberger (et al.) found that the pairing of an op-ed piece with an editorial cartoon helped to solidify meaning on the editorial pages. In these arguments, satire viewing and reading can be useful in discussing American politics.

But apparently, people are worried about the children. There is an abundance of scholarship that has been written examining the effect that modern political satire has on young voters. This emanates from a Pew Research Center study from 2000 that reported 47 percent of voters under 30 were "informed at least occasionally" by late night humor shows about the 2000 presidential election (Jones 2007). This information nugget was released, and the public began to freak out. The press, academics, and popular writers all pointed to the research study as evidence that the youth of America was learning about the world from *The Onion*, in lieu of the *New York Times*. It makes for a good and frightening narrative where young people are far dumber than older ones, but it may not be very accurate. Donnagal Young addressed this in her article "Dispelling Late-Night Myths," where she makes several excellent points about the Pew Center study: first, there is nothing in the research that states younger Americans only get their news from late night programming; second, the "late night" audience is not one single entity, but rather spans a wide demographic variety. These two points do take some of the bang out of the concern for our kids; however, the concern persists because there is some truth to it. In two different studies, Jody Baumgartner analyzed the influence of online political humor seen in flash animation and political cartooning, and in both studies concluded that the candidate depictions found here had a negative effect on political trust, especially among college students (Baumgartner 2007, 2008). Satirical conceptions of candidates during political campaigns can be especially important, particularly if they present an entirely different construction of a candidate image than the candidate himself or herself would like to impart. Since it is possible that young voters consume more political satire than their older colleagues, these are worrisome conclusions. By learning about candidates from relatively superficial depictions, voters miss the opportunity to truly understand the candidates' policy positions. Additionally, younger voters who are still developing their political socialization will learn skepticism, distrust, and doubt about the American political system before they have the opportunity to fully participate in it or understand it completely. To quote former president George W. Bush: "Rarely is the question asked: Is our children learning?" This literature answers yes, the children *is* learning, but they is learning from a variety of sources, several of which eschew any desire to teach or responsibility to inform. So that's a problem.

Research on voting behavior asks a two-part question: first, what happens once the messages are received? And second, do voters change their voting habits or do they vote differently because of exposure to political satire? Starting with the first part of the question, scholars have asked about whether people vote more or less often because of exposure to entertaining news. The answers are wildly divergent. The aforementioned 2006 article from Baumgartner and Morris that argued *The Daily Show* breeds cynicism also made the argument that this cynicism leads to decreased voting rates (Baumgartner and Morris 2006). But Cao and Brewer have a very different view, and they argued that those who have watched satire shows become more engaged in political participation as a result of their viewing. Proving a correlation between satire consumption and voting levels is somewhat difficult, which is why there is relatively little research done in this area. One idea that germinates in much of the literature posits the theory that someone drawn to *The Daily Show* or *Colbert Report* is more inclined to be interested in politics to begin with, and thus will vote more often regardless.

The question of voting decisions (meaning, do voters vote differently because of exposure to satirical programming?) has been addressed as well. Harvard professor Matthew Baum takes the position that exposure to candidates on late night comedy shows and entertainment-oriented television programs can lead politically unengaged voters to cross party lines, or to at least see a candidate from an opposing party in a more positive light (Baum 2005). Baum has conducted other research that takes a similarly positive spin on entertainment programming and political behavior, in which he makes a good point: on entertainment shows, candidates are not challenged on difficult policy questions, but rather are asked to talk about their personal lives or share humorous anecdotes that help define them. Unless a politician is going on these shows to apologize for something or to try and get ahead of a joke, these appearances are tightly constructed and upbeat. Politicians on these entertainment shows get to paint a pretty picture for voters watching late night television who may not be C-SPAN junkies, and who may not be aware of the candidate. As a result, these are all very positive representations made through funny or self-deprecating stories, and viewers come away from these shows liking the candidates quite a bit. I wrote a bit about the blending of politics and entertainment in 2010, but I took the position that this personalization was negative and encouraged superficiality that was harmful for political discourse (Dagnes 2010). I could have been wrong, though.

American University professor Danny Hayes wrote an interesting paper in 2009 asking the question, "Has Television Personalized Voting Behavior?" to which he answered: not really. Using data from the National Election Survey (NES), Hayes found that "personal attributes are no more likely to be mentioned now as reasons to vote for or against a candidate than they were half a century ago" (Hayes 2009). Instead of television being the leading influence in voting decisions, Hayes argued, party adherence plays a far more significant role:

> Candidates' attributes are by no means irrelevant. But given the growing ideological distance between the parties, it is not stunning that little evidence exists of the kind of "personalization" of voting behavior that might have been expected in an era where television has come to dominate the media landscape... The medium's power to prime candidates' personal attributes has been diluted by a rising tide of partisan politics, and perhaps by the fact that issues have continued to be a prominent feature of candidates' political advertising (Hayes 2008).

So even though we would like to point to television as the reason candidates have become more shallow and superficial in their campaigning, we really cannot. Thus, it follows that television satire cannot have too much of an effect on voting decisions if we are not, as a public, easily persuaded by the medium itself.

Program analysis is the third type of academic research conducted, and (not surprisingly) much of this is done on *The Daily Show* and on the *Colbert Report*. Interestingly, unlike the first two categories of research, this one lends itself toward a flattering and positive examination of satire. In short, the authors love themselves some Stewart.[iv] Geoffrey Baym from the University of North Carolina at Greensboro has paid special attention to *The Daily Show*, and in two separate publications examines the format of the show. In one paper, Baym lauded the program for its "experiment in journalism":

> The blending of news and satire confronts a system of political communication that largely has denigrated into soundbites and spin with critical inquiry. The use of parody unmasks the artifice in much contemporary news practices, while the interview segment endorses and enacts a deliberative model of democracy based on civility of exchange, complexity of argument, and the goal of mutual understanding (Baym 2005).

See? *The Daily Show* is actually good for you! Along these same lines, George Washington University professor Michael Cornfield made the argument that the technique of blending comedy and information in *The Daily Show* is good enough to be considered revolutionary—a game changer, if you will (Cornfield 2005). And this means that not only is this brand of TV satire not harmful, but it's also leading the charge in changing the other forms of news around it.

So all of this research, and a significant amount not mentioned here, lend credence to the idea that political satire plays a significant and influential role in modern American politics. If political humor is so influential, then the scarcity of conservative voices may be of concern. But in the end, the character of the satirists and the nature of political humor makes sure that no damage is done. Anyone in power is a potential target, and in the end, as influential as *The Daily Show* may seem, these satirists and writers are not political activists but comedians who place more importance on laughter than on politicking.

[iv] And really, what's not to love?

The rest of this book goes into much more depth. The history of satire, the temperament of the satirists and comedians, and the very nature of political humor are all explored to show why there are so few conservative satirists today. This scarcity may be troublesome to many, but it should not be so concerning. Even though satire plays an increasingly significant role in our political messaging, it remains true to its mission of entertainment. This is not necessarily a bad thing, because in our highly mediated political environment, political comedy is a respectable salve for modern problems. Additionally, this form of political criticism can be extremely instructive, even when it does not try to be. In our increasingly polarized political climate, laughter may be one thing that can bring us together, as long as the comedy is not dismissed as a reason to keep us apart. The next chapter explores how the jokes we laugh at are aimed at the powerful, and why this is a good thing.

CHAPTER 2

Data, Experiments, and Proof

There is an important separation between the satirist and the material he or she produces. Satirists are a people with opinions, but their material may not convey all of their beliefs. Are there more liberal satirists than conservative ones? Yes. Does modern political satire have a leftist bias? Perhaps, but this needs to be determined. This chapter examines satirical material from a variety of angles to gauge whether or not the political humor itself is ideologically prejudiced.

Both humor and ideology are somewhat subjective concepts. A joke will not be funny to everyone, nor will everyone agree on what it means to be "liberal" or "conservative." And when these two concepts are blended into one question, there is room for interpretation. For example, three academics from Ohio State University investigated the way *The Colbert Report*'s audience processed the jokes and information featured on the show (LaMarre, Landreville, and Beam 2009). *The Colbert Report* features comedian Stephen Colbert acting as a very conservative pundit, his characterization based almost entirely on Fox News pundit Bill O'Reilly whom he refers to as "Papa Bear." The Ohio State scholars examined two things. First, they looked at whether or not a viewer's political ideology affected their perception of Stephen Colbert: if someone was conservative, did they think Colbert was truly conservative as well? Also, they examined the way the general satire from the show was processed: did an audience member's personal beliefs color how they processed the messages? The answers to both of these questions were the same. The results indicated that "political ideology influences biased processing of ambiguous political messages and source in late-night comedy" (LaMarre et al. 2009). In other words, people will see what they want to see, and this is a psychological phenomenon called "confirmation bias." Heather LaMarre, one of the authors of the study, said this about Stephen Colbert (the character):

> Liberals will see him as an over-the-top satire of Bill O'Reilly-type pundit and think that he is making fun of a conservative pundit. But conservatives will say, yes, he is an over-the-top satire of Bill O'Reilly, but by being funny he gets to make really good points and make fun of liberals. So they think the joke is on liberals (Drutman, 2009).

While the idea that a viewer's political philosophy might color his or her view of satirical material is interesting, it is genuinely alarming that a sizable portion of those surveyed by the Ohio State crew genuinely thought Stephen Colbert was really a conservative. More importantly, the ideological lens that each of us wears as we devour political humor is definitely going to color the way we respond to a political joke. Accordingly, this chapter sets term definitions in the hopes of demarcating the boundaries of the data and then runs several small experiments to establish whether there is a bias in satire.

American Political Ideologies

In its most basic definition, ideological bias means that there is a slant in a product where one ideological side is favored over another. Ideological bias is alleged and refuted in the news (Jamieson et al. 2008; Goldberg 2003; Alterman 2003), in academia (Horowitz 2009; Mattera 2012), and in the entertainment industry (Hirsen 2005; Ross 2011; Simon 2011), where more often than not, conservatives charge that there is liberal control and authority to the exclusion of right-wing opinion or thought. There has been ample research that proves these contentions false, but I do not want to delve into this debate too much; so, if this is a sticking point for readers, I urge them to seek out this scholarship elsewhere. This book examines political comedy where it is alleged that conservatives are victims to left-leaning jokesters, so that allegation covers the "bias" part. But what is political ideology? Political ideology is a complicated subject, one that many political scientists have spent volumes of research exploring. Put simply, political ideology is a set of political beliefs that a person possesses. People develop their political ideology after years of political socialization, the process by which we learn about the world around us. Some people are exposed to politics at a young age because of their parents, their environment, or the media they enjoy. Others are not so exposed, and go on to develop their ideological beliefs through acquired experience and exposure to the political system. Some people have a strong interest in politics and feel equally soundly about their ideological leanings, and some don't care at all about either. In the United States, we like to draw an overly simplistic spectrum where liberals are on the left and conservatives are on the right. This is a decent place to start, but it doesn't quite get to the heart of our political divide in America. Essentially, American political ideology centers around two basic questions: how much government do you want, and what do you want that government to do?

In very broad terms, the definitions of the primary American ideological groups fall along four lines, conservatives, liberals, libertarians, and communitarians.

Conservatives, who want small government to take care of what is written in the preamble to the Constitution: national defense, defense of liberty, justice. Conservatism comes with a dedication to tradition and an antipathy toward change. According to political theorist Michael Oakeshott, the general characteristics of conservatives are thus:

> They centre upon a propensity to use and to enjoy what is available rather than to wish for or to look for something else; to delight what is present rather than what was or what may be (Oakeshott, 1962).

Conservatism has varying forms. There are social conservatives, who are more concerned with morality; fiscal conservatives, who are more concerned with the budget; and neoconservatives, who are more concerned with government power and external threats to the nation. But in general, conservatives would like to shrink the size and scope of the federal government, move power to private industry and the states, and protect individual rights. They do not think it is the government's job to further social justice; the result of this is, if programs are few in number, taxes are kept low.

Liberals follow the other ideological line; they want a government big enough to help the people who President Roosevelt referred to as the "neediest among us." This involves not only the promotion of the general welfare (stated in the preamble to the Constitution) but also the expansion of social justice. Liberalism, according to political scientist Nathan Grimes in 1953, has the following characteristics:

> [Liberalism] represents a system of ideas that aims at the realization of the pluralistic society, favoring diversity in politics, economic, religion, and our cultural life. It is opposed to uniformity; it is opposed to conformity...It is essentially antiauthoritarian, and represents the claims of those who are out of power and thus lacking in authority; but who, had they the power, would not impose authoritarian solutions on others (Grimes 1956).

Liberalism is the ideology that aims to do the most for the most people, which means these liberal social groups end up competing against one another for attention and resources. This also means that there's a great deal of fighting within liberalism, which helps to explain the Democratic Party.

Libertarians want as little government as possible, taking the Henry David Thoreau line "That government is best that governs least" pretty far. Libertarians side with both conservatives and liberals on different matters: they feel conservative when they side with the National Rifle Association to make sure the government does not regulate firearms, but then they feel more liberal when they side with Planned Parenthood to make sure abortions are not legislatively prohibited. From the Libertarian Party:

> Libertarians believe in, and pursue, personal freedom while maintaining personal responsibility...Libertarians strongly oppose any government interfering in their personal, family and business decisions. Essentially, we believe all Americans should

be free to live their lives and pursue their interests as they see fit as long as they do no harm to another. In a nutshell, we are advocates for a smaller government, lower taxes and more freedom (Libertarian Party 2011).

Libertarians simply want the government to stay out of their business. Oh—and they don't like the Federal Reserve or wars of empire much either.

Communitarians want strong government to regulate public life to create a community of equals. According to *Washington Post* journalist Dana Milbank:

"Communitarianism," or "civil society" thinking (the two have similar meanings) has many interpretations, but at its center is a notion that years of celebrating individual freedom have weakened the bonds of community and that the rights of the individual must be balanced against the interests of society as a whole. Inherent in the philosophy is a return to values and morality, which, the school of thought believes, can best be fostered by community organizations (Milbank, 2001).

While not as practically pronounced as the previous three philosophies, there is a great deal of modern political philosophy dedicated toward this school of thought, and I urge interested readers to explore the writings of Michael Sandel and Michael Waltzer.

Within these overly broad definitions, the political parties align themselves. It is important not to confuse party with ideology, because all Democrats are not liberal, nor are all Republicans conservative. That said, in general terms, conservatives *tend* to be Republicans or Libertarians, and liberals *tend* to be Democrats or Communitarians. In the current political climate, we see a divided conservative electorate pulled between the libertarian and Republican camps. And big tent liberals are just pulled among themselves most of the time anyway. This, by the way, provides ample fodder for satirists to make fun of the parties and of the ideologies they espouse. Take, for example, satirist Will Durst's take on the battle lines:

Conservative voices dominating center stage today can be divided into three groups. The Greedy. The Mean. And the Stupid. They live in a black and white land where compromise equals defeat and discussion means you taking notes while they talk. Liberals can be distilled into three groups as well. The Pompous. The Weak. And the Stupid. Their world is a rainbow of colors where the government provides everyone with that big box of 64 crayons encouraging them to write on the walls. Anybody's walls...Another odd thing is the two sides continue to play the game under entirely different narratives. Liberals act like associate producers at a folk fair trying to choreograph the welcoming dance of converging cultures failing to notice the ragged band of Conservatives lighting torches and running headlong towards them up the castle hill armed with pitchforks (Durst, 2011).

In a two party system (sorry Tea Partiers), these battle lines are drawn for a reason: they help us determine winners and losers, and they help those winners and losers organize themselves. We have a procedural political system, which means that the rules apply to everyone but the political winners have more opportunities to lead than the losers do. Please note that "losers" here is not a disparaging remark, only the factual aftermath of an election. While smart politicians strive for balance by aiming at the middle (after all, elections are won by winning 50 percent plus one), rarely are politicians neutral. They are not supposed to be—the whole point of running for office is to stand for something. Hence, it would follow that standing for something would be a good goal of a political satirist—and neutrality would be avoided. If a satirist neutered his or her material to the point of safety, it would negate the whole point of the art form.

This is why there is no "neutral" satire, but satirists can aim for impartiality. Can political cartoonists and stand ups and radio/ TV show hosts ply their craft if they are so conscious of ideological aim? Many argue they are impartial, despite the satirical imperative to criticize. They can (as politicians do) strive for balance, and one way to do this is to balance barbs on both sides. Several satirists admitted to this technique, especially on predominantly nonpolitical shows such as *Saturday Night Live* (*SNL*). Said *SNL*'s Doug Abeles:

> I think we kind of have our own internal barometer of trying to, you know, not trying not to go too far one way or the other...we can't do three "Bush is dumb" jokes in a row and not take some kind of shot on the left, you know, or the opposition.

I think there is a sensibility here of not wanting to be unbalanced ... That being said it is not like we are ... really doing a count: For every, you know, joke that we take at the expense of the Republicans we must have a joke that makes fun of the Democrats. But we ... try the best we can to try to keep a balance in there (Abeles, 2010).

It seems that making sure that both sides were hit would be a fair way to do political material, but other satirists rejected this idea. They argued that since satirical jokes are event-driven, there is little control over the targets. Said *Wait, Wait*'s Peter Sagal:

I am very skeptical of false equivalencies in the sense that you say to yourself: "Oh we are making fun of the person with an R after his name then we have to say the same thing after a person with the D after his name." You see this in the general media and it makes me nuts. It doesn't work that way. Sometimes only one side screwed this up and you need to talk about that ... You always have to be careful to be sure of things. That said, you try to be balanced on a perspective. One question we ask is: Would we make the same kind of jokes about a person if they had a different letter after their last name, D instead of an R or an R instead of a D? We ask ourselves that question and the answer is no, like we are making fun of them because they pissed us off or did something we don't like and then we back off (Sagal 2010).

The Daily Show's Kevin Bleyer agreed with Sagal and argued that once you focus on equality, the mission of satire is lost:

We respond to the news of the day ... We do, of course, have discussions in the room about how to address something and sure, those inevitably come from different individual perspectives, but it is never: 'Oh, well, it is about time we do something conservative or it is about time we do something liberal?' Not at all ... It is never to make course corrections for our previous shows. It is always to be honest on the show we are about to do (2010).

Certainly, political satire is only funny when it hits a mark, and that mark is only funny when it is foremost in an audience's conscious. As mentioned, this is why many funny political jokes go untold: not because it has a slant to it, but because the average audience wouldn't get it. Some comedians eschew the political entirely in order to gain and maintain audiences. Says Ned Rice, who used to write for Jay Leno, "Jay does not have any political agenda at all. He takes a lot of pride in, literally, 'If I do eleven Democrat jokes tonight, I am going to do eleven Republican'" (Rice 2010). This makes a great deal of sense, since most Americans have little interest in American politics. Truly, most comedians in general stick to observational humor or jokes about celebrities because when they are funny, the majority of their audience will laugh. So with the understanding that political satire must be accessible enough to get a general audience to appreciate it, how much actual *bias* is at play? The rest of this chapter aims to answer this question.

Claims of Bias, Types of Bias

People feel very comfortable tossing around accusations of bias, especially in a political media environment where bias actually exists. Even worse than actual bias existing (and perhaps this is more to the point of this book) is the harm done by attaching bias claims to specific media entities. One study from Western Kentucky University's Joel Turner found that the accusations of bias against news outlets such as Fox News and CNN were so strong that even mentioning the news organization in relation to a story colored the reception of the story itself (Turner 2007). Consequently, the very accusation of bias has tremendous significance in our current political culture: hence this research project. This book is built around the question of why there are so few conservative satirists, but the underlying issue concerns the satire that the American public consumes. It is one thing to have a preponderance of liberal satirists, but quite another to have satire that only strikes in one direction. Conservative satirists and comedians argue the bias begins with the satirists, extends to their material, and is regulated at the very top, by those who run the entertainment business in Hollywood. They argue that the leftist slant of Hollywood denies any conservative programming, in any form, from news to entertainment. Perhaps this is true, perhaps this is not, but it does beg an important question: what would a bias in political humor look like? This is complicated, since people tend to have varied ideas about what bias is and how it affects society.

There are several different forms that bias could take if there is an ideological slant in the political humor itself. Satirists could poke at one side over another, completely excluding those with whom they disagree. Conservatives allege this kind of prejudice on Stewart, Colbert, and their ilk, saying they hit President Bush (43) pretty hard but pull the punches on President Obama. This kind of satirical bias would mean very little criticism of the left on the part of modern satirists; when asked about this, satirists tended to disregard the allegation. *Wait, Wait*'s Peter Segal addressed this:

> A lot of people say to me, "You should make fun of Obama." Granted. What should we make fun of? "Well, you should make fun of his healthcare policy because it is going to ruin healthcare in America. You should make fun of that." And, I say, okay, I don't know if you are right, maybe it will, maybe it won't, but why is that funny? Tell me how/why healthcare is funny and I would be glad to make that joke. They always look at me and they say: "But it is dangerous, it is dumb." [Shakes head] Not funny (Sagal 2010).

Without doubt, the bulk of the satire of the first decade of the twenty-first century was aimed ferociously at Bush (43), but then again, he was in the ultimate power position. Additionally, his administration gave up some formidable ammunition for comedians and satirists. Bush himself was prone to the verbal gaffe, giving the impression that he was at best ineloquent, and at worst unintelligent. Life during wartime is never fundamentally funny, but the Bush administration's policies beyond the invasions of Afghanistan and Iraq also provided some occasional comic relief from the challenging times, especially when Bush announced in his 2006 State of the Union address that he advocated a ban on animal/human hybrids. It also didn't help that Vice President Cheney maintained a shadowy appearance to the outside world, emerging into the culture only sporadically, such as the time he shot a lawyer during a hunting trip. So when critics complain about satirists who brutally mocked George W. Bush, it is important to remind them that the president is always the most prominent target of political humor, and that the Bush administration was occasionally an easy target. Truthfully, most administrations are easy to mock. Certainly, Clinton and his administration proffered some fertile satirical material; even before the Lewinsky affair, he had a huge comedic target on his back. Critics maintain Bush (43) had it worse.

One possible reason for this perceived disparity arises thanks to the technological development of the media. Cable satellite technology, which had roared to life in the 1990s, was in full bloom in the 2000s. Internet technology developed beyond slow dial-up service to high-speed transmission. The devices for calling, texting, and surfing became smaller, faster, and more affordable. As a result of all of these changes, the media have become more ubiquitous, and messaging has fundamentally changed. Before Bush (43), President Clinton had provided more than ample satirical material, but the technology wasn't there to spread it as quickly and as easily to so many people. When Bush (43) rolled into town, the media were changing at such an alarming rate, it was difficult for politicians to keep up with the pace. Comedian Lewis Black agreed with this assessment: "Cable creates the *Daily Show* and the *Daily Show* creates the *Colbert* show" (Black 2010). And the Internet helps spread it around like wildfire even to those who do not watch cable.

So this helps to explain the fertile field of Bush (43) satire in the 2000s, but what, then, of the administration that came next? Did satirists hold Obama in such high regard as to give his administration a free pass? This would indicate bias in that particular form; to gauge this possibility, I turn to the Center for Media and Public Affairs at George Mason University in Virginia. In 2010, scholars there conducted a thorough examination of thousands of jokes about public figures from the late night comedy shows, and they looked specifically at the targets of these jokes. They judged the partisan balance among the comedians and analyzed the material to see if ideological bias existed. This was an expansive study, and it helps to definitively conclude the presence (or not) of bias among some of the most influential political satirists of the modern age.

Bias could also come in the form of selecting certain guests for certain programs in order to highlight one side's strengths or the other side's weaknesses. This would manifest itself in a guest-list imbalance or, even more obviously, in a partisan mandate to avoid certain biased programs. The *Huffington Post* addressed this question in a 2011 article about Sarah Palin, and *The Daily Show*, arguing that many of *The Daily Show*'s guests since the 2008 election have been conservatives:

> Though he leans left, host Jon Stewart has coaxed plenty of Republicans—including potential 2012 contenders Tim Pawlenty, Mike Huckabee and Newt Gingrich, Tea Party leader Dick Armey and even longtime punching bags like former Defense Secretary Donald Rumsfeld and former RNC Chair Michael Steel—to appear on his show and engage in lively debate with one of the most well-respected interviewers on television (Baram 2011).

If *The Daily Show* does book a sizable number of conservatives, a follow-up issue might concern how those guests are treated. If conservative guests were lambasted and humiliated, then having a balance wouldn't matter much. But if conservatives were treated poorly, then why would they continue to appear on the show? One obvious answer comes from the old adage "no publicity is bad publicity," and certainly that may apply. But it seems that in many cases, conservative guests on these shows enjoy themselves. Former defense secretary Donald Rumsfeld appeared on *The Daily Show* to promote his book, and even though the show had used him as a comic foil for most of his tenure in office, after the interview, Rumsfeld tweeted, "Just wrapped up one of the most thoughtful interviews of book tour with @thedailyshow" (Baram 2011). But the possibility of bias does exist in guest selection, as noted by comedian Nick DiPaolo who spoke about guest booking on Fox News Channel:

> I know people laugh at the 'fair and balanced' but I do watch the enemy. I do flip over to MSNBC and watch idiots like Keith Olbermann, and Rachel Maddow's very smart, but do you ever see a conservative with any credentials on MSNBC? I mean, you know, O'Reilly and Hannity, they'll have anybody on from the left to debate. You don't see that...I really believe the left, they insulate themselves, and they have for years with people who think just like they do and whether you're talking about show business or the news industry (DiPaolo 2011).

If only left-leaning guests are booked on TV and radio satire shows, then certainly a bias in the material can result. I compared the guests lists from *The Daily Show*, *The Colbert Report*, and *Wait, Wait...Don't Tell Me!* to determine whether there is an imbalance in the booking process.

The final examination of bias in political humor is gauged through conduct content analysis of several popular satiric forms. *The Daily Show* is one obvious vehicle to analyze, but since satire extends beyond electronic media, I also examined political cartoons from several prominent cartoonists, and columns from two political humorists. This will help measure, to a certain degree, the ideological angle of the satiric material within a specific period. All put together, the jokes told, the guests booked, and the aim of the material will help to determine the veracity of bias claims in the political humor consumed by the American public. The end result (spoiler alert!) is, while there is some left-leaning partiality, it is certainly not exclusive nor is it hostile to the right. This makes sense because of the nature of satire.

But the biggest potential indicator of bias concerns the central question of this book: why are there so few conservative satirists? Of the dozens of satirists I interviewed, so few were conservative, it was noteworthy. After all of my hours of discussions about ideology and comedic material, I came away with a firm opinion that a satirist is separate from his material. So before I investigate the reasons for the scarcity of conservative satirists, I have to determine whether or not the satire itself skews left. The conservatives I interviewed reflexively argued that it does, but the liberals I interviewed argued just as instinctively that it does not. The data help determine the actual answer to this question.

Partisanship in Late Night Jokes

The Center for Media and Public Affairs (CMPA) at George Mason University (CMPA) examined late night political humor from January 1, 2010, to September 6, 2010, to determine the most popular joke targets and to see if the comedians were slanted in their humor (Lichter 2010). They studied every specific joke told about a public figure during this time on four late night shows: *The Tonight Show with Jay Leno*, *The Late Show with David Letterman*, *Late Night with Jimmy Fallon*, and *The Daily*

Show with Jon Stewart. The sheer number of politically partisan jokes was significant (1,625) because "public figure" was not limited to those elected to public office but instead extended to newsmakers and partisans of all stripes. Several important facts emerged from the study.

First, the president was the biggest target of the jokes, and during this study the president was Barack Obama. This was consistent with past studies of joke targets; during the 2000s, Bush (43) was such a prime foil. The president is the most obvious joke-butt because of his position of prominence, and this makes sense—the American president is the leader of the free world, arguably the single most identifiable politician around the globe. According to the CMPA study, all four comedian hosts told around the same number of jokes about Obama (Leno told 68; Letterman told 92; Stewart told 72; and Fallon told 77), but the jokes varied in their political attention. The report notes: "Fallon told fewer partisan jokes than the others. As a result, his totals were more influenced by the relatively large number of jokes he told about President Obama" (Lichter 2010). This indicates a varying degree of satire on these shows, three of which are purposefully not political shows. Additionally, the study's authors compared the number of Obama jokes to the number of Clinton and Bush (43) jokes told in those presidents' second years in office. Because *The Daily Show* was nonexistent in its current form during Clinton's second year and fledgling during Bush's (43), the study looked at Leno, Letterman, and Conan O'Brien instead. Clinton won by a landslide. In 1994, Leno, Letterman, and O'Brien targeted Clinton 15 percent of the time they told jokes about public figures, and in 2002 they told jokes about Bush (43) 10 percent of the time. In 2010, their total was 9 percent for Barack Obama, which shows that comparatively, President Obama did not garner as much comedic attention as his predecessors. But it was pretty close. The fact that Clinton was a target 50 percent more than Bush (43) indicates a deficiency of ideological bias in this material.

Another important finding from the study is that the targets of the jokes were event-driven. For example, Tony Heyward, CEO of BP, made the list as the fifth most frequent target because of the Louisiana Gulf oil spill and his incredibly poor reaction to the disaster. Also making the list was US Representative Eric

Massa, a New York Democrat who resigned from the US House of Representatives after being accused of sexually inappropriate conduct with his staff, and Massachusetts Republican Scott Brown, who won a special election to fill the US Senate seat of the late Ted Kennedy. None of these men would necessarily garner much attention independent of these newsworthy events unless a comedian had a special affinity for the target. This appears to be the case for Jon Stewart using Glenn Beck as an object of ridicule; Beck made it to number eight on the list of Stewart's most frequent humor targets. But during the time period analyzed by the CMPA, Beck was organizing and advertising a large march on Washington, which was newsworthy in itself, and according to the CMPA, Stewart told 44 of the 50 jokes about Glenn Beck during this time period (Lichter, 2010). Additionally, several comedians told jokes about politicians who were no longer in office [Leno about Al Gore, Letterman about Bush (43)], which might also indicate some sort of bias. And they did find a slant. Stewart and Letterman each had Barack Obama as their top target, but after that directed the majority of their jokes at Republicans. Stewart's top targets after President Obama were (in order) Glenn Beck, Sarah Palin, John McCain, and Michael Steele. For Letterman, his next four targets were George W. Bush, Sarah Palin, Scott Brown, and Michael Bloomberg (Lichter, 2010). That Letterman made fun of the mayor of New York was not surprising, since his show is filmed and so rooted in the city. The Sarah Palin and John McCain references could also be explained because of her reality television show being filmed at the time and his race for reelection to the US Senate. Together, these two comedians had a similar partisan slant with a rate of Republican-targeted jokes running around 60 percent to Democratic-directed jokes around 40 percent. However, Leno and Fallon (who also hit President Obama the hardest) then directed most of their jokes at left-leaning political actors. Leno's top four foils after Obama were Al Gore, Joe Biden, Sarah Palin, and George W. Bush. Jimmy Fallon followed Obama with jokes about Biden, Palin, Eric Massa, and Bill Clinton. Leno aimed 67 percent at left-leaning targets and Fallon aimed 78 percent. The Biden jokes stemmed from his position as vice president and his occasional verbal missteps. Gore and Clinton were well worn and easily identifiable joke targets. All of this meant that there was ideological leaning on the part of these shows when it came to the political jokes told by the hosts.

The study found that the jokes about Obama mostly addressed his "personal demeanor," which is largely consistent with other political jokes told. Policies and sinking popularity ratings were also food for the comedians, but personal demeanor jokes were dominant. This is because (as mentioned) the average American does not know very much about public policy, nor do they necessarily follow the news closely enough for a political joke to work. This means that satirists and comedians have to use existing impressions of politicians with which people are familiar, or they have to use current events so widely understood as to be accessible to a lay audience. This could be one reason George W. Bush received so much more comedic attention than Obama has (thus far): there are more personal quirks to Bush than there are to Obama, who is one tightly wound president. Said actor Keegan-Michael Key about Obama satire:

> He keeps himself close to the vest. And so it has been very difficult for us, for any of us, to find a way to chip away at the veneer. You know, when you do a sketch about him it is never satirical it is always putting him in a comedic position. There is no comedic engine... The only thing I have found is a couple of mobile signatures, but they don't lead us to anything satirical so it falls back into the land of parody (Key 2010).

In all, the study found that certain shows did lean more left than others, as CMPA president Dr Robert Lichter noted: "Just as conservatives get their political news from *Fox* and liberals from *MSNBC*, conservatives are getting their political humor from *NBC* and liberals from *Comedy Central*" (Lichter, 2010). But that said, these leanings were not particularly strong, nor did they stray from targeting the president the most often.

Guest Lists: Who Is Invited to the Party?

I interviewed comedian Jimmy Tingle in Cambridge, Massachusetts, and asked him about a possible leftist bias in satire. He was defending *The Daily Show* by making the argument that Republicans go on that show all the time, and he suddenly suggested: "You should look at the guest lists" (Tingle 2010). This was, in my opinion, a flash of brilliance. So I did look at the guest lists to gauge the liberal-to-conservative ratio of the guests who were booked on *The Daily Show, The Colbert Report,* and *Wait, Wait...Don't Tell Me!* This turned out to be a useful exercise, but only to a certain extent because the show formats and purposes are so incongruent. Comparing these shows to one another wasn't even comparing apples to oranges—it was comparing apples to pick-up trucks, but here is what I found: these shows are, in the main, entertainment driven. This means that the vast majority of the guests on satire programs are Hollywood celebrities hawking books, movies, music, or tickets to their sporting events. When politicians appear on the shows, they are also pushing their wares—either something tangible such as themselves (for election) or something more amorphous such as ideas (for policy making). The following includes the breakdown by show, starting with *The Daily Show.*

The Daily Show with Jon Stewart

In 2010, Jon Stewart taped a total of 160 shows and sat with 160 guests. The format of the shows remained, with a few notable exceptions, remarkably consistent: the first half of the program included a monologue by Stewart and fake interviews from his pretend-journalist staff. The second half of the show consisted of an interview with a newsmaker, author, journalist, or entertainer. I took the guest list from this second half of the show and sorted the guests into four general categories: book authors, journalists, entertainers, and politicos. These are broad categories, and several times a guest bridged more than one of them, so I sorted according to dominant occupation. If the guest was, say, Jimmy Carter, I figured his job as US president was more significant than his role as an author and, so I put him in the politico category. This was more art than science, and there were four guests who bucked my system entirely (two businessmen and two scientists), but overall it worked fairly well.

The Daily Show Guest List Totals By Category

32 Authors	21 Journalists	
63 Entertainers	40 Politicos	4 Others

Stewart's 2010 guest list brought up several important points. As Stewart himself has argued, this is an entertainment show. The vast plurality of guests were entertainment figures, and while it's great that *The Daily Show* featured interviews with two former presidents and one current one, at the end of the day Stewart chatted most frequently with those from the Hollywood A-list. This is taking a fairly broad use of the term "A-list" because it includes Snoop Dogg, but you get my point. Second, without exception every guest had something to sell, which was why they were on the show to begin with. The entertainers had movies, TV shows, or albums to hawk. The journalists had their stories or media outlets to push. The authors were selling their books. And the politicos were selling themselves (or, in the case of administration officials, their boss). The combination of these two points results in the somewhat obvious conclusion that a symbiotic relationship exists in booking guests for *The Daily Show* (*TDS*): the show wants an audience and the guests want the audience to buy whatever they're selling. This may be the case for all the shows, but what emerged most profoundly from the guest list of *TDS* was that Stewart's claims that his is just an entertainment show are valid. Additionally, since the interview segments ran under ten minutes in total, there was very little time for Stewart to dig deeply enough to criticize too much. As a result, even the most political interviews were slightly superficial, the fault not of the interviewer but of the format.

This evaluation of *The Daily Show* guest list makes it hard to see an ideological partiality, since so many of the guests were apolitical celebrities. However, a review of the politicos on the guest list sheds a bit more light on this possibility. Jimmy Tingle and the *Huffington Post* are generally correct in their assertion that *TDS* books plenty of Republicans, but most of these guests were out of office. The guests who were incumbent politicians were, in the main, Democrats. The show does attract former Republicans such as Donald Rumsfeld, Condoleezza Rice, and John Yoo, but all of these former politicos also had books to sell. Forget the assessments of *The Daily Show* audience by these former politicos—more likely they assumed that Stewart's audience adored him and (in order to sell more books) decided to play nice with the host. There are clear advantages to an appearance on these shows: access to a young demographic who are politically engaged, combined with the ability to frame yourself in a political light. Win-win. Out of 160 guests in 2010 on *The Daily Show*, only 7 incumbent politicians appeared on the show, and 5 of them were Democrats. This helps to illustrate several things, most significantly the reticence of incumbent politicians to appear on satirical programs, for fear of being mocked. This is a pretty reasonable fear, although Jon Stewart is, as noted by Rumsfeld himself, renowned for his thoughtful interviews. But Stewart's acumen as an interviewer could also pose a threat, and, in today's hyper-mediated atmosphere, one slip up by an incumbent is far too easily turned into an unflattering opposition ad. Going against a professional comedian is a risky proposition, and, for someone currently up for reelection (because all politicians are constantly up for reelection), this might be too daunting a task. So, *TDS* political guests were Democrats in the main, although a five-to-two imbalance does not a sweeping condemnation of bias make.

The Colbert Report

A spin-off of *The Daily Show*, *The Colbert Report* takes a satirical approach to the punditry that is so pervasive in modern political media. Stephen Colbert, who had once been a "correspondent" on *The Daily Show*, started *The Colbert Report* in 2006. His show follows the format of a pundit show, with a wide variety of segments that allow Colbert to pretend to be a bloviating, egomaniacal loudmouth. The show tapes immediately after *TDS* but from a different New York studio, which lets the two hosts maintain separate writing staffs, personas, and formats, but it also allows Stewart to "throw" to Colbert in keeping with the parody of the cable news channels themselves. The shows air on Comedy Central back-to-back in the late night time slot (11 and 11:30 p.m. EST respectively) with Colbert following Stewart's mock newscast. The two shows are conceptually very different, and *Colbert* features many more guests than *The Daily Show*, which only includes one interview per show.

As a result, although *The Colbert Report* taped 161 shows in 2010 (only one more than *The Daily Show*), it featured segments and interviews with 197 guests, 20 percent more than *The Daily*

Show. Because his segments last anywhere from three to ten minutes, Colbert frequently has more than one guest on each program, and occasionally he brings on several at one time to have a more layered discussion about a specific topic. As in *The Daily Show*, these guests were also largely entertainment figures; however, in Colbert's case, this included a large number of athletes because the show taped for two weeks in Canada during the 2010 Winter Olympics. Where *Colbert* deviates from *The Daily Show* is the expansiveness of his guest list. While the author, journalist, entertainer, politico categories were the largest, Colbert also invited a significant number of scientists and academics onto his show to act as experts and foils of his satire.

The Colbert Report Guest List Totals By Category

29 Authors	38 Journalists
57 Entertainers	38 Politicos
15 Scientists	14 Academics
5 Business Leaders	1 Other

Colbert stays in his character throughout the program and acts as a pundit, encouraging his audience to act out or support his various causes. For example, Colbert stepped in to help fund the US men's speed skating team which had lost its sponsorship, and he urged his viewers to donate money for the team. Colbert made the news by testifying on Capitol Hill (in character) about illegal immigration and about campaign finance reform. He created a Colbert Super PAC which raised real money for fake candidates, and thus Colbert has run his satire into the "real world" more so than any other satirist. *The Colbert Report* differs from *The Daily Show* in format but not in purpose: both shows are forms for satirically criticizing the modern broadcast and cable news systems. The format difference means that the two programs are viewed quite differently by their audiences. As host of *The Daily Show*, Jon Stewart does break from character occasionally, laughing at material, which gives cues to his audience to laugh along with him. *The Colbert Report* never breaks from its strict satirical format and as a result does not provide the same kind of instruction for the audience to laugh. As noted by several scholars from Ohio State University: "Colbert's deadpan satire and commitment to character do not provide viewers with the external cues or source recognition that Stewart offers" (LaMarre et al. 2009). This is an academic way of saying that by staying so strictly in character, Colbert (the man) does not give the same kinds of cues to his audience that Stewart does, which instructs the audience to laugh. This means that a *Colbert* audience member who does not understand the material will also not understand that a joke is being made (hence the Ohio State University study on confirmation bias).

Colbert also treats his guests far differently than Stewart does. While Stewart's interview style is more similar to that of a broadcast journalist, asking fair questions and analyzing the answers, Colbert acts (on purpose, remember) more as an O'Reilly-style pundit who is hostile to those with whom he disagrees. And oftentimes, he ramps up the disagreement in order to make a broader satirical point, but because of the aforementioned confirmation bias, some audience members will not see inside this form. The interviews range from terribly funny to deeply, deeply uncomfortable,[i] and throughout Colbert continues to use this satirical form to make a point. Even when he is interviewing a distinctly nonpolitical person whom he admires, he tries to remain in character so as not to breach the form. For example, the real Stephen Colbert is an actor who loves musical theater. He is a big fan of Stephen Sondheim, who was a guest on *The Colbert Report*. This is what Colbert said about the Sondheim interview to NPR's Terry Gross:

> I have to stay in character. Even though I like [Sondheim], I have to try to stay in character, and it was very hard for me because I didn't want to go in attacking Stephen Sondheim or really even be that ignorant about Stephen Sondheim, which is another sort of tactic on the show. I can either sort of be hostile toward my guests, or I can be ignorant of what they know and care about, and it was hard for me to do that with him because I care so much about him and—or his work, that is (Colbert 2011).

Accordingly, to judge Colbert's guest list, one also must take into account his show's persona and the way he holds the interviews. And so he did interview 38 politicos, the majority of whom were Democrats (21), but he also included voices across the ideological

---

[i] See the interview with Henry Kissinger.

spectrum, even loud ones such as Mary Matalin and Laura Ingraham. The fear of incumbent politicians to appear on the show is palpable because of his segment called "Better Know a District" where he interviews representatives from the 435 US congressional districts. When he began his show in 2006, politicians were eager to be segment guests for the free publicity, but they did not realize the satire involved. This led to some of the more awkward interviews in the history of Congress, with Colbert asking wide-flung questions and verbally jousting his guests into odd responses. For example, Colbert interviewed Representative Brad Sherman, a Democratic House member from California:

> *Colbert:* Are people ever shocked when they find out this mild-mannered man represents the largest porn industry in the United States?
> *Sherman:* Sir, I don't know what you're saying. If you're claiming that the San Fernando Valley has a pornography industry, I have no idea where you got that.
> *Colbert:* What was the name of your first pet?
> *Sherman:* My dog, Sandy.
> *Colbert:* And what was the name of the first street you grew up on?
> *Sherman:* Teller.
> *Colbert:* So your porn name is Sandy Teller. My porn name would be Caesar Honey Bee.
> *Sherman:* Why would I want a porn name?
> *Colbert:* Because you wouldn't want to be doing porn as Congressman Sherman (Writers 2006).

In 2006, Representative Lynn Westmoreland (R-GA) cosponsored legislation that would mandate that the Ten Commandments be displayed in Congress. When he appeared on the "Better Know a District" segment, Colbert asked him to list all Ten Commandments, and he could only name three. After that, and after more embarrassing appearances on *Colbert* by other lawmakers, Congress pulled the plug. According to Politico:

> Lawmakers and their aides are repeatedly turning down requests for "The Colbert Report," political advisers are suggesting members avoid Colbert like the plague and the infamous "Better Know a District" segment that put Colbert on the map on Capitol Hill appears to be dying out (Lovley 2010).

Because Colbert's verbal jousting was leveled on representatives from both sides of the aisle, no one has claimed bias against him. Additionally, beyond the "Better Know" guest list, the rest of Colbert's guests are, as in the case on *TDS,* mostly entertainers. While Colbert addresses a wider variety of topics than his Comedy Central counterpart, it appears the most important influence in guest booking is amusement.

Wait, Wait...Don't Tell Me!

Wait, Wait is the NPR quiz show hosted by Peter Sagal, where a panel of professional writers and comedians answer questions about current events. The hour-long show is based in Chicago but travels around the country and is performed live each week. The guest panelists on the show are selectively picked for their ability, as Sagal says, to "juggle through this obstacle course while we shoot bows and arrows at you" (Sagal 2010). The show relies on the improvisational skills of the panelists to respond quickly (and with great wit, of course) to one another and to the show as it unfolds. *Wait, Wait* adheres to a strict program format which involves listeners calling in to play games with Sagal and his panelists; additionally, a single celebrity guest is featured for an interview and trivia game which lasts a total of about ten minutes. Each week a different famous person appears on the show, and unlike *The Daily Show* or *The Colbert Report* guests, these celebrity guests are often residents of the city to which the show has traveled, meaning they are selected in part for their geographic desirability as well as their fame. The celebrity guests play the game called "Not My Job" where, according to the *Wait, Wait* website: "We invite famous people onto the show to see what they really know." The *Wait, Wait* guest list reads less like a hit list of A-list celebs and more like the NPR line-up itself: very diverse, eclectic, and varied along types, ages, and areas of expertise. Reviewing the guest list, one gets the impression that many of the celebrity guests are people Sagal wanted to interview, which is not a bad thing considering Sagal is a terrifically smart and inquisitive guy with (one might guess) a serious interest in music.

The show breaks for vacation four times a year which means that a total of 46 live shows are taped annually. As with *The Daily Show,* the sum of entertainers far outnumbered the authors, journalists, and politicos who were show guests. There were also four scientists or businesspeople who appeared on the program, whom I categorized as "other."

Guest List Totals By Category
3 Authors   4 Journalists
30 Entertainers   5 Politicos   4 Others

The *Wait, Wait* guest list illustrates the entertainment function of the show, just as those for *The Daily Show* and *Colbert* do, but *Wait, Wait*'s entertainment category included more obscure and diverse musicians and actors than the others. When a show includes members of the Village People and football quarterback Kurt Warner as guests, the word "eclectic" comes to mind. Of the five politicos booked on the show, three were Democrats (I am including NYC mayor Michael Bloomberg in this assessment, although he is technically an Independent), one was Megan McCain (daughter of GOP Senator John McCain), and the other was the superintendent of the US Air Force Academy (who has to remain party-neutral). Even with this list, however, one gets the impression that, for instance, Houston mayor Annise Parker was booked because the show traveled to Houston, rather than because of her political leanings. It is incredibly difficult to see any kind of bias (or even consistency) in the *Wait, Wait* guest list, and, because Sagal seems to genuinely excited to interview every guest on the show, there appears to be zero partiality here. The hesitation that celebrity/political guests may have in appearing on the show probably stems not from a bias concern, but from (once more) a reasonable fear of being made to look foolish, either by Sagal and company's quick wit[ii] or by the offbeat trivia questions they ask. Another reason for possible concern could be the demographics of the NPR audience, since it is widely assumed[iii] that NPR has a leftist slant. Nonetheless,

---

[ii] One example involves Austin Goolesby, the former chairman of President Obama's Council of Economic Advisors; he appeared on the show in September 2011. He said to Sagal, "You are aware I've been spending time thinking about the economy for the last three years," and Sagal responded, "Oh really? I wasn't aware" (Goolesby 2011).

[iii] Although never academically proven.

it is hard to see a bias in the *Wait, Wait* guest list, because it is hard to see an agenda of any type in their guest selection at all.

After examining these three programs, it is difficult to find much partisan or ideological bias in the guests lists. Nick DiPaolo's aforementioned contention that Fox News features guests from both sides goes for these programs as well. And while liberals may argue that the left-leaning guests on Fox are not featured as prominently or as fairly as those on the right, the same cannot be said for *TDS*, *Colbert*, or *Wait, Wait*. On *The Daily Show*, Jon Stewart appears to interview the biggest names he can land, and, in a nation with such an emphasis on entertainment, most of his biggest names are those coming from Hollywood. On the *Report*, Stephen Colbert appears to make sure he is cast as the idiot over his guest, and while this may be a mechanism for criticism, it's such a complex criticism that is difficult to conclude as partial. And on *Wait, Wait*, the guest list seems so varied, and almost too assorted to be deliberately biased. The biggest difference between Fox News shows and these programs is that while Fox delivers the news, these shows all mock it. Accordingly, their primary purpose is (once more) entertainment rather than influence. As a result, the people they book as guests on their shows are not meant (or often able) to inform. They amuse.

Content Analysis: Partisanship in the Material?

In order to generally gauge whether there was bias in the content of the satirical material produced by these comedians, I took one specific week with a partisan event and examined the humor content available during this specific time period. Humor most often comes out around a crisis of its own making, and this explains why shocking tragedy is rarely funny but someone's pants falling down to their ankles almost always is. In order to most accurately gauge bias, I looked at a significant (but avoidable) crisis for material. I chose the week of July 26, 2011, because this was the week before an impending budget crisis would potentially force the United States to default on its foreign loan, which would then potentially send the world economy into crisis. This was a crisis of the country's own making, and the two sides fought loudly about whose fault it was. The

Republicans argued that the Democrats had taxed and spent the deficit into stratospheric heights, and the Democrats argued that the Tea Party was obstructionist and economically blind. So a self-constructed catastrophe ensued, riddled with the kind of polarizing talk emblematic of our times. To adequately and fairly recap these events, I turn to the *Washington Post* for its explanation of this situation:

> The debt ceiling is the legal limit on borrowing by the government. Before 1917, Congress had to approve each issuance of debt as it came up. To give the Treasury more flexibility in borrowing, lawmakers established a limit covering nearly all government debt. The ceiling has been raised almost 100 times since then. Under George W. Bush, the national debt soared with the costs of wars in Iraq and Afghanistan, the new tax cuts and higher spending on government programs. The debt has climbed even higher under President Obama, fueled by a massive $814 billion economic stimulus package and the collapse of tax revenues during the recession.
>
> Today, the United States is facing a debt limit of $14.3 trillion. Treasury Secretary Timothy F. Geithner has warned that if the limit is not raised by early July the nation may default on its debt obligations, roiling global financial markets. Republican lawmakers say they need a commitment from the White House for more spending cuts in exchange for voting to raise the limit. The White House has rejected the inclusion of spending caps or other changes to the budget process in legislation, arguing that ensuring the government's solvency is too important to be held hostage to other issues (Cha 2011).

Put simply, this became a showdown between a Democratic president and a Republican-controlled House of Representatives, and the fighting escalated as we drew closer to the August 2 deadline. The mainstream media treated this as an impending disaster, and the face-off dominated the headlines in the weeks prior to the deadline. Both partisan teams were on the attack against one another, and leaders from both sides took to the airwaves to make their cases to the American public. Since this was a very straightforward case of partisan divide, if there was bias in the political humor dealing with this set of events, it would be easy to identify.

The Daily Show titled its coverage "Armadebtdon 2011: The End of the World As We Owe It."[iv] During his Monday night show, the week before the August 2 deadline, Stewart began the discussion: "Our country moved ever closer to self-inflicted economic collapse. Something we have known has been coming for as long as we've been told . . . *it's coming*" (Stewart 2011). This led to a clip-montage of news coverage arguing that the August 2 deadline was predicted, repredicted, and was probably an arbitrary date. Stewart went on to lambast Congress for not avoiding a financial meltdown, arguing that the debt ceiling has been raised more than a hundred times in the past. To illustrate this point, Stewart put up a graphic showing that Congress has raised the debt ceiling 33 times in the past four presidencies. He cemented his criticism of Congress with this: "I'm not saying they're bad at their job . . . I'm just saying that this Congress is equivalent to a skunk with its head in a jar of Skippy peanut butter," and then showed a video clip of a skunk with its head in a peanut butter jar (Stewart 2011). He ended his scathing lament against Congress with this:

> My question to Congress, and I think a question that many Americans may be sharing as of tonight, is this: Do you want out of this relationship so bad but don't have the balls to leave so you all have decided to act like such giant assholes that you force us to break up with you? 'Cause if so, just get the fuck out (Stewart 2011).

His analysis made both sides look ridiculous; he did not single out Republicans for his wrath. On his Tuesday broadcast, one week to the day before the August 2 deadline, Stewart continued the "Armadebtdon 2011" coverage and examined President Obama's previous evening national address. Stewart took shots at the "educator in chief" and mocked his "austerity speech," which was made in a lavish background, arguing that Obama was ineffective and weak. He mocked the process and the Democrats for backing down. Then Stewart turned to the Republicans and called Speaker Boehner, who spoke to the nation after the president, the "world's saddest tangerine."[v] He

---

[iv] A tip of the hat to REM.

[v] Boehner has, at times, appeared to tan orange.

took on Boehner use of clichés and of his stand against the debt ceiling raise. When Boehner made the claim that the stimulus package gave more benefits to "late night comedians" than to the nation, Stewart went on the attack and argued that a current sex scandal involving a Democratic House member was far better fodder for comedians than the stimulus package.[vi] And then he broke for a commercial. The rest of the week's programming did not include further coverage of the political crisis, but two things were clear from Stewart's two-day coverage of the debt ceiling crisis: first, he displayed a fairly low regard for Congress in general. Second, he preferred the Democratic side of the debate. While he certainly went after both sides equally, his criticism against Obama was levied at the president's inability to stand up to the opposition party, while his criticism against the GOP was levied against its policies. In this case, Stewart's comedy originated from a leftist perspective. Although he took aim at both sides, his criticism of the Democrats argued that they were not firm enough in their resolve to do the right things, and that the GOP was in the wrong. More striking, perhaps, was the brief amount of *TDS*'s crisis coverage, which helps illustrate the difference between comedians and journalists. This was big news, but when it ceased to generate comedic material, the program's crisis coverage ceased as well.

Congress' inability to get anything done was a major point in other satire, and many satirists avoided specific finger-pointing in order to stick to it Congress as a whole, as did Will Durst:

> Both parties are now striding histrionically across the stage pronouncing in loud mellifluous tones how determined and proud they are to stick to their core principles while demanding that the other side be the first to compromise. The theory being the other side is more likely to abandon their core principles because, let's be honest, they aren't really core principles at all, so much as they are reelection talking points. And you know what, they're right. Who? Yes (Durst 2011).

[vi] Representative David Wu, a Democrat from California, was accused of unwanted sexual advances toward an 18-year-old woman, shortly after he sent pictures of himself in a tiger costume to his staffers. So, yes. It would have been better fodder for comedians.

Durst sent out another newsletter, called "Gibberish and Manure," which covered the ongoing crisis; it lambasted Congress for its incompetent behavior, and he took shots on both partisan sides for their sheer inability to make progress. Then he took special aim at the Tea Party who was, arguably, the most obstinate faction in the entire crisis:

> Tea Party members have evidenced their ideological purity by not only refusing to consider any bill that features revenue enhancement, but also shunning anyone who has ever been in a room where revenue enhancement might once have been mentioned. Their mantra is cuts, cuts, cuts. Then sell the blood, blood, blood. They claim to be practicing tough love, with emphasis on the adjective and a void near the noun (Durst 2011).

Durst's antipathy toward the Tea Party was clear, but he still blamed the larger Congress for the problems. Frustration at Congress is an overall easy joke to make since the public (even during good times) has such low regard for the institution. Because during this calamity Congress was the *reason* for the crisis, it made sense to cast blame widely. And because most Americans could not explain the debt ceiling, the imminent predicament, or the proposed solutions on either side, blanket condemnation made sense. In his coverage of the debt crisis, satirist Andy Borowitz went more personal with an ad hominem attack against House Republican Leader Eric Cantor:

> In what members of both parties are hailing as an important first step on the road to a deal on raising the debt ceiling, President Obama and House Speaker John Boehner today came to an agreement that Rep. Eric Cantor (R-VA) is a douche. Mr. Obama and Rep. Boehner made the dramatic announcement in the East Room of the White House late Sunday afternoon. "Speaker Boehner and I have come to an agreement that Eric Cantor is a douche," the President said. "We'll see if we can build on that." The breakthrough reportedly came Sunday morning, but both sides spent several hours hammering out the language before agreeing on the word "douche." "Boehner had been pushing hard for 'dickwad,'" said a source familiar with the discussions. "He was concerned that using a like 'douche' could be alienating to his base because it's French" (Borowitz 2011).

This writing demanded that readers know who the House majority leader was, have knowledge of the rift between Cantor and Boehner, and have an inside understanding of the machinations of Washington political life in 2010. As the crisis continued, Borowitz sent another more broadly focused report titled "Debt Ceiling Crisis: Like Y2K With Assholes Instead of Computers," which has an anti-Congress slant instead of a personal one. In another report, titled "China Puts U.S. on Ebay," Borowitz fantasizes the sale of the country, with "government sold separately":

> Showing its impatience with the debt ceiling stalemate in Washington, China today took the extraordinary step of putting the United States of America on eBay. Officials at the online auction site said they believed it was the first time a major Western nation had been listed for sale there "if you don't count Greece" (Borowitz 2011).

Here, Borowtiz used the same kind of reporting used by *The Onion* to make his argument and his joke. This report was free of partisan slant, because wholesale denunciation of Congress can be partisan-free and still stinging. But in his next missive, Borowitz aimed his attention at the right. He went after Fox News in a writing titled "*Fox News* Reports: Obama Starting to Wonder Why He Moved to U.S.—President Nostalgic for Land of Birth, Fox Says":

> According to the Fox News Channel, President Barack Obama is so weary of the debt ceiling stalemate in Congress that he is beginning to wonder why he moved to the United States in the first place. *Fox News* anchor Shepard Smith broke the story today, reporting that "sources close to the President say he's increasingly nostalgic for the land of his birth."
> "To someone like President Obama, this wrangling in Congress must seem very foreign," said Mr. Smith. "In Kenya, debt ceilings are raised automatically by the village elders, who then celebrate with a ceremonial feast of cabbage, mangoes and goat" (Borowitz 2011).

This satire included an attack on the media coverage of the crisis, especially from the right-leaning Fox; Borowitz's position on the situation was clearly left-leaning. Bringing up the patently absurdist idea that Obama is Kenyan made Fox look ridiculous, a contention that is definitively liberal. In his final posting about the debt crisis, titled "Debt Ceiling is Raised Before Tea Party Understands What It Is—GOP Begins Hard Work of Creating Next Crisis," Borowitz went directly after the Tea Party and the Republican Party:

> In an historic eleventh-hour bipartisan accord, the United States' debt ceiling was raised Sunday night before the Tea Party understood what it was. In an effort to gain as many Tea Party votes as possible, the debt ceiling bill was drafted entirely in one-syllable words, congressional aides said. But even as the final agreement was being put to bed, Senate Minority Leader Mitch McConnell (R-KY) urged his Republican colleagues not to rest on their laurels: "Now, let us begin the hard work of creating the next crisis." According to those close to the negotiations, the GOP in Congress were under pressure to get a deal done before the observance of the official Republican holiday, Shark Week (Borowitz 2011).

Like Stewart in his humor of the debt crisis, Borowitz took on the Democratic Party, but only for caving in to the Republicans. In a report titled "Democrats Accept Major Cuts to Their Balls: Outcome Surprises No One," Borowitz makes the familiar argument that the Democratic Party is feeble and pathetic:

> After weeks of wrenching negotiations that went right up to the wire, Democrats in the House and Senate today accepted major cuts to their balls. The cuts, which are expected to pass both houses of Congress on Tuesday, will give Republicans' total custody of the Democrats' cojones through the next election cycle (Borowitz 2011).

Are any of these examples biased? You bet. What started as anti-Congress criticism quickly became an argument about the Democrats being weak, which originates from the stand that they should have won in the first place. It could be argued that these satirists perhaps wanted an even fight, to consist of reassured and vigorous debate in an attempt to attain the best solution. While possible, it is more likely that these humorists found the Democratic weaknesses unpalatable because they wanted the Democrats to win.

The anti-Congress argument continued in *The Onion*, which also threw a criticism of weakness against President Obama similar to the one made by Jon Stewart and Andy Borowitz, but in this case the satire was not condemning Congress but the absurdity of the self-made crisis:

Members of the U.S. Congress reported Wednesday they were continuing to carefully debate the issue of whether or not they should allow the country to descend into a roiling economic meltdown of historically dire proportions. "It is a question that, I think, is worthy of serious consideration: Should we take steps to avoid a crippling, decades-long depression that would lead to disastrous consequences on a worldwide scale? Or should we not do that?" asked House Majority Leader Eric Cantor (R-VA), adding that arguments could be made for both sides, and that the debate over ensuring America's financial solvency versus allowing the nation to default on its debt—which would torpedo stock markets, cause mortgage and interests rates to skyrocket, and decimate the value of the U.S. dollar—is "certainly a conversation worth having." "Obviously, we don't want to rush to consensus on whether it is or isn't a good idea to save the American economy and all our respective livelihoods from certain peril until we've examined this thorny dilemma from every angle. And if we're still discussing this matter on Aug. 2, well, then, so be it." At press time, President Obama said he personally believed the country should not be economically ruined (*The Onion* 2011a).

In this case, *The Onion* writers crafted their piece entirely on the assumption that a credit default would cripple the global economy, an assessment made by most public intellectuals, politicians, and economists but derided by those on the hard right. Specifically, the Tea Party coalition in Congress clearly felt that disaster was not a foregone conclusion, or else they would not have obstructed the vote in the first place. According to author Robert Draper, who had been following the debt crisis negotiation on Capitol Hill, it was not that the Tea Partiers thought there was no problem, but just that they could not trust the Democrats on their predictions of crisis:

A lot of the more conservative members [of Congress], certainly including the freshmen, weren't buying the notion that a default was going to be a grave thing, and they certainly weren't buying the Tim Geithner August the 2nd deadline. And I think that part of what crept into this was a view that if the White House says it, it must be untrue, and if anyone else echoes the White House, then they're essentially, you know, in cahoots with the White House (Draper 2011).

And here is where ideology demands a bit of finesse. Moderate and even conservative Republicans seemed to understand the gravity of the situation, but those on the farthest right mistrusted their ideological counterparts so much they held the outcome of the situation in doubt. So was it biased of *The Onion* to assume global catastrophe when the majority of American politicians (on both partisan sides) agreed this would be the outcome? Tea Partiers will call "bias" but most others will call "fact." This leads to Stephen Colbert's theory of "truthiness": where fact is up for debate. Although Daniel Patrick Moynihan said, "Everyone is entitled to his own opinion, but not to his own facts," we live in a time when people arm themselves against others' purported facts, and allege bias when confronted with their own truthiness.[vii]

As the arguments about the debt ceiling crisis reached a crescendo on op-ed pages of the newspapers, political cartoonists drew their anger at the situation. The first target, again, was Congress. One cartoon showed the US Capitol with the dome held up by a deck of cards. Using the standard donkey and elephant characters as metaphors for the major political parties, other political cartoonists depicted Obama walking delicately through a minefield with an elephant on a pogo stick behind him. Cartoonist Daryl Cagle drew the US Capitol being lifted by thousands of balloons with the word "Up" next to it, to parody the Disney film of the same name. Other cartoonists used drawings of hostage situations to mock the events that were unfolding on Capitol Hill, with Obama either taking a hostage or being one, or the economy being the hostage between the two sides. Tom Toles drew Uncle Sam in his living room with his wife answering the door to an armed House Speaker saying, "Honey! John Boehner is here to take you hostage again!" (Toles 2011). Dan Granlund drew Cantor with a Boehner hand puppet saying, "Yes,

---

[vii] This occurs on both sides of the ideological divide, and liberals are as guilty of their own truthiness as well.

I have a hand in the debt limit talks" (Granlund 2011). Granlund also drew a donkey and an elephant blasting each other with fire hoses while the debt burned behind them (Granlund 2011).

Many of the cartoons took the view that Congress was generally in the wrong, or that the Democrats were being weak or railroaded, but conservative cartoonists took aim at Obama. Michael Ramirez parodied Michelangelo's Sistine Chapel ceiling using the *Creation of Adam* painting to portray Obama, surrounded by Democrats, reaching into Uncle Sam's pocket in order to pick it (Ramirez 2011). Erin Bonsteel drew Obama riding a debt bomb falling through the skies yelling, "No debt-limit here! Yeee-Hoooo!!!!"; it's a parody of the Slim Pickens bomb ride at the end of *Dr. Strangelove* (Bonsteel 2011). Eric Allie drew Obama's mouth on a gigantic man-eating plant about to swallow Uncle Sam (Allie 2011). In these cases, showing Obama to be gleeful about the economic disaster cast the accusation that he was inept in his role as president, that he was to blame for the crisis. Again, the liberal cartoonists originated from the place that the Republicans were in the wrong, and the conservative artists drew from the place that Obama was incompetent (or worse). In the main, they focused on the inefficiency of Congress, but these satirists had the difficult job of using symbols and very little verbiage to make their arguments about the extremely complex situation.

Similarly, the late night humorists were somewhat hamstrung in their jokes, since it can be fairly assumed that the majority of the American could not sufficiently follow the crisis. As a result, most of the jokes centered around the idea that we were out of money:

> "They say that the United States might default on its loans and China might foreclose. We'll have to move into a cheap rental country or something."—Jimmy Kimmel
>
> "The government is less than a week away from not being able to pay its bills. We may have to move in with Canada for a while."—Conan O'Brien

Other jokes took aim at Congress and at the players who were dominating the debate:

> "John Boehner told Republicans to 'get in line.' He was very angry. His face turned from orange to mandarin orange."—Jimmy Kimmel

"Rumor has it that Lindsay Lohan and Paris Hilton are friends again. There you have it. Lindsey Lohan and Paris Hilton are now more mature than President Obama and John Boehner."
—Jimmy Fallon

"A record 46 percent of Americans think Congress is 'corrupt.' The other 64 percent think Congress is 'extremely corrupt.'"—Jay Leno

The humor waged in the course of the debt ceiling debate went beyond television and print to the Internet. A Washington, DC, actor nicknamed "Remy" created a rap song (and accompanying video) called "Raise the Debt Ceiling" that included lyrics such as "Drive all kinds of cars, got all kinds of whips. People ask me how I get 'em, I tell 'em 'stimulus.'" And, "Security surplus . . . guess what? Aw it's gone. I've got my hands on everything like Dominique Strauss Kahn."[viii] The interesting thing about Remy's video was that it was posted by ReasonTV, the Internet and YouTube TV channel of the Libertarian organization of the same name. The video clearly mocked the government's efforts to boost the economy, an argument consistent with Libertarian philosophy. But since the video was called "Raise the Debt Ceiling," the sarcasm of the message might have been lost among the many who saw it. The video got more than three hundred thousand views on YouTube, and garnered almost two thousand comments which is quite a bit for a piece of homegrown comedy about complicated economics.

By the time Congress did vote to raise the debt ceiling, there had been so much discussion about the stalemate in Washington the jokes had gone sour. The majority of the humor surrounding the impasse was levied at the legislative body; the next largest target was the Tea Party, who were widely viewed as the instigators of the entire crisis. Will Durst first took aim at Congress, and then moved to the Tea Party and to Democrats who, in his opinion, caved:

The Tea Party held the government hostage, and the President fell victim to a wicked case of Stockholm Syndrome, bonding with his captors, until at last, he was able to successfully convince the kidnappers to accept more than they originally asked for.

[viii] Former IMF chief accused of sexually assaulting a hotel housekeeper in New York City in 2011.

The administration called the deal a compromise. The same kind of compromise the Titanic arranged with that iceberg. Like how Nagasaki and Hiroshima compromised with Fat Man and Little Boy. Brokered as many concessions as New Orleans got from Katrina. The financial equivalent of handing over Czechoslovakia after extracting a vague promise to possibly leave Poland alone (Durst 2011).

There are several ways to analyze this humor. From a conservative standpoint, the satire went squarely against the Tea Party, who acted as a blockade against a compromise between the president and Congress. Certainly, the humor did take the Tea Party to task for its obstruction in the crisis. This impression was not only dominant on the left, but also on the right. Many conservatives and Republicans looked to the first-term Tea Partiers in the House as the cause (for better or for worse) of the impasse. No less than FreedomWorks, the interest group behind much of the Tea Party action, published this statement once the debt ceiling debate concluded:

The so-called historic debt-ceiling deal passed the Senate 74–26 yesterday and quickly landed on President Obama's desk. He immediately signed the lousy compromise to raise the debt ceiling by $900 billion...The Tea Party drove the debt-ceiling debate. Even though we face a democratic-controlled Senate and White House, the Tea Party was a central player who managed to control the narrative. Even Sen. McConnell (R-Ky.) admits that Congress wouldn't have had such a debt-ceiling debate without the Tea Party (Borowski 2011).

So, even the group behind the Tea Party proudly cops to its obstructionist behavior. Is the humor that alleges this behavior biased? Not exactly, because being obstructionist was the primary tactic of those who opposed raising the ceiling. More problematic was the starting point that most of the comedians came from, which was that the obstruction was incorrect or erroneous. That said, even uncompromising conservatives like Charles Krauthammer found flaws in the Tea Party's political barricade:

I have every sympathy with the conservative counterrevolutionaries. Their containment of the Obama experiment has been remarkable. But reversal—rollback, in Cold War parlance—is simply not achievable until conservatives receive a mandate to govern from the White House. Lincoln is reputed to have said: I hope to have God on my side, but I must have Kentucky. I don't know whether conservatives have God on their side (I keep getting sent to His voice mail), but I do know that they don't have Kentucky—they don't have the Senate, they don't have the White House. And under our constitutional system, you cannot govern from one house alone. Today's resurgent conservatism, with its fidelity to constitutionalism, should be particularly attuned to this constraint, imposed as it is by a system of deliberately separated—and mutually limiting—powers. Given this reality, trying to force the issue—turn a blocking minority into a governing authority—is not just counter-constitutional in spirit but self-destructive in practice (Krauthammer 2011).

The upshot of this Tea Party blockade was victory for the Republicans, who did win the vast majority of what they wanted from their negotiations with President Obama. Speaker Boehner even boasted to CBS newsman Scott Pelley: "When you look at this final agreement that we came to with the White House, I got 98 percent of what I wanted. I'm pretty happy" (2011). So it is not a biased statement to say that the Republicans won or that the Tea Party acted in an impeding manner in order to effect this victory. Is it biased, then, of comedians to mock the left for caving in to the GOP? An alleged 98 percent victory is not exactly indicative of collaborative negotiations, but if the initial thought is that the Democratic view was more virtuous than the Republicans', then some bias may be at play. But all of that said, the comedians *still* made fun of the left for rolling over, and their criticism of the right was not based on policy as much as it was on strategy. If the idea of satire is to mock those in power, then mocking the Tea Party for running the game is perfectly understandable. And, therefore, mocking the Democrats for not doing their part in the power structure is fair game as well. As Will Durst told me in an interview well before the debt ceiling crisis:

> Well, I do pick on both sides. I've got to admit my jabs at the left are for an entirely different reason than my jabs at the right. My jabs at the right is that they are horribly insensible and they are greedy, mean, stupid and angry and my jabs at the left are they are spineless and weak and disorganized (Durst 2010).

Because of the timing of this interview, Durst's criticism of the left was prescient of his future condemnation during the debt ceiling crisis, but it also showed a consistency in his critique since he has panned the left for this kind of behavior in the past.

This brief content analysis helps to prove that the ideological bearings of the satirists may launch the jokes, but in the end these comedians take shots at both sides of the aisle and do not discriminate solely against politicians on the right. Casual viewers of the late night shows or readers of the political cartoons on the op-ed page will find a far more damning condemnation of the governmental institutions in general (i.e., Congress) than they will specific politicians. When specific people are assailed by satire, such as President Obama or Speaker Boehner or Majority Leader Cantor, their wrongdoings are ensnared in the larger problems that are occurring. So is there a bias? Sort of: the origination of the material begins on the left but works its way around to shoot at all sides—a metaphor that can also be used for the Democratic Party. Only they tend to shoot themselves in the process.

Conclusions

After examining the political joke targets on late night television, the guest lists of three different satire broadcast shows, and the ways different satire forms addressed the 2011 debt ceiling crisis, it becomes clear that while there are some partisan biases at play in the satire produced, none are particularly glaring. In the main, satirists and political comedians took shots at the establishment predicated on events that demanded attention. This is consistent with the political humor throughout American history which has sought to bring down institutions and actors a peg while amusing the public. But before we get to the long and rich history of satire in American culture as one possible explanation for this bias, I would like to end this chapter with one observation: even the most ardent satire discussed in this chapter also took aim at the left. There was not one example that congratulated the Democrats at the same time it condemned the Republicans, and in the review of joke targets, every single comedian took shots at both sides. I am certainly not saying that this fact negates the partiality on the part of the writers and artists, but I am saying that this contention of bias must be more nuanced than unswerving. The ability of left-leaning satirists to take aim at their own political side should be recognized as one very important component of political satire. More on that will be discussed in Chapter 4, but first, a walk back through history.

CHAPTER 3

Mirroring the Political Climate: Satire in History

We would like to think today's satire is fresh, ground-breaking, original, and different in the age of *The Daily Show*—but it's not. In fact, there is a history of satire that extends as far back ancient Greece (see Aristophanes) and Rome (see Juvenal).[1] The Age of Enlightenment was a fecund period for satire in Britain (see Pope and Gay[2]), and we look to Jonathan Swift as the hero of historical satire.[3] The success of our modern satire has produced imitations abroad; there is a version of *The Daily Show* that airs in, of all places, Iran. In short, there is a tremendous amount that has been written about the history and expansion of satire. This study is going to stick to American satire, not for any jingoistic reasons but for practical ones. I encourage interested readers to go back and go abroad to get a handle on the amazing satirical precedent that has been set and the remarkable imprint satire is making internationally. To help point readers in the right direction, I footnote often.

The significance of political satire throughout American history is dependent upon two variables: the first is the political climate of the times, and the second concerns the media available to disseminate the satire to a national audience. If the political culture is not amenable for humor, because of national fear, sadness, or ennui, an effort to get laughs will fall on deaf ears, or even be considered socially unacceptable. Think of the post–September 11 declarations that irony was dead. Additionally, there needs to be an effective mechanism to spread the satire to a national audience. Tip O'Neill's proclamation that all politics is local notwithstanding, for large-scale political satire to work, it has to reach a national audience. This means that the increasing development of media technology that moved the media to its current state of ubiquity today has also aided the progression of satire and encouraged its popularity. In other words, in order for an audience to get the joke, they actually have to *get* the joke, which is where the modern media come into play. This happy combination of national/political culture and media technology has meant that satire's potency and popularity has waxed and waned throughout our history. American politics is steeped in a tradition of debate, and from the very inception of American democracy, an emphasis on free expression has driven our ability to criticize elected officials through serious deliberation or through humorous parody. As the American public grows more comfortable with satire and relies on new satirical forms as information sources, satire becomes increasingly important both as an area of research and as a practical influence in modern society. The satire we see today emerged from an impressive history of American political humor stretching back to our founding. The "Join or Die" drawing from the Revolutionary era led to Thomas Nast; Twain led to Mencken; Mauldin to Trudeau. Many forms of satire set the stage for the satirical forms we have today, and without past precedent our modern satire would not exist. By examining the past, we can better understand the present significance of American political satire.

Satirists do add fun to the observation of American politics, but at the same time they also allow us to criticize those in power and highlight the imperfections in our political system, all with the hopes of remedying the problems that plague us. Satire has been, and remains, a way to sharply criticize political leaders, which is a pretty important component of democracy. Satirist Paul Provenza writes that the power of satire is because of its audacity, daring to state the controversial and critical: "[Satirists] are talking about things so many others are afraid to talk about, and they tell you the truth as they see it...Most of them see politics in general as worthy of rage and mockery. I think they stole that from Mark Twain. Who stole it from Jonathan Swift. Who stole is from Aristophanes" (Provenza 2010).

As political scientist Robert Hariman wrote, "Political humor may be necessary to ensure that public discourse is destabilized beyond the prevailing standoff, that competing parties are equally accountable in their race to the bottom, and that a sense of discursive agency is distributed broadly" (Hariman 2008). And so we begin with the Revolutionary period in America and work our way through to the present. Not everything will be covered, but hopefully this retrospective will help show how American political satire has developed, why it grew stronger and weaker throughout time, how it has always been antiestablishmentarian in nature, and why we have the satire we do today.

Revolutionary Period

The lengthy build-up to independence meant that the two sides battling against one another were fighting for quite some time. During the pre–Revolutionary War period, those who were Loyalists to the British throne argued vociferously against rebellion, and the Patriots, who wanted freedom from royal power, argued just as stridently for it. These fights occurred in the public realm, and much of the humor at the time was aimed at either deflating the existing power structure or at delegitimizing the rebels who wanted a new government. As David Francis Taylor writes, "The American Revolution, and the prolonged not-quite-civil, not-quite-imperial military conflict it precipitated, challenged—indeed threatened to collapse—a whole array of cultural and political taxonomies on both sides of the Atlantic" (Taylor 2009). The satire during this time paralleled this challenge. Oftentimes, the arguments played out in the public in pamphlets that conveyed serious messages and in other forms that took a more humorous take. Each argument, be it satirical or solemn, was made with the same level of weightiness and sincerity, for it was the future of the republic that was at stake.

No less than Benjamin Franklin, publisher, diplomat, inventor, statesman, and genius of the American founding, used satire in his writings.[4] One such example was from the *Pennsylvania Gazette*, which Franklin himself published. In the piece called

"On Sending Felons to America," Franklin criticized the British authorities for the practice:

> We may all remember the Time when our Mother Country, as a Mark of her parental Tenderness, emptied her Jails into out Habitations, "*for the* BETTER *Peopleling*," as she express'd it, "*of the Colonies.*" It is certain that not due Returns have yet been made for these valuable Consignments. We are therefore much in her Debt on that Account; and, as she is of late clamorous for the Payment of all we owe her, and some of our Debts are of a kind not so easily discharg'd, I am for doing however what is in our Power. It will show our good-will as to the rest. The Felons she planted among us have produc'd such an amazing Increase, that we are now enabled to make ample Remittance in the same Commodity (Bakalar 1997).

Using humor to criticize the crown added one more weapon to the fight for independence, and it brought a bit of well-needed levity at a difficult time. Franklin's was classic satire, as defined by *SNL*'s Alex Baze, which is when an author takes on the position of those with whom he disagrees in order to make a point. By co-opting the role of the British throne, Franklin illustrated its weaknesses.

Historian Alison Olsen has broken the American Revolutionary era into two time periods in order to characterize the political humor used then: "In the first phase, 1765 to 1773, the production of humor grew very slowly, what did appear was usually strikingly unfunny, and it could have had very little effect on deferential attitudes at all" (Olsen 2005). Olsen explains that during this first period, the colonists opposed the British oppression that threatened them, but "not enough to go to war" over it. The problem for satirists was that most of the objectionable oppression came from abroad, and the local targets of satire were few in number. Those who were available (meaning accessible to the public) for ridicule were not a major source of humor (Olsen 2005). This changed after 1773 when the British Tea Act triggered the Boston Tea Party, the First Continental Congress was followed by the second, and the Declaration of Independence was signed. The split between the Loyalists and Patriots manifested itself in a sharply divided press—perhaps the first partisan press structure in American history—where Loyalist writers were excluded from Patriot newspapers. According to Olden, "In any year between 1774 and 1783, between twenty-five and forty-two papers circulated in the colonies, only five to eight of which were Loyalist" (Olsen 2005). Even though the Loyalists were significantly outnumbered, they still managed to make an impact with the undecided public through humor. Loyalists attacked the Patriots as unsophisticated and unskilled in the area of politics, while the Patriots attacked the Loyalists as "Anglified dandies and fops" (Olsen 2005). Within these characterizations came the overarching argument that the opposing side was ill-suited for leadership, their followers deluded in their adherence to the power structure. While there were fewer newspaper outlets for Loyalist humor, the targets for the humor were local persons, who easily accessible. The Patriots' primary targets were far away across the pond. Though smaller in number, the Loyalist satirists were considerable in impression.

There was a wide variety of humor forms used during the later Revolutionary period, making it a time rich in political satire. Pamphlets, plays, songs, poems, and newspaper articles all contributed to the satirical landscape at this time. The Revolutionary mood led to a strong emphasis on expression, and satire flourished within this atmosphere. Because the time period was so heavy with debate and argument, political writers were amenable to new outlets for their craft: "Like all markets, this one relied on both its consumers—an informed readership now aware of what government was up to and how it ran—and its producers: political writers seeking a public forum for their views on government controversies" (Olsen 2001). Pamphlets were an important component of political communication of the time, expressing opinion through a form easy to disseminate and quickly spread. One such pamphlet, titled *Monster of Monsters*, was written in 1754 in opposition to an alcohol excise tax. This was one of the first examples of satire and the pamphlet set the stage for more political humor thanks to its popularity and consequential fame (Olsen 2001). Prior to this time period, satire had not been particularly popular or lucrative in the colonies, but it flourished as the immensity of the conflict grew and the debate became ubiquitous—and the forms of satire were varied.

Taylor writes of "antigovernment pamphlets in dramatic form" that were never performed, but were instead published and disseminated among the colonists (Taylor 2009). There were songs published by the Patriots and the Loyalists in their efforts to sway public opinion, and satirical poems, such as "The Battle of the Kegs" by Francis Hopkinson, which spoke of the British mistakenly shooting beer kegs floating down the Delaware River (Ridge 2003). All of these satirical forms combined to create the very beginning of American political satire, the use of humor engaged in an effort to sway public opinion, demonstrate perceived wrongs, and criticize the power structure that so many were fighting against. Satirists during this period honed their craft with the understanding that there would be consequences if caught—most notably the retribution of the crown and the Loyalist powers that tried to control the movement toward independence. There were legal threats to Revolutionary satirists as well, since they could have been taken to court with libel charges against them. The eighteenth-century court definition of libel read as follows: "Defamation, tending to expose another to public hatred, contempt or ridicule" (Olsen 2001). This resulted in a satirist having to disguise the object of his attention so he could avoid legal entanglements, but not so much that the audience would not see who the intended target really was.

Since the fight during the Revolutionary era centered around the power of the British monarchy and the debates raged about freedom, the satirical attention was squarely on the power hierarchy that existed at the time. This varied between the powers in Great Britain or the powers of the Patriots fighting for independence. As Hariman writes, "Premodern laughter is all about maintaining and subverting hierarchy, as hierarchy is the most important social fact of premodern societies" (Hariman 2008). This is academic speak for the idea of critiquing the existing power structure, not in any amorphous way but very concretely. Since the fight for independence was predicated on the subversion of hierarchical power, this meant that the satire during this period was doubly formidable. And since the political environment was abounding with debate, satire was welcomed and accepted as a legitimate and entertaining form of political expression.

One can envision how the Patriot-originated satire was received by those who wanted to fight against Britain for independence—as a refreshing take on their difficult deliberations—and also how the Loyalist-originated satire was greeted by those who were resistant to revolution—as a funny reprimand against their rebellious neighbors. Drenched in debate, the Revolutionary era was fertile ground for all sorts of argument, and thus American satire (along with the nation) was born.

The Jacksonian Era & the Gilded Age

Political cartoons made a halting start at the outset of the Revolutionary War, and it was Benjamin Franklin's conception of "Join or Die" that brought the colonists their first political cartoon. The woodcut drawing accompanied Franklin's editorial in the *Pennsylvania Gazette* which "bemoan[ed] a lack of unity among the colonies on the question and warning of Iroquois attacks within the context of looming hostilities between England and France" (Dewey 2007). This cartoon was refashioned later on to fit the argument in favor of going to war against Britain. Cartoons were not the primary source of satire during this time period, although the first political cartoon depiction of a president came with the very first president's inauguration. While George Washington had wide support, he still had detractors:

> All the world here are busy in collecting flowers and sweets of every kind to amuse and delight the President...Yet in the midst of this admiration there are skeptics who doubt its prosperity, and wits who amuse themselves at its extravagance...A caricature has already appeared, called "The Entry," full of very disloyal and profane allusions" (Dewey 2007).

One important reason for the scarcity of political cartoons was the difficulty in producing them, since publication of these cartoons during the earliest days of the republic mandated wood carvings or copper engraving. Thus, when lithography was presented in the United States during the early part of the nineteenth century, the number of political cartoons increased dramatically, and so did their popularity. As lithography caught on later in the century, the very nature of cartooning changed as well.

According to historian Donald Dewey, the *United States Telegraph* was the first newspaper to regularly include political cartoons and specifically did so for electoral purposes. The paper opposed Andrew Jackson, and so in 1832 used illustrations to complement the editorials against Jackson. Further anti-Jackson sentiment was seen in other forms of satire, to include fictional stories that mocked "Old Hickory." Alan Miller writes of Seba Smith's literary creation: the fictional "Jack Downing" character who appeared as an unkempt supporter of Jackson in the *Portland (Maine) Daily Courier* (A. R. Miller 1970). Smith's Major Jack Downing character became such a popular fictional foil in American culture that it was used to symbolize Jackson's inadequacies and the feeblemindedness of his supporters, and cartoonists began to draw the fictional Major Jack in their pictorial critiques of Jackson. Even after Jackson left office, Major Jack continued to be portrayed in the papers as a national symbol opposing Jacksonian politics: "If not the very first, the relentless attacks by cartoonists on Jackson and his administration were an important early example of how northeastern media centers conditioned impressions of what vox populi was saying across the country" (Dewey 2007). Here, satire criticized the politician and his supporters, and spread across to differing media forms.

The most lasting legacy of the Jacksonian era cartooning was the creation of the donkey as the symbol of the Democratic Party. While cartoonists first used the "Jackass" symbol against Jackson, he turned this on its head, using the donkey for his own campaign purposes to show his "mule-like dedication and stubbornness in fighting for his policies" (Dewey 2007). This may have been one of the first (and most effective) cases of political spin control. However, after Jackson left office and continued to wield power within his party, cartoonists used the donkey (jackass) as the symbol for the Democratic Party instead of as the symbol for Jackson, and it remains so to this day. Yet again, the sources and nature of debate reflected the political mood of the time. The Jacksonian era, while vital in the creation of party politics and other significant advancements in American political development, was not one that lent itself toward satire and Sullivan notes that during this time, much of the satire fell flat. The temper of the nation was not amenable to snark or wit, the debate reflecting, perhaps, how the citizens were beginning to identify themselves as Americans. The political cartoons that blossomed once lithography took root sparked an interest in this form, but it still took some getting used to. Writes Sullivan:

> Indeed the literal interpretation placed on the most famous of the satirical pieces employed in the 1828 campaign...typified the Jacksonian attitude toward this form of argument. Their refusal or inability to deal with such works of "imagination" led one anti-Jacksonian to ask if one must write out "this is irony" in capitals before the Tennessean's friends could comprehend such an attack. (Sullivan 1973).

Certainly, the lack of appreciation of satirical forms of criticism speaks to the time period, and to Jackson's supporters themselves: "Those who placed a premium on the people's ability to discover the truth had little regard for sophisticated argumentative forms. The man of action, not the man of words or of the brush, was most admirable in their world view" (Sullivan 1973). Thus during this time period, satire was not as rich in content or as popular as it once had been, or as it would be again. The example of Major Jack is the exception within the Jacksonian era, one that showed the possibilities of satire in a time lacking much humorous social and political criticism.[5]

If satire was finding its footing during the early part of the nineteenth century, it gained tremendous traction toward the end of the century when the strength of political humor and the force of political cartoons inspired entire magazines that were dedicated to political and social satire. America at this time had become a nation of immigrants, and many of the publications distributed at the time were published in the European languages of the émigrés. Also at this time, the advancement of lithography was continuing to change the way magazines were printed. The combination of these two factors meant that there grew an abundance of magazines available throughout the burgeoning country and so the American-style of satirical magazine resulted from copying established foreign publications. Two of the most prominent satire magazines, *Punch* and *Puck*, each began as European versions of themselves before they became Americanized. *Punch* came from England, *Puck* from Germany, but both had to remake themselves in a distinctly American style before they became the powerhouses that they were.

Originally a German-language magazine, *Puck* failed initially as an English-language publication but then was revived through a herculean effort by its most well-known cartoonist, Joseph Keppler (West 1988). Keppler drew his cartoons first in St. Louis, but then moved to New York City and partnered with Adolph Schwarzmann to relaunch *Puck* in 1877. After a difficult three-year adjustment period, *Puck* began to wield the kind of influence that Stewart and Colbert carry today. The title, *Puck*, comes from the mischievous character in Shakespeare's *A Midsummer Night's Dream*, and the official motto of the journal was from the play: "What fools these mortals be" (Thomas 2004). The magazine strived to make its mortal targets look especially foolish. *Puck*'s cartoon attacks on religion and politics made it a formidable force in American society, and the magazine is credited with publishing cartoons that helped sway elections and make bold stands against corruption. *Puck* emerged within the partisan age of the Jacksonian era and, instead of taking political sides, it fought against the patronage that riddled the American political systems with fraud. Writes Samuel Thomas, "In an age of extreme partisan politics, *Puck* moralistically and boldly proclaimed a nonpartisan crusade for good government and the defense of American constitutional ideals against machine politicians" (Thomas 2004). The magazine had wide influence, and was successful enough to generate competition: artists from *Puck* left the magazine to form their own humor magazine in 1881 called *Judge*. Together, these magazines published political cartoons that aimed to entertain, but to criticize the establishment as well. Wrote one biographer of *Puck* cartoonist Joseph Keppler:

> He saw that the duplicitous and greedy tendencies of those who exercise political and religious leadership must be monitored; [that] the callousness and lack of humanity of those with money and those who seek it must be moderated; and [that] the suffering of the poor and discriminated against must be alleviated (Lamb 2004).

This was the common thread among the cartoonists of the time, and their work is widely viewed as a golden era of print satire and *Puck* in particular fit in extremely well within the reform- driven sentiment of the era. It came at a time when Americans were increasingly angered by the political corruption of the Reconstruction era politics and the scandals that emerged during industrialism. Repeated political disgraces scarred many crooked politicians at the same time they inspired others to fight for reform. Machine party politics led to enormous corruption, and all of this led outraged Americans to demand governmental transformation. The sleazy and fraudulent politicians were ripe for judgment and condemnation, and because of this, political cartoons became a prominent form of humorous—but stinging—disapproval. The culture was not only amenable for such satire, but was hungry for it and satire flourished as a result.

Keppler had many imitators and competitors, but no one was as influential as Thomas Nast. Considered to be "America's first great cartoonist," Nast worked for *Harper's Weekly* during the Civil War and in its aftermath. His cartoons exemplified his Republican political stands: he assailed the Democrats for their racism, he supported voting rights for African Americans, and he supported the Union. Nast was also buoyed by the publication revolution that widely distributed his cartoons. According to Dewey, Nast gave the Republicans enough support to garner significant political attention:

> Both Lincoln and Grant explicitly acknowledged the support they received from Nast's work in Harper's Weekly, the first mass weekly largely sold through subscription on a national level. For Lincoln, the cartoonist was "our best recruiting sergeant" for the drawing he did from the battlefields of the Civil War (Dewey 2007).

Alongside his kudos from party leaders, Nast is also credited with creating the elephant symbol for the Republican Party. Most famous, however, were Nast's cartoons that went after New York City's Tammany Hall boss William Marcy Tweed (Lamb 2004). Tweed was the New York City commissioner of Public Works, and he effectively controlled the city's operations and politics. The corruption under the Tammany Hall gang was fodder for Nast's cartoons, and using animal imagery, combining creativity with searing political commentary, Nast assaulted Tweed for his dishonesty and his graft. Nast's cartoons were so effective,

Tweed is reported to have stated: "Let's stop them damned pictures. I don't care what the people write about me—my constituents can't read; but damn it, they can see pictures!" It is reported that Tweed offered Nast a bribe to stop publishing his cartoon—a bribe that Nast rejected. After Tweed was convicted of fraud, he escaped to Spain where he was found on the lam, identified because of his cartoon imagery courtesy of Thomas Nast. Nast's Tweed cartoons not only lampooned the man, but also the culture of graft within Tammany Hall, and at the same time, they assailed any complicity on the part of the public, the satire inherently demanding far more and better from the politicians.[6]

Even as literacy rates grew in the late nineteenth century, thanks to the advent of the printing press which produced an abundance of reading material, the American public still liked to look at the pictures. Nast's great skill was in his vivid imagery, his ability to convey a great deal of outrage in his cartooning. Wrote Charles Press about Nast's abilities:

> The Nast cartoon is great because of the emotional impact of its presentation. It continuously goes beyond the bounds of good taste and conventional manners. Nast is like the man who rings your bell and, when you open the door, guns in shouting insults at you and throwing rocks and mud at you and your wife and on your front hall walls. Your reaction is that what excites him must be a grievous wrong you somehow unwittingly committed (Fisher 1996).

Because of Nast's immense popularity and ability to incite a reaction, political cartooning became more popular and American newspapers around the country began to hire cartoonists of their own (Lamb 2001).

Political cartoons helped to influence the presidential election of 1884, when *Puck* published a series of cartoons called "The Tattooed Man" which opposed Republican politician James Blaine. Blaine was well-known for his fights against the Democrats, Grover Cleveland especially. The *New York World* published "The Royal Feast of Belshzzar Blaine and the Money Kings," which opposed the candidate and emphasized his corruption (Lamb 2004). The pro-Cleveland *Puck* published the first "Tattooed Man" cartoon in April and after its success, went on to publish 21 more cartoons that depicted Blaine with tattoos of his offenses spread all over his body. These cartoons are credited with swinging the very narrow election to Cleveland, and this influence helped secure political cartoons as a significant force in satire and American politics (Thomas 1986).

While political cartoons were a powerful form during the Gilded Age, so too were satirical novels, and during this period the work of Mark Twain and Henry Adams served to truly embody political and social satire. Their novels poked fun at the political establishments of the time, but they also shed light on the imperfections of man, of the depravity of individuals, and of society's misfortunes. Both Twain and Adams sat in judgment of others, but used humor as a way to soften the blow. In the case of both authors, their devil was in their details; both used language to explain and prove a point; both used description to make an argument.[7] This is evident in explicitly political Twain writings, such as "Banquet for a Senator," and the less obviously political writings, such as *The Adventures of Tom Sawyer* and *Huckleberry Finn*. Twain's obvious concern for social justice was found directly in his writings and indirectly through his use of satire to make a larger argument about the political system through which the country navigated. In one antiwar writing, "The War Prayer," Twain penned a fictional prayer to God for soldiers about to enter battle:

O Lord our Father, our young patriots, idols of our hearts, go forth to battle—be Thou near them! With them—in spirit—we also go forth from the sweet peace of our beloved firesides to smite the foe. O Lord our God, help us to tear their soldiers to bloody shreds with our shells; help us to cover their smiling fields with the pale forms of their patriot dead; help us to drown the thunder of the guns with the shrieks of their wounded, writhing in pain; help us to lay waste their humble homes with a hurricane of fire; help us to wring the hearts of their unoffending widows with unavailing grief; help us to turn them out roofless with little children to wander unfriended the wastes of their desolated land in rags and hunger and thirst, sports of the sun flames of summer and the icy winds of winter, broken in spirit, worn with travail, imploring Thee for the refuge of the grave and denied it—for our sakes who adore Thee, Lord, blast their hopes, blight their lives, protract their bitter pilgrimage, make heavy their steps, water their way with their tears, stain the white snow with the blood of their wounded feet! We ask it, in the spirit of love, of Him Who is the Source of Love, and Who is the ever-faithful refuge and friend of all that are sore beset and seek His aid with humble and contrite hearts. Amen (Bakalar 1997).

Twain was the most accomplished satirist of his time, and one of the best of all time, but he was not without a peer. Henry Adams, author of *Democracy*, served up one of the most trenchant critiques of political manners ever published about life in Washington. Although it was published after his death, Adams's sardonic take on the political establishment was a cutting form of satire. Recognizing the potential power of the novelist, editor, and writer William Dean Howells exemplified the idea that a writer was not merely an entertainer, but an artist with a higher purpose: "'Something like that of a physician or a priest.' The office of the novelist was closely related to that of a teacher, an instructor who could make men realize their kinship and help make the race 'better and kinder.' The sense of mission is as clear as that set forth in any political document" (Payne 1980).

American political culture was ensnared in the fight between corruption and the counterbalancing reform of the post–Reconstruction Era, and during this time satirical critique was hugely popular and enormously influential. Hariman writes, "To take humor seriously, one has to be prepared to step outside the norms of deliberation, civility, and good taste" (Hariman 2008), and the late-eighteenth century was a time when humor was taken seriously and consumers of political satire stepped far outside the norms of civility. Political humor in this time illustrated for many Americans that the troubled politicians were not only corrupt, but morally flawed as well. The cartoons and books that angrily mocked the shady and dishonest leaders for dereliction of duty and betraying the public trust did so in a way that peeled back the layers of their artifice and exposed their deficiencies for all to see. This brought laughter, obviously, but it also began a cynical approach to examining American politics. Twain once wrote, "The human race is a race of cowards; and I am not only marching in that procession but carrying a banner" (Twain 1940). When before had the nation heard such cynicism? As the twentieth century approached and the norms of American life began to dramatically change, so too did the ways that the public regarded their political leaders. The popularity, strength, and quality of the satire during this time reflected this new and careful regard.

Early Twentieth Century

World War I brought a new type of conflict to the global landscape, and during this time there was very little political humor or satire in the popular culture at all, but this changed after the war and the time between the wars was fertile for entertainment. New technology had emerged and allowed Americans to listen to their radios and go to the movies, which had morphed from silent films to ones with dialogue. Will Rogers, who began as a cowboy and rodeo performer, became a performer with the Ziegfield Follies and then became a film star.[8] He was also a prolific writer who wrote often about American politics, and his critical observations conveyed his annoyances with parties and politics using humor. Maintaining a folksy tone, Rogers established himself as one of the people, and his reflections were immensely popular. One such example of his satirical writing style was an observation of the 1928 Democratic National Convention: "Ah! They was Democrats today, and we was all proud of 'em. They fought, they fit, they sip and adjourned in a dandy wave of dissention. That's the old Democratic spirit! A whole day wasted and nothing done. I tell you, they are back to normal" (Bakalar 1997).

Other writers at the time, fueled by the muckraking journalism that had emerged during the Hearst/Pulitzer newspaper battles (themselves subjects and consumers of political cartooning), began to employ the use of humor in their columns as well. The work of editor and writer Henry Louis (H. L.) Mencken serves as an example of both satire's success and its failure.[9] Although Mencken was predominantly a literary critic, he turned his attention to politics and wrote some famously scathing critiques of American life. His coverage of the Scopes evolution trial, which he named the "monkey" trial, ran in the *Baltimore Sun* in 1925, and with wit, sarcasm, and irony, Mencken reported on developments in the historic case between Clarence Darrow and William Jennings Bryant. In an article titled "Homo Neanderthalensis," Mencken set the stage for the trail ahead:

> Such obscenities as the forthcoming trial of the Tennessee evolutionist, if they serve no other purpose, at least call attention dramatically to the fact that enlightenment, among mankind, is very narrowly dispersed. It is common to assume that human progress affects everyone—that even the dullest man, in these bright days, knows more than any man of, say, the Eighteenth Century, and is far more civilized. This assumption is quite erroneous. The men of the educated minority, no doubt, know more than their predecessors, and of some of them, perhaps, it may be said that they are more civilized—though I should not like to be put to giving names—but the great masses of men, even in this inspired republic, are precisely where the mob was at the dawn of history. They are ignorant, they are dishonest, they are cowardly, they are ignoble. They know little if anything that is worth knowing, and there is not the slightest sign of a natural desire among them to increase their knowledge (Mencken 1925).

Mencken went on to write about anti-Semitism, an essential and yet unpopular topic at the start of the Holocaust, of American Asian relations before the start of World War II, and of the New Deal, which he sharply criticized. Writer Gore Vidal wrote of Mencken, "Like *Puck*, Mencken found most mortals fools," which goes far in explaining his deep cynicism toward both the American public and the political establishment (Vidal 1991). Of the former, he coined the phrase the "booboisie," and of the latter, he wrote, "The best of [politicians] seem to be almost as bad as the worst" (Vidal 1991). Yet while Mencken's satirical critique of American politics (and of the American public) made him widely admired and well-read at the start of the twentieth century, it did not sit well amidst the popularity of FDR's New Deal, and so when his political observations fell flat during FDR's more popular period, he abandoned satire and instead wrote three volumes of memoirs. This proves—again—that satire works best with a receptive audience.

A more prescient obstacle for print satire at this time concerned the competing forces that fought for audience attention. The technological developments that broadened the American entertainment experience also drew attention away from the print media that had once had a lock on the American public. According to historian Donald Dewey:

> The cartoonist working between World War I and World War II was anything but the last word in political satire. One big reason was that he was no longer working in the mass medium with the strongest audience pull. With the establishment of national radio networks and the advent of motion picture "talkies," polemical humor had more popular wells than the written word and the illustrated figure (Dewey 2007).

And thus, with the American audience distracted by other media and unreceptive to establishment-critiquing satire, the immediate run-up to World War II was not a particularly prolific time for satire. Neither was war-time itself.

American humor in times of conflict tends to be a rare thing, and one can imagine that during the run-up to and start of World War II there was little appetite for humorous denigration of American political leaders or American patriotism. Certainly, the political cartoons during World War I were not mocking but rather reinforcing; James Montgomery Flagg used himself as the model for the legendary Uncle Sam "I Want You" poster used first in WWI recruiting (Dewey 2007). A similar lack of humor emerged during World War II, and although important political cartoons were published with great acclaim, most notably from Bill Mauldin, Herb Block, and Theodor Seuss Geisel, they were not what we would define as satirical in nature.[10]

Bill Mauldin won the Pulitzer Prize when he was only 23 years old for his political cartoons about soldiers in World War II, which exemplified (rather than satirized) the courageous life of the troop in war time. Said fellow cartoonist Jules Feiffer about Mauldin's work:

> He showed us how these soldiers really lived, and he showed us truth in the form of a cartoon. It was one of the few times that a cartoonist had found a way of very simply and very directly showing us how people lived exactly at a certain time, and getting through to a mass audience at the same time. He had a remarkable gift (Feiffer 2003).

Mauldin certainly used the cartoon form to make political statements, but it was in support, rather than in critique, of the establishment and of the political powers. Quite the contrary, in showing the gritty life of the soldier, Mauldin was able to make a profound statement about the war that mirrored the public sentiment: that the boys abroad were to be supported, that the war effort was a noble one, and that the politics that put them there—in sharp contrast to the evil of Nazi Germany or the deviousness of the Japanese forces—were to be heralded. Much of the cartooning was aimed at demonizing the enemy, and what is now viewed as racist depictions of Japanese political leaders led the way. Similarly insulting caricatures of Hitler and Mussolini were also the rule and although these criticized an establishment, they certainly did not criticize *our* establishment. Mauldin's work was a break from the cynicism that had begun to take root earlier in the century, and certainly a break from the skepticism and distrust that had persevered during the reform movement and the Progressive Era. Similarly, cartoonist Herb Block (also known as Herblock) earned prominence for his critical cartoon assailing Father Coughlin and Huey Long, and then won acclaim for his searing antifascist cartoons that pictorially denigrated Franco, Mussolini, and Hitler. Herblock won the Pulitzer Prize in 1942 and eventually moved to Washington, DC, working for the *Washington Post* for more than 50 years. His political cartoons reflected his liberal stands on a variety of issues, including "supporting civil rights measures, gun control, campaign finance reform, funding for education and democracy for residents of the District of Columbia" (Katz 2001). Although Herblock's later work, most notably the cartoon of Richard Nixon crawling out of a sewer, was clearly satirical and strived for the humorous in addition to the critical, his work in World War II was not meant to be funny. Reflecting the solemnity of the time, Herblock's WWII cartoons were analytical and judicious, forceful and patriotic. But they weren't meant for laughter. Neither were the cartoons of Theodore Geisel, who preceded his children's illustrations with more serious work. Theodore Geisel (also known as Dr. Seuss) was a noted political cartoonist during the war years, drawing for a liberal newspaper published in New York called *PM*. Dr. Seuss's political cartoons, like Mauldin's and Herblock's, were serious illustrations that served as editorial pieces rather than as jokey artwork. The founder and editor of *PM*, Ralph Ingersoll, sent a memo to the magazine's staff after the outbreak of the war: "That today we begin a new task. That this task is WINNING THE WAR" (Minear 1999, emphasis in the original). This memo had to include the understanding of a seriousness of purpose, a dedication to patriotism in a time of conflict.

Both Mauldin and Herblock served in the war, and both were trendsetters in the field of political cartoons. According to Chris Lamb, the important cartoonists inspired imitation from others in the field: "Beginning with Nast, the profession has always had its leaders and its followers. In post–World War II America, several cartoonists drew as Bill Mauldin or Herblock did" (Lamb 2004). This imitation, therefore, had an additional influence on the cartooning of the time, emphasizing patriotism over criticism, and satire did not emerge as a force of humor until after the war's end. The mood of postwar America changed dramatically from the years in conflict, and although there were serious matters at hand with the Cold War and the anticommunist movement, there was the possibility of levity among the significant. This brought on an onslaught of humor that gained traction as the twentieth century progressed, working well within the social mood of the counterculture and antiestablishmentarianism that prospered during this time as well.

Modernity and Humor

As Hariman writes, modern society differs from its premodern ancestor in its rejection of identity and norms. While premodern satire took aim at the established order, modern satire took a different focus: "Modern public culture has to be defined against kinship, clan, or ethnic identity or other hierarchical structures. Laughter in those structures is used to enforce domination, resist and endure it, and negotiate its gaps and slippages" (Hariman 2008). Historian Arthur Schlesinger stated in 1965 that the 1950s was "the most humorless period American history," and historian Arthur Dudden writes, "By the early1950s political humor walled dead in the water, becalmed like a vessel without a breeze" (Dudden 1985). Dudden goes on to quote the writer Malcom Muggeridge:

> The enemy of humor is fear. Fear requires conformism. It draws people together into a herd, whereas laughter separated them as individuals. When people are fearful, they want everyone to be the same, to accept the same values, say the same things, nourish the same hopes, to wear the same clothes, look at the same television, and ride the same motorcars. In a conformist society there is no place for the jester. He strikes a discordant tone, and therefore must be put down (Dudden 1985).

This fear was rooted in the atomic age, in the anticommunist era, and in the readjustment period following the end of the war, and this fear was certainly palpable. This time also saw the birth of modern American consumer culture, something that progressed to be a subject of satire and a very clear presence in American life.

> Unique socioeconomic factors—governmental preparedness, sharp increases in marriages, households, purchasing power, and savings, along with the eruption of general advertising volume and its influence upon the magazine format—testify to the fertile bed of commercial potential evident during the post-World War II period. That any such changes occurred at or around the end of World War II is no coincidence. In addition to being a time of weaning the economy and the nation away from rationing and state control over commercial output, this was also an opportunity to "win the peace" through the reconversion of the adult population back to the ideals of commodity fetishism. The postwar period also proved to be a propitious time for the induction, conversation, and baptism of the only undeveloped consumer class remaining in the capitalist church. These last obstructionists to a national unanimity of consumer consciousness were the children of America—heirs to the then-nascent mass consumer culture (Viser 2001).

To summarize, then, the time period immediately following World War II was not one that would be particularly fertile for comedy. Humor and satire were not present as the nation recovered from a war that had lasted more than five years, with more than four hundred thousand Americans killed in action and more than two million wounded. And thus, it was amidst a distinctly unfunny time that satire began to bud, although it was less prevalent, covert in its nature, and found in more remote places. The comic book began in the prewar era but, according to scholar Nathan Abrams, during the last years of World War II and the years immediately following the war it took flight, to the point that by 1947 comic books were selling at a rate of more than 60 million per month (Abrams 2003). The idea of comic books in postwar America was a controversial one, probably because of their immense popularity. Since many of the comic books included graphic depictions of sex and violence, opponents argued that they were a pernicious influence for the American youth. Their immense popularity posed a cultural problem, and in a 1949 article in *Commentary* magazine, Norbert Muhlen wrote, "Comic books prime American youth for totalitarianism." This antipathy toward the medium should have dissuaded magazines from launching, but in 1952, *MAD* appeared on the landscape as a four-color comic book even though, Abrams writes, "*MAD* Magazine was born in an anti-comic era" (Abrams 2003). Two years after its creation, a review body called the Comic Code Authority (CCA) was established calling for comic book decency standards; the following year *MAD* progressed to magazine format. Said *MAD* editor Harvey Kurtzman about this transition, "Could we live under the censorship of the Comics Code? We decided absolutely *no*. We could not go on as a comic book" (Abrams 2003). But *MAD* continued as a publication and grew exponentially as a print force. One scholar argued that *MAD* was so influential that it "revolutionized the field of comic-book satire" (Abrams 2003). This satire was politically poignant, something the magazine's leadership tried to eschew. *MAD*'s postwar publisher, William Gaines, consistently rejected the claims of his magazine's politicization stating, "We reject the insinuation that anything we print is moral, theological, nutritious, or good for you in any way, shape or form. We live in the midst of a corrupt society and intend to keep making the best of it" (Matthews 2007). And yet, according to scholars who examined the magazine and its impact on American life, *MAD*'s satire was indeed nutritional, using "the comic magazine medium to challenge totalizing rhetoric within the American cultural, intellectual, and political establishment, and to call for readerly autonomy" (Matthews 2007). Building upon the success of the political cartoonists who came before it, *MAD* used comic book form to challenge authority. While it featured mostly social commentary, the magazine did turn political, and in the 1950s it took aim at Senator Joseph McCarthy's red baiting. Political satirists (notably cartoonists) had to be careful during the early anticommunist years, for fear of being sent up on charges of un-Americanism and of being blacklisted. But *MAD* punched at the anticommunist paranoia that was sweeping the nation, and it railed against the injustice of the Red Scares. Stephen Kercher has written an exhaustive exploration of liberal satire in postwar America and writes that *MAD*:

> struck at the commercial practices, social conventions, and cultural institutions that underwrote postwar consensus ideology and the Great American Way. At its best, *MAD,* particularly in its earlier incarnation, invited a spirit of skepticism toward institutions . . . and dramatically broadened the range of subjects open to satiric scrutiny (Kercher 2006).

MAD struck at the heart of a burgeoning satirical movement as Americans increasingly turned away from a constructed dichotomy of "right and wrong."

> [*MAD*] pried open a cultural territory which became available for radical transmutation . . . *MAD* certainly pre-empted or paved the way for the satires of the 1960s that are usually credited with helping to understand the conformity of the Eisenhower years (Abrams 2003).

It also turned an entire generation on to satire and comedy. The baby boomers were young when *MAD* reached popularity, and as a result they were exposed to antiestablishmentarianism in a very new way:

> Mad liberated a generation by ripping every institution, organization, and idea that out parents, teachers, priests and rabbis held out to us as deserving of our respect and obedience. School, and any other form of government, the military, organized religion, life in the suburbs, the rich, the middle class, the poor, all of it was fodder for satire and parody (Noonan 2007).

MAD may have paved the way, but it was certainly not alone in this new era of humorous criticism, as editorial cartoons made a similarly significant impact with their analysis and commentary. Herblock and his fellow cartoonist Walt Kelly used their drawings to make sharp political criticism. According to Bill Maudlin, their job was to

> peel back the veneer of hypocrisy and deception, stick pins in pompous windbags, puncture inflated egos, comfort the afflicted and afflict the comfortable, in a word, carry on the fight of the "little guy" against greedy and vested interests, bigots and fakers, potential Caesars and misguided do-gooders (Kercher 2006).

Editorial cartoonists had set a patriotic precedent during World War II, penning nationalistic depictions of our troops abroad and xenophobic illustrations of our enemies in wartime. After the war had ended, cartoonists turned their attention to such topics as the Cold War, the Eisenhower presidency, and the foreign policy stands of the United States. Herblock, Mauldin, and Kelly all espoused liberal philosophies, and Kelly in particular was vocal about the cartoonists' role in spreading their ideology. Walt Kelly himself said that humorists

> must be relentless and ruthless... quick of mind, light of hand, and fleet of foot... [The] satirist or humorist—as opposed to a jokester—is a liberal, against all the redundancies and stupid conservatism of the big landowners. To be a real humorist you must have skirted the edges of poverty. You must be able to look at the entrenched and say we don't like these guys (Kercher 2006).

Thus begins the idea that satire is, at its most basic form, antiestablishment and thus liberal.

Satire in postwar America took several different forms and most of these forms were liberal ones steeped in antiestablishmentarianism. On the stage, political comedy from satirists such as Mort Sahl prospered; his edgy comedic commentary thrust him onto the national stage. Sahl began in California as a stand-up, but thanks to his popular articles in *Playboy* magazine, he garnered a national audience. He broke all the older conventions of stand-up comedy with an irreverence and informality that challenged conservative social norms:

> Indeed, the loose, jazz-inflected performing style Sahl began to develop on the hungry i's stage in 1954 represented as big a departure from the conventions of modern stand-up performance as did the Compass's break with mainstream commercial theater (Kercher 2006).

Using current events as the foundation for his comedy, Sahl spoke about the world around him in a way that was funny, irreverent, and boundaries-pushing, and in this manner he "revolutionized the comedic form":

> He wasn't interested in cute observations about airline meals, mothers-in-law, or family pets. What he was interested in—passionately—was the world at large, political events, the currents of state dressed in casual slacks and a V-neck sweater, he'd take a newspaper up on stage and use various stories to riff off the absurdities and criminal incompetence of our elites...Sahl didn't tell jokes so much as he offered a form of lacerative comic analysis (Posner 2007).

By calling himself a radical, he entered American culture as a humorous antidote to the conservative culture of the 1950s, and in doing so, he led the way for comedians to come. As Woody Allen noted, Sahl was but the "tip of the iceberg" and "underneath were all the other people who came along: Lenny Bruce, Nichols and May, all the *Second City* players" (Kercher 2006). All of these comedians were establishment-bashing liberals, and proud of it. Flying in the face of conservative convention, they took great pride in their rebellion and their criticism of the politicians around them. One of the most mutinous comedians of the time was Lenny Bruce, who not only voiced the rebellion but became the standard of revolt by which other comedians and satirists measured themselves. Wrote British arts critic Kenneth Tynan, "Others josh, snipe, and rib, only Bruce demolishes" (Zoglin 2008). Bruce was a brutal performer, one who liked to push the boundaries of decency and norm as far as possible. According to *Time Magazine* critic Richard Zoglin,[11] "He liberated stand-up from the old rules and gave them an enormous new sandbox to play in. Bruce made fun of old show biz and lashed out at Hollywood phonies... Bruce uttered forbidden words and dared the audience to walk out" (Zoglin 2008). In doing so, he opened the door for those who followed to push the boundaries even further. Bruce was arrested for indecency after using words on stage that had not been spoken on stage before, and spoke about topics once deemed taboo. Bruce addressed race in some of his most scathing satirical material, intermingling the issue of civil rights with his most voracious attacks on religion:

> For Bruce, the failure of American Jews and Christians around the country to recognize the rights of African Americans or to urge a more aggressive path toward racial recognition was symptomatic of the glaring contradictions and moral failures plaguing modern-day religion (Kercher 2006).

He spoke during the civil rights movement about the injustice of racial inequality in his routine "How to Relax Your Colored Friends at Parties," which served to open the door for black comics to address race as well. Amidst the 1960s antiwar, social revolution backdrop, satirical arguments became increasingly angry and more popular. Writes Dudden:

> Eventually the civil rights struggles of the 1960s reconstituted political humor's vitality by escalation the intensity of confrontation. Skepticism about segregation's prolonged absurdities bubbled up comically from deep, underlying veins of doubt, disillusionment, pessimism, cynicism and moral indignation, thought not simply from any superficial or temporary indisposition. Laughter began to succeed once again where other weapons were failing (Dudden 1985).

Mirroring the political climate, political comedy began to rebel as society revolted against the conventional norms.

The Protest Era

The progressive arguments of the 1960s civil rights movement were found in humor as comedians of all races used wit to make a far stronger point, but more importantly it led black comedians such as Dick Gregory and Richard Pryor to forge groundbreaking humor. According to one historian at the time who wrote about this subject, this was part of a larger effort by African Americans to define their own culture and their own stands on civil rights. With the Black Power push for ethnocentricity, the comedy of the time also worked to define what it was to be black:

> Because Negroes have become less negative about their heritage even, in fact, to the point of being proud of it, they are able to create their own "public" humor. It is self-conscious, but in a new

way, self-conscious because it is image-creating. Now the group permits a sharing of its humor with the outside group, while continuing to perpetuate and enrich its own private in-group humor. Because of television many Negro comics and humorists have gained a new national audience... Today many of the Negro comics most popular with white audiences use their ethnocentricity as a source of material (Arnez 1968).

One important commonality between the Jewish comedians of the 1950s and the black comedians of the 1960s was their shared experience as outsiders. Truly, this type of antiestablishment satire was an outsider art, one made more powerful by the underdog position of the humorists. As the 1960s turned into the 1970s, comedy and satire about race began to have a therapeutic element to it. Writes Zoglin about Pryor:

> For white America, emerging from an era of racial strife, Pryor's comedy was harsh but healing. The black comics who reached out to white audiences before him tried to foster racial understanding by stressing how much alike we are. Pryor rubbed our noses in the differences—and yet made us feel their universality (Zoglin 2008).

But it took more than a decade to get to the place where this comedy was so universally acceptable, and during these years as the satire sharply criticized the political, social, and cultural upheaval of the times, it was viewed as subversive and daring.

The improvisational cabaret troupe The Second City was established in Chicago in the late 1950s and used skits, songs, and dance numbers to assess the political environment and the players involved. This kind of improvisational comedy was the perfect format for political satire, since the players could freely express their own opinions and play off one another in the same kind of free-form comedy that Sahl and Bruce were making so popular. It was a tough art, since success rested entirely upon the skills of the improvisers doing the work. According to comedian Robert Klein, "For performance, technique, and everything there was nothing like *Second City*. It was a year in the most grueling training ground, in front of audiences, learning the nuances of getting a laugh" (Zoglin 2008). The Second City grew from the minds of several University of Chicago students, including founding member Bernie Sahlins. I spoke with Mr. Sahlins about The Second City in particular and satire in general. He observed that since satire was speaking truth to power, a satirist has to know the power in order to mock it and be ready to criticize.

The Second City attracts young writers and performers today as it did when it was founded in 1959 because, according to Sahlins, the young have a natural rebelliousness that lends itself to satire. When The Second City first began, the remnants of McCarthyism were overshadowing the nation, and Sahlins argued that early political material from the improv troupe was a "reaction formation" to fight the conservatives. He made the distinction that all people in power were fair game, that the primary goal of satire was to speak truth to power and not to make a partisan argument. But inherent in 1950s and early 1960s satire was an ideological argument against the established order, making the satire sharp, angry, and very liberal. As Lenny Bruce was being arrested for indecency at a time when popular culture was shifting toward rebellion, The Second City was pushing the boundaries of political critique. Audiences were ready for such condemnation. What is interesting is that during this time there were tried and true "conservative" entertainment outlets available for those uninterested in satire, and thus those who were drawn to such sharp social analysis were undeniably interested in a liberal viewpoint. TV shows such as *I Love Lucy* and *Gunsmoke* appealed to what Nixon would later call "the silent majority" of Americans, while seedlings of dissent began to grow. The satire that emerged from Lenny Bruce, The Second City, and others during this time began an entertainment movement that mirrored the political culture.

Tom Lehrer, the Harvard-trained mathematician, became one of the most renowned social satirists of this period, using parody in his songs to make pointed political commentary. His songs satirized war, consumer culture, and politics, and in doing so he commented on the public at large. Interviewed by Paul Provenza, Lehrer described the era in which he performed:

> There was, as I call it, a "liberal consensus" back then among everybody I knew and everybody in my audience. On the Left, there was general agreement about what was good and what was bad. Adlai Stevenson would make a better president than

Eisenhower; most everyone agreed on that. One got the impression, as I certainly did, that anybody who would come to my performances would already be on my side (Provenza 2010).

That the audiences were self-selecting liberals should not be surprising, since the line was drawn between the boundaries-pushing left and the establishment-supporting right. No wonder satire is so deeply rooted in liberalism.

The early seedlings of liberal satire began to grow into a larger movement, and two decades after the end of World War II brought a wider variety of political humor. In literature, Kurt Vonnegut and Joseph Heller's absurdist work on the perils of war took hold of the American attention and satirized the war in ways that had not been done previously.[12] Vonnegut wrote a piece on the 1972 Republican National Convention called "In a Manner That Must Shame God Himself":

If I were a visitor from another planet, I would say things like this about the people of the United States in 1972: "These are ferocious creatures who imagine that they are gentle. They have experimented in very recent times with slavery and genocide" . . . I would say: "The two real political parties in America are the *Winners* and the *Losers*. The people do not acknowledge this. They claim membership in two imaginary parties, the *Republicans* and the *Democrats*, instead. Both imaginary parties are bossed by Winner. When Republicans battle Democrats, this much is certain: Winners will win. The Democrats have been the larger party in the past—because their leaders have not been as openly contemptuous of Losers as the Republicans have been. Losers can join imaginary parties. Losers can vote" (Bakalar 1997).

The country was ripe for such criticism, and thanks to the early stand-up comedians and political cartoonists who helped set the precedent of such critique, more voices began to join the satirical cacophony. All of these forms combined to criticize the established norms, the political culture, and the American citizenry as the country moved from staid acquiescence to a more questioning disposition. In short, although the period immediately following World War II saw a scarcity of satire, the years that followed were a fecund period, a time when new media forms were being utilized and the public was more amenable to laughter and to political criticism that stretched beyond the established social boundaries. At this point, satire expanded both its scope and its audience, and as the nation came to accept this type of political criticism, the very nature of political satire grew and matured as the nation worked to redefine itself. During the 1960s culture of America, the differences between groups began to stretch and strain the American public's convention. Satire, the vehicle for separating the existing from the possible, had found the perfect time to reemerge in public culture. Here began a new era in political satire, which emerged at a time when the American public was ready for such commentary, engaging in political criticism itself. Not only was the public amenable to satire, the media helped political humor by expanding dramatically, showcasing satire in innovative ways that felt fresh, groundbreaking, and very relevant to the changing social climate.

One of the developments in postwar America that assisted in the growth of political satire was the expansion of the American media system from print and radio to television. The cultural and political revolutions of the 1960s ran concurrent to the stratospheric rise in popularity of TV. The 1960s was a period of "industrial, social, and cultural upheaval" (Carr 1992), and thus it follows that satirists and comedians would take up the revolutionary charge as well. In Britain, the variety show called *This Was the Week That Was* (TW3) ran in 1962 and 1963, and an Americanized version ran in the states in 1964 and 1965. Writers for the American program included Calvin Trillin, Buck Henry, Tom Lehrer, and Gloria Steinem, and the show aimed to be edgy at a time when edgy was just being tolerated. It ran against two of the most popular shows at the time, *Petticoat Junction* and *Peyton Place*, both of which had a much more conservative sensibility about them. Writers on the show pushed the limits of their satire by submitting material they knew was "too far" by network standards. They did it in spite of the reaction, or because of it: that's what satire was all about. According to historian Stephen Kercher,

> The troubles Lehrer and other TW3 contributors encountered with their material were exacerbated by the institutional conservatism of network television, but they were hardly new to

liberal satirists working in the fifties and sixties. Nearly all liberal satirists at one time or another tested the limits of irreverence (Kercher 2006).

Concomitant with the rise of TV was all that the medium brought, to include network censors, those corporate entities who would watch satirical television programming for controversial content and force suppression and editing before airtime. As a result, some of the most pointed and outraged satire of the time never aired on television, leaving many of the most prominent satirists of the time frustrated, angry, and despondent. When a show was censored by a broadcast network in the days when there were only three channels, it probably felt a good deal stronger than if a cartoon as pulled quietly by a newspaper or a comedian was heckled on stage. This thunderous condemnation of liberal political humor only served to add fuel to the social fires that were growing larger during the 1960s.

Picking up the gauntlet of "edgy" was *The Smothers Brothers Comedy Hour*, which ran on CBS from 1967 to 1969.[13] Guest stars on the *Comedy Hour* were among the most famous from that era's television, music, and film. The brothers' very first show was introduced by Ed Sullivan himself, giving the impression that the Smothers brothers were average, unchallenging performers, whom Sullivan called "typical American kids" (Bianculli 2009). The first episodes remained noncontroversial, but as the show grew in popularity, the brothers were able to push the boundaries set at the time. Tommy Smothers especially was eager for his show to make a strong political statement, and the brothers worked hard to get material past censors and even harder to book guests who would make similarly strong political statements. While others were making such strong statements elsewhere in the media, the Smothers brothers figured out that comedy was an insurgent way of making an argument. Interviewed by Paul Provenza, Tommy Smothers said:

> I saw Jane Fonda on *The Tonight Show* around this time, and she was talking about burning babies in Vietnam and workers' rights . . . and all the things I *agree* with. And I'm going "What's wrong with his?" Epiphany: no *joy*. There was no joy, she had no sense of humor! And I realized I'd been doing that for two years

at that point. And I just realized: to have a message, you can't be deadly serious or they're not gonna hear you; you're just an advocate of a point of view (Provenza 2010).

And so the Smothers brothers used satire and humor to make some very sharp points about the Vietnam War, race relations, and other targets. One segment, called "Smothers Polls," had Dick Smothers asking cast members and program guests about current events. Comedian Pat Paulsen, a regular on the show, announced his satirical presidential candidacy on the program (Bianculli 2009). But with this boundaries-pushing came the inevitable push-back from CBS, and the management began to censor the show. Every component of the program, from the written skits to personal appearances by celebrities, was subject to censorship, either because of the content itself or because the reputation of the guest stars preceded them (Carr 1992). Two such instances occurred around folk singer Pete Seeger, who had been black-listed by network television executives for 17 years. Seeger was first booked in 1967, breaking his 17-year blacklisting, but the booking began the biggest censorship controversy for the show (Bianculli 2009). Fights began between network executives and Tom Smothers, who argued that he had total creative control over the show. The antiwar sentiment that was circulating throughout the country was finding a home on entertainment television—if only barely. By the time Seeger was famously censored for his song "Knee Deep in the Big Muddy" the Smothers brothers' anger toward political figures was palpable:

> *Tom*: Even right here in this country, if there's something we don't like, we have the right as members of this country to stand right up and throw the government right out! March right over and throw them right out!
> *Dick*: Wait a minute, Tommy. You *love* this country.
> *Tom*: I know I love this country. I'm just not too sure about the government (Bianculli 2009).

This distinction was a political necessity of the time because making sure a performer was not seen as anti-American was culturally important in the 1960s, in the time following the Hollywood blacklists and the Red Scares. Antigovernment declarations were more readily accepted during this time. As a result, the Smothers brothers' liberal arguments against the war and the political system (most famously their hard-hitting political allegory called "A Fable for Our Time") were popular with their audience. George Fox in the *Saturday Evening Post* wrote, "The Smothers Brothers are obviously at war...The enemy is that familiar old bugaboo 'the Establishment'—that world of powerful, frozen-minded, aging cynics out to destroy the creative young" (Carr 1992). While this fit in well with a certain demographic, it also was lighting-rod antagonistic toward others. The brothers' insistence to push the CBS censor limits made for exciting and ground-breaking television. They brought Pete Seeger back to the program a year after he first appeared, and he was able to sing "Knee Deep in the Big Muddy" on prime time, appearing in 13.5 million homes. Said Seeger in David Bianculli's book:

> Singing on *The Smothers Brothers* was one of the high points in my long life. I look back on it with pleasure. It was one thing to criticize the establishment when you're just with yourself and a few friends. But to do it on prime time and get away with it- that was an extraordinary achievement. They did it by being extraordinarily honest (Bianculli 2009).

The brothers' extraordinary honesty only carried them so far with the CBS management, which demanded that tapes of the shows be sent to CBS headquarters in advance of the airings in order to judge their adequacy. The brothers acquiesced to the demands for previews, but not without tweaking the management at the same time. Said Fred Silverman, who was a CBS programmer at the time, "It was always kind of a cliffhanger whether the tape would even get there. Those were irritating ploys. And I will say one thing, and this I can say firsthand. The executives in New York got angered. I mean *really* angered" (Bianculli 2009). After a particularly nasty showdown concerning a show that contained a sermonette from comedian David Steinberg, the *Comedy Hour* was cancelled and virtually nothing else took its place as a televised satirical outlet for political anger. *Laugh-In* aired as a comedic replacement, and *The Tonight Show* featured comedians who did political material, but nothing during that time period had the sharp edges of *The Smothers Brothers*

Comedy Hour. It did, however, set the stage for satire to flourish elsewhere and mirror an increasingly cynical view of the government and the political establishment.

During this period, satirists took aim at the Vietnam War, at racial injustice, and at unequal rights for women, and added wit to the discordance of protest voices yelling at the time. Thus, the turmoil of the 1960s was the perfect milieu for angry and strong criticism of the government, which grew into satire as humor was found to be another outlet for discontent. Satire spread to the theater, and several satirical plays were produced during this time including *MacBird!* a play about Lyndon Johnson written by Barbara Garson in 1967, and *An Evening With Richard Nixon* written by Gore Vidal in 1972. *MacBird!* made the satirical argument that LBJ was responsible for the assassination of John Kennedy; it was fervently denounced by the critics as thin, weak, and inappropriate. Writes Stephen Whitfield, "The satiric attacks on Lyndon B. Johnson...were open, unabashed, often sadistic and scatological—and expressed with utter impunity" (Whitfield 1985). The play was also popularly successful for the same reasons, and it recouped its substantial production costs. Theatrical productions had, for obvious reasons, a limited audience. So while satire spread across the medium, the dearth of satire on television was pronounced. This began to change with a change in administration.

The satire opposing LBJ was subdued compared to the next big target: Richard Nixon. Cartoonists have historically let loose their ire for the occupants of the White House, but in Nixon they had an old enemy: he had been around since the 1950s, associating with Joseph McCarthy, serving as vice president to Eisenhower, losing a close 1960 presidential election, and announcing he wouldn't be there to kick around anymore. Additionally, Nixon was physically mockable, all jowls and eyebrows, and his voice was easily imitated. When Nixon returned to the world stage and Herblock drew Nixon campaigning by crawling from a sewer, political cartoonists had already had plenty of experience in drafting the blistering caricature of the president and the public effortlessly recognized the target of their criticism (Whitfield 1985). Cartoonists David Levine and Jules Feiffer also made an art out of depicting Nixon as exaggeratedly evil: "Even if one knew little about Nixon's policies, there would be something scary about Levine's drawings of him" (Whitfield 1985). By the time Nixon had entered his second term and the Watergate scandal was breaking bad around him, he had become to the American people a caricature of himself by virtue of his political cartoon persona. The fact that his true personality buoyed those drawings only added fuel to the fire. Gary Trudeau's *Doonesbury* strip took on the Watergate scandal early in its run, and was a highly effective opinion maker. According to Will Kaufman in the *Journal of American Studies*: "Gerald Ford was to admit the importance of Trudeau's targeting when he observed, 'There are only three major vehicles to keep us informed as to what is going on in Washington: the electronic media, the print media, and *Doonesbury*—not necessarily in that order'" (Kaufman 2007). The Watergate affair was a gold mine for cartoonists, or as cartoonist Patrick Oliphant called it, "bloody good fun":

> There was drama, detective work, skullduggery, secret filed, paranoia and (bless them both for humorous relief), Martha Mitchell and Al Haig. Cartoonists need villains and, in those happy times, there were villains galore. The political cartoon responded to this wonderful circumstance by producing satire of exceptional quality—as Bill Mauldin remarked soon after. 'Even the bad cartoonists were drawing good cartoons.' It is no stretch to claim that the political cartoon had a distinct influence on the termination of the Nixon presidency (Oliphant 2004).

The satire that mocked Nixon was found in literature (Philip Roth, Robert Coover, Kurt Vonnegut), on the stage, in stand-up comedy (David Frye, George Carlin), and on television. The Vidal play titled *An Evening with Richard Nixon* took a strident tone, with George Washington narrating the play which accused Nixon as, essentially, a war criminal (Altschuler 2009). But the political cartoons had the real strength for several important reasons: first, the satirical literature of this time was fairly high-brow stuff, which meant its audience was what we would today consider to be a solid blue-state, metropolitan readership. Philip Roth's *Our Gang* (1971) took aim at "tricky Dick" and Robert Coover's *The Public Burning* (1977) used the execution of Julius and Ethel Rosenberg as a platform for excoriating Nixon, but this was not considered mainstream literature, although it was considered shocking at the time. The plays about Nixon were performed in New York City, Los Angeles, and Chicago, where Judith Wax wrote sharp satire about Nixon and his posse. She wrote that John Erlichman looked like he "ate babies for dessert," and penned a piece for *New York Magazine* called "The Love Song of G. Gordon Liddy." The stand-up comedy performed in clubs or on college campuses by Sahl and his cohorts was equally sharp but inaccessible, which all together means that none of these mediums were easily reached by mainstream America. Additionally, television was still an emerging medium, albeit one that Nixon was well acquainted with. Nixon had both successfully used the medium (his "Checkers" speech in 1952) and disastrously been victim of it (the 1960 presidential debate which launched the joke, "He sweat more than Nixon"). Nixon tried to show his funny bone on *Laugh-In*, but that was not truly satirical—it was barely self-deprecating. TV satire was not pronounced during Nixon's term, and really only came of age after he left office with the introduction of *Saturday Night Live* in 1975. And so political cartoons were the satirical art of choice, and several infamous drawings have lasted throughout the decades. Mike Peters penned a cartoon that showed George Washington saying, "I cannot tell a lie," Richard Nixon saying, "I cannot tell the truth," and Jimmy Carter saying, "I cannot tell the difference."

Early satirical depictions of Nixon were harsh, stemming from the reputation that preceding him combined with his personal characteristics that led to a damaging portrayal, especially in cartoons. Throughout the course of his presidency, Nixon became increasingly disdained by more than just the artistic elites that held him in constant disregard. For the general public, Nixon eventually became a caricature, which meant that the satirists whose work was to caricaturize political figures had an especially ripe target. By the time the Watergate affair exposed the horrendous truths about Nixon, the country was fairly united against him and as a result there was little for satire to rebel against. This, combined with the mood of the country post-Watergate, led to very little new satirical material about Nixon immediately after his downfall. Nixon's fall from grace was dramatic, public, and some fodder for the satirists who had been arguing against the establishment all along. But once Nixon was truly gone, satirists had nowhere to go with him: "Humorists were thrown back onto mundane events and their own devices with no fresh break-ins or cover-ups to inspire them. Political cartoonists, Communists, and comedians reverted to routine comments on the news from day to day" (Dudden 1985). Interestingly, just as satire's strength seemed to crest, it went into a bit of hibernation.

The mood of the country, bruised following Watergate and the end of the Vietnam War, was not initially amenable for satire, but that changed pretty quickly. Nixon proved to be a hard act to follow, the nation was still reeling from the scandal, and it would probably be difficult to be funny about being anti-establishment when the entire country was antiestablishment. President Ford was not a likely target, especially after Richard Nixon: Gerald Ford has been an all-American football star at the University of Michigan, a former House minority leader, and was vice president without ever slugging through a national election.[i] He was on the Warren Commission,[ii] for heaven's sake—not exactly a target-rich satire environment.[iii] And so the satirical criticism against Ford was lacking at first, but Ford wasn't perfect and a few notable physical gaffes left him wide open to mockery. During this time, Garry Trudeau's *Doonesbury* cartoon was tremendously influential, rising to great heights during the Watergate scandal. Trudeau won the Pulitzer Prize for editorial cartooning in 1975. The strip was so influential that politicians read it daily to keep a beat on what was happening inside the Beltway. The post-Watergate years may not have been necessarily the happiest of times in America, but they were fertile ground for the progression of satire. *Saturday Night Live* (*SNL*) was born

---

[i] For those too young to remember, Nixon appointed Ford as his vice president after Spiro Agnew resigned in disgrace. Ford moved up to the Oval Office when Nixon became the first president to resign (also in disgrace). This meant that once Ford ascended to the White House, he had never been elected to national office. Pretty cool, huh?

[ii] The congressional commission that investigated the John F. Kennedy assassination.

[iii] Perhaps a poor choice of words.

during the Ford administration and cast member Chevy Chase embodied the parody of Ford that stuck in the cultural zeitgeist. Chase's Ford impression made the president look utterly incapable—mistaking a water glass for the phone, stapling his forehead, tripping over his desk, thinking his stuffed dog was alive. Was this actual satire? Not by the strictest definition—it was more mockery than argument-making, more parody than anything else. But Chase's fictional Ford was a disaster because it was distributed to millions of viewers every week, thanks to *SNL*, and thanks to this distribution the impression stuck.

Saturday Night Live began broadcasting on NBC in 1975 and brought a mix of mainstream comedy and political humor to the viewing public. *SNL* was the first late night entertainment show to feature an administration official when White House press secretary Ron Nessen appeared on the program. According to Ford's chief of staff, a young, eager upstart named Dick Cheney, Chevy Chase's portrayal of President Ford as a bumbling klutz became the public narrative for the president. Cheney complained about the influence of Chase's Ford: "Once you get to the point at which something becomes a stock gag on Johnny Carson's *Tonight Show* or one of those kinds of TV shows, that label sticks and you can't get rid of it" (Rollins and O'Connor 2005). As the political cartoons turned Nixon into a charicature, so too did emerging late night television do the same to Ford, and it was this ripe television environment that spread the depiction so readily. But rather than angry condemnation, the satirical representation of Ford was laughably slapstick. Even Ford himself didn't seem to mind: he held a "Humor and the Presidency" conference at the Gerald R. Ford Museum in 1986 with remarkable magnanimity. It was one of the first cases where the electronic media showed such power in cementing a political impression. But even if the parody was not intentionally malicious, the Ford narrative was damaging.

The humor aimed at Jimmy Carter was also tame compared to that aimed at Nixon, for two reasons: the ammunition wasn't there and the mood of the country was again not amenable. Probably more quickly than Ford would have liked, the Ford presidency changed to the Carter administration, and Carter's physical characteristics proved to be fodder once again for the political cartoonists, who took aim at his ears and teeth in their depictions—but the Carter satire lacked the anger seen before. Even *SNL*'s treatment of Carter was viewed as gently mocking, instead of angrily attacking. Dan Aykroyd's depiction of what one critic referred to as Carter's "gluey sanctimoniousness" was almost endearing (Rollins and O'Connor 2005). One Carter-themed skit featured a radio call-in program at the White House where Aykroyd as Carter answers caller questions on an absurdly wide variety of topics in what becomes increasingly technical and challenging terms. The skit began with Aykroyd's Carter answering a mechanical question about a mail sorting system used by the US postal service and then moved to the President helping a 17-year-old named Peter who was tripping on acid:

> President Jimmy Carter: Alright, Peter, just listen. Everything is going to be fine. You're very high right now. You will probably be that way for about five more hours. Try taking some vitamin B complex, vitamin C complex . . . if you have a beer, go ahead and drink it.
> Peter (on phone): Okay.
> President Jimmy Carter: Just remember you're a living organism on this planet, and you're very safe. You've just taken a heavy drug. Relax, stay inside and listen to some music, Okay? Do you have any Allman Brothers?
> Peter (on phone): Yes, I do, sir. Everything is okay, huh Jimmy?
> President Jimmy Carter: It sure is, Peter. You know, I'm against drug use myself, but I'm not going to lay that on you right now. Just mellow out the best you can, okay? (*SNL* 1976).

Carter did not engender the kind of animosity that Nixon did, but by the time he was up for reelection in 1980 he was far from beloved—the economy was in the crapper, American hostages were held in Iran, and supporters could, at best, muster a burning indifference for the candidates running for president. Comedian Mort Sahl said that Americans voted against Jimmy Carter instead of for Ronald Reagan: "If Reagan had been unopposed he would have lost" (Nilsen 1990). Both Ford and Carter did not provide the satiric material necessary for outrage, but with the Reagan administration came an entirely different national mood, and at the same time new satiric formats and new media modes began their ascendancy into our political discourse. *SNL* and *SCTV* were on the air, *The Tonight Show* was still bringing stand-up comedy to the masses, The Second City was still delivering satire on the stage in Chicago, and political cartoonists were on op-ed pages of newspapers that were still read by the general public. But the technology was on the verge of a developmental explosion which would change everything. And so onto the scene emerged on old-school satirical format (cabaret), and one very new media technology (cable television). The first format catered to an influential group of political elites and the second catered to everybody.

Mark Russell began to sing his political satire songs during the Nixon administration, but his star rose during the Reagan era when he appeared on national television on a number of different programs. Sitting at a piano, Russell sang somewhat milquetoast political songs about politicians and current events and became a darling of the Beltway elite. You don't ascend to this position unless you lob softball jokes at your targets, and Russell did. But he was popular, and on the heels of his success came another cabaret act, The Capitol Steps, which was founded in 1981. Elaina Newport, one of the founding members of the Steps told me that the group began as Senate staffers performing for holiday parties, and they were continuously booked, although always slightly afraid of getting fired from their day jobs. The reason that they did not get fired? Because the politicians liked that they were the center of the entertainment attention:

> It took many years for us to discover that the politicians were good-natured about it, that was our biggest surprise. The politicians that we worked for didn't seem to mind, in fact, they would invite us to perform and do shows for them. You know, Senator Percy, in particular, invited us to do a lot of shows at his house and for various parties and things. His daughter, Sharon Percy Rockefeller, still comes to the show occasionally. So, nobody told us to stop and we are still doing it almost 28–29 years later (Newport 2010).

Both Russell and the Steps hit upon an important point: politicians enjoyed the attention. They probably didn't much like vicious depictions as incompetent evildoers, but self-deprecating humor can be useful in politics, and as someone once coined the phrase: there is no such thing as bad publicity. The Reagan years (unofficial motto: you can never be too rich or too thin) were fertile ground for humor that specifically targeted elites. The decade that brought Reagan also brought Gordon Gekko[iv] and Leona Helmsley,[v] and the Reagan era policies that favored the rich supported the sentiment that money, power, and greed were all excellent qualities. The satire that mocked Reagan sometimes aimed at this elitism, and in the case of the political cabaret, it did so in front of elite audiences. Ironic, no? The Steps released albums that aimed at Reagan's policies ("We Arm the World"), his napping schedule ("Workin' 9 to 10"), and his political blunders ("Thank God I'm a Contra Boy"). Much of the satire pointed at Reagan's ability to avoid blemish, and to that end, Herblock drew Reagan propping up a huge cardboard version of himself, commenting: "Through all this, Reagan remained popular, and his image was upheld" (LOC n.d.).

But also at this time, new technology burst onto the scene. Cable satellite technology, which was born in the 1970s but matured in the 1980s, expanded the television line-up from 3 channels to 16 and then to 34 (and eventually to 300), and satire was able to grow along with it, thanks to the pay cable channels such as HBO, Cinemax, and Showtime, and the niche programming found on Comedy Central. HBO, very early in its existence, began to run comedy specials that featured stand-up comedians who occasionally dabbled in political satire. In 1986, Cinemax featured a comedy special called "Spitting Image" which featured human-sized puppets imported from Britain. According to a *New York Times* write up of the show, it was described as such:

> An NBC press release gingerly describes "Spitting Image" as irreverent. Actually, the show, created and produced in London, is scathing—outrageously and hilariously scathing...Now, brought to this country by NBC for two half-hour specials, the "Spitting Image" puppets focus their refreshingly unfettered

---

[iv] A fictional elitist character with discriminatory tendencies and an inflated sense of superiority.

[v] An actual elitist character with discriminatory tendencies and an inflated sense of superiority.

satire on a host of American notables, with Ronald and Nancy Reagan at the head of a contingent that includes both Republican and Democratic luminaries, supported by an all-star cast of this year's ensconced celebrities. It's as if the Muppets had gone somewhat grotesque and rather nasty (O'Connor 1986).

The expansion of the television landscape made for a wider breadth of satire available for the American audience. HBO had a corner on the comedy market with its own dedicated programming and MTV had a cable channel called Ha! which competed against one another, until they merged in 1991 as Comedy Central. *The Daily Show* first brought dedicated political satire to the network in 1996, which has since exploded in popularity and reach. Satire and comedy was found across the cable spectrum, and for the first time there was an abundance of political humor outside of *Saturday Night Live*.

All of this occurred just as American politics shifted. As Reagan left office, George Herbert Walker Bush entered, offering a "kinder, gentler nation"; he brought with him the motherload of fodder for satirists of all stripes: vice president J. Danforth Quayle. Before this goes any further, please let me say that I am certain Dan Quayle is an intelligent, kind, and good man. He probably was a decent Senator from the great state of Indiana, and I am sure that in some circles he was considered an able vice president—but you sure wouldn't know this from the coverage he got, and from the political satire that he generated. Forget the fact that he looked incredibly young, and within this youthful appearance he also sometimes looked lost or confused. Forget the fact that in 1988, he ran against Lloyd Bentsen, an older, seasoned, and towering Democratic vice presidential candidate from Texas who, in comparison, would make the most stentorian octogenarian look frivolous. Forget all of that: Dan Quayle was the king of the malapropism. Yes, perhaps George W. Bush could mangle the English language with aplomb, but Dan Quayle was able to take well-known phrases and destroy their syntax, able to take obvious occasions to make the exactly wrong statement, able to make a verbal gaffe heard around the world before the Internet was there to forward it. He was a gift to comedians and satirists, who were thrilled with the possibilities of four years of Quaylisms. There was literally a publication devoted entirely to the verbal blunders of our forty-fourth vice president called *The Quayle Quarterly* which was published on a desktop computer and sent around the country by mail. It had a circulation of twelve thousand. Said publisher Deborah Weksman, "Quayle is the only thing that this administration has done to help the economy. He's spawned an entire cottage industry" (Kadetsky 1992). He was a one-man band of satirical targeting. Don't believe me? Here are but a *few* quotes:

- I am not part of the problem. I am a Republican.
- I have made good judgments in the Past. I have made good judgments in the Future.
- The future will be better tomorrow.
- We have a firm commitment to NATO, we are a *part* of NATO. We have a firm commitment to Europe. We are a *part* of Europe.
- What a waste it is to lose one's mind. Or not to have a mind is being very wasteful. How true that is.
- [It's] time for the human race to enter the solar system.
- One word sums up probably the responsibility of any vice president, and that one word is "to be prepared."
- Illegitimacy is something we should talk about in terms of not having it.
- Mars is essentially in the same orbit...Mars is somewhat the same distance from the Sun, which is very important. We have seen pictures where there are canals, we believe, and water. If there is water, that means there is oxygen. If oxygen, that means we can breathe.
- The Holocaust was an obscene period in our nation's history. I mean in this century's history. But we all lived in this century. I didn't live in this century.
- We're going to have the best educated American people in the world.
- For NASA, space is still a high priority.
- If we do not succeed, then we run the risk of failure.
- I stand by all the misstatements that I've made.

See what I mean? Pure comedy gold. And the best part was that by his own admission Quayle stood by all the misstatements he made. Gary Trudeau drew Quayle as a feather. *SNL* had a child actor play him in one skit. But even as a treasure trove of comedic fodder, Quayle's boss, G.H.W. Bush, was a target as well. Bush (41) suffered from his own verbal faux pas and his devotion to sound bite statements. It didn't help matters that on *Saturday Night Live*, comedian Dana Carvey nailed his impression of Bush and, once again, exaggerated his missteps and ineloquence to parody perfection:

> Tomorrow is Earth Day. Environment, a difficult problem—gotta be prudent! [motions wildly with hands] Now, I'd love to just take care of the Greenhouse Effect in one fell swoop up here. Not gonna sacrifice jobs down here. Nah gah dah! Wanna do something bold about the rainforest here—gotta breathe, everyone's gotta breath! Don't wanna pin Brazil down here—they're a democracy. Don't wanna be at cross-purposes—wanna get together! Not out here, right here! A thousand points of light (*SNL* 1990).

In one skit from the 1988 race against Massachusetts governor Michael Dukakis, Carvey stumbled through a debate statement and was countered by John Lovetz playing Dukakis: "I can't believe I'm losing to this guy." As the 1992 election approached, Carvey was tasked with two presidential candidates, since in addition to the Bush impression he also perfected his send-up of Texas billionaire H. Ross Perot. Up to the *SNL* stage came the Bill Clinton parodies as well, first from Phil Hartman and then from Darrell Hammond, and with Clinton there was an abundance of material at the ready. Since political humor extended beyond *SNL* at this point, it was an especially ripe time for satirists to take aim at the political establishment. Yes, the nation had been at war, but the war was short and the parades were big. A presidential campaign was waging between three caricatures with big personalities and humorous facial features to match. The 1992 presidential campaign was seemingly made for political humorists across media types. According to one book, called *Campaign Comedy*:

> 1992 also offered something special—a billionaire with big ears and a funny haircut who started his own party. There was also the ever-appealing George Bush and his teenage running mate,

providing a reliable target for whimsy or malice. And best of all, there was a Democrat who, unbelievably, showed signs of *winning*. For a long period, Bill Clinton thoughtfully provided voters with a scandal a week involving those perennial favorites: sex, dope, and the draft (Gardner 1994).

Bush's consistent verbal gaffes were fodder, as were Perot's odd syntax and his public statements alleging a Republican conspiracy to ruin his daughter's wedding. Clinton was assaulted by what GOP operatives Mary Matalin and Torie Clarke termed "bimbo eruptions," the recurring proclamation of sexcapades between Clinton and a variety of women-not-his-wife. When asked about past drug use, he claimed to have tried marijuana without inhaling. Although Clinton was a relative unknown prior to his presidential run, his physical characteristics, his home base of Arkansas, his herculean appetite for fast food, and the "bimbo eruptions" were like a welcome mat inviting satirists to poke fun at the man referred to snidely as "Bubba." *SNL* continued its Carvey-led assault on George H. W. Bush, made Perot out to be a leprechaun, and portrayed Clinton as a pot-smoking hippy. Political cartoonists had an easy time drawing Perot's gigantic ears and Clinton's bulbous nose. The three-way presidential race, with such an abundance of material, was comedic gold. Clinton eventually won a plurality and hopped right from the frying pan into the fire. The Capitol Steps discography accurately depicts the progression of Clinton humor: their 1994 album is called "The Joy of Sax"; their following album is titled "Lord of the Fries"; and then they moved on to "Unzippin' my Do-Dah!" Clinton was yet another gift for satirists, but unlike his predecessors Ford and Carter, he came at a time when satire was perfectly acceptable in American culture. Bush (41) and Quayle had primed the pump, and the nation was ready. We were at peace, the economy was emerging from a difficult recession that would bloom into a full-blown economic orgy of spending and good times, and two rock loving, handsome baby boomers were in the White House inviting Aretha Franklin to state dinners. Good times all around—let the humor begin.

Clinton inspired a visceral reaction in most people—you either loved him or you really, really hated him. Many on the right fell into that latter category, and what Hillary Clinton eventually (and rather unfortunately) termed a "vast right-wing conspiracy" was born. Republicans couldn't stand the guy: he was accused of dodging the draft and smoking pot, and he had a smooth (or sly) way about him that eventually engendered the nickname "slick Willie." Said Dennis Miller about Clinton in the early years of his presidency:

> This guy has hung off more cliffs than an Austrian with an inner ear infection. He is the modern day Prometheus, picked apart by the media vultures each day only to become whole again to weather yet another scandal. Maybe we root for him because he is our Rocky, taking punch after punch after punch, round after round, and always calling out for his Adrian. The only difference is, you know this as well as I do, Clinton is also trying to nail all the ring girls (D. Miller 2001).

The first President Clinton skits on *Saturday Night Live* had him jogging into a McDonalds and eating the other patrons' food while explaining foreign policy. Political cartoonists drew him skating through indignity, all bulbous nose and big hair. But as the right's dislike of him grew stronger and the accusations of corruption began to grow in earnest, satirists had more to play with. When both Bill and Hillary Clinton were accused of financial misconduct in regards to a real estate investment, the calls for Clinton's impeachment began. The "Whitewater scandal" occurred after associates of the Clintons broke the law in the land deal, which led to the question of whether the Clintons obstructed justice in the investigations. It was complicated and unwieldy, and most Americans could not explain the questions that surrounded the investigation. But the "slick Willie" moniker made Clinton look like he was weaseling out of something, which led satirists to take aim. Wrote the *Washington Post*'s Tony Kornheiser:

People ask, "Can Clinton survive Whitewater?" Survive it? Can he explain it?

> Wouldn't that be something—if some two-bit land deal brought Clinton down? Here's a guy who has been so coated with Teflon you could fry an egg on his big behind. He survives dodging the draft. He survives that preposterous story about not inhaling the marijuana. He survives repeated allegations about a

sex life that would make Heidi Fleiss blush. He survives the general impression that right before he became president, he was pledge master at Delta House; I mean, if there were a story tomorrow involving Bill Clinton, a vat of lime Jell-O, two orangutans and the June Taylor Dancers, almost everybody in America would:

a. believe it; and
b. not care.
He survives all that—and this might get him? (Kornheiser 1994b).

Satire in the Clinton era tried to make sharp points about leadership, character, and morality but it was generally harmless stuff because it almost always resorted to sex jokes. Again, this was perhaps not the best example of satire, but more along the lines of humor or parody. It was accessible to almost everyone: liberals could get on board with it because generally Clinton attacks did not criticize his polices, conservatives liked it because it struck Clinton at his furtive and ostensibly untrustworthy core, and everyone got a big chuckle out of the Southerner who was way smarter than we were but who also made some colossal mistakes. He was such a target for criticism and humor that at the 1996 Radio/TV Correspondents Dinner, radio shock jock Don Imus referred to the president's hound dog behavior in front of both Clintons:

When Cal Ripkin broke Lou Gherig's consecutive game record, the President was at Camden Yards doin' play by play in the radio with John Miller. Bobby Bonilla hit a double, we all heard the President in his obvious excitement holler "Go Baby!" I remember commenting at the time, I bet that's not the first time he's said that. [Turns to President] Remember the Astroturf in the pickup? And my point is, there is an innocent event, made sinister by some creep in the media (Imus 1996).

Please note: this was *before* the Lewinsky affair, which, of course, hit the American culture like a bomb. There have been enough examinations of the Lewinsky affair for the affair to earn its own place in the cannon of presidential literature, and I direct readers there for more information on this scandal and the political effects of the impeachment threat. For the purposes this exploration, there are a few important points to note. First, the scandal was the first of its kind to be uncovered by an Internet blogger. The technology was still so new and so raw that few politicians had wrapped their heads around the political repercussions of the medium. Second, the surrounding political climate was in such good shape that a sex scandal of that magnitude (The president! In the Oval Office! With an intern!) was almost too big, but it was comprehendible by the public which had been treated to this narrative of Clinton for years. Because of this preexisting knowledge, there was seemingly little hypocrisy to criticize (always a stalwart of satire) until the tape was released of Clinton wagging his finger in denial of the affair, but even then the scandal simply supported everything that had already been thought, said, or joked about. Third, the satire that resulted had a variety of targets: it was aimed at Clinton, at Lewinsky, at Hillary, and at the Clinton apologists who stood by their man. Maureen Dowd of *The New York Times* was awarded no less than the Pulitzer Prize for Commentary for what the committee called her "fresh and insightful columns on the impact of President Clinton's affair with Monica Lewinsky" (Pulitzer 1999). In one column, Dowd wrote:

> After the President's prime-time confession, the news media were abuzz about whether Mr. Clinton could repair his damaged relationships with his wife and daughter.
> Suddenly, That Woman stamped her feet. Like the Glenn Close character in "Fatal Attraction," Monica Lewinsky issued a chilling ultimatum to the man who jilted her: I will not be ignored. She let it be known that she was wounded that the President had failed to apologize to her and had dismissed their grand, 18-month romance, their shared passion for books and laughs, as trivial—a mere mechanism for relieving Oval Office tension (Dowd 1999).

The late night talk show hosts had too much material to perform. Political cartoonists used Clinton's physical attributes and combined them with Lewinsky's own physical characteristics to draw scathing critiques of the affair. *SNL* had so many skits about the Lewinsky scandal they released a special video devoted entirely to the subject. And even as the Clinton administration wound down, the assaults kept coming. As he was scheduled to release his memoirs, cartoonist Mike Lester drew a "White Wash" machine that cranked out Clinton's autobiography. As Clinton left the White House amidst a flurry of other scandals (allegedly stolen furniture, purchased presidential pardons), he remained in the peripheral vision of the public eye as a target of political humor, but satirists shifted their focus to the incoming president, George W. Bush, after a tumultuous election that lasted weeks and was satirical feed as well. Initially, Bush (43) appeared to be an easy target—as occasionally inarticulate as his father but with a new kind of religiosity—but events conspired to shorten his satirical shelf life. And thus, for a while, Clinton was the last presidential target of humor. This would change, of course, but for several years, it was hard to laugh at all.

Conclusions

The new millennium brought a new president, a national crisis, and a wide variety of new media formats to distribute political humor once people were ready for it. This, understandably, took a while. Following September 11, there were proclamations that "irony was dead," and it took a long time for the late night humor shows to get back to work. I spoke with comedian Jimmy Tingle who, quoting another comedian, Jonathan Katz, said that "sincerity is the death of comedy" (Tingle 2010), and in the days following the attacks, the nation was notably sincere: sincerely sad, scared, and unfunny. Said Doug Abeles, who was then a brand-new writer at *Saturday Night Live*, of experiencing his very first show immediately after the September 11 terrorist attacks:

> When Giuliani came out, there was Lorne [Michaels] ... Giuliani really did give, I felt like, permission to laugh and it was incredibly moving ... [It] was one of those moments where you feel like whether it is valid or not, you feel like, this is the center of the universe right now, like what is happening here is kind of historic and I am witnessing an historic moment, or at least a special moment (Abeles 2010).

Because *SNL* was broadcast (live, if you will) from New York, its first episode after the attacks was watched with special attention.

The show avoided political humor and went instead for the goofy. Many of the humorists I interviewed who were writing for late night shows during this time indicated that the industry waited for Letterman to return to work, and then the other shows followed suit. While *The Tonight Show* airs from Los Angeles, the other programs broadcast from new York City, which meant that the writers and performers were more personally connected to the tragedy of September 11. On his first show back, Jon Stewart wept openly about the attacks, mirroring the nation's mood at the time. So, it took a while to get the satirical groove back, which is where *The Onion* played such an important role. First published by two University of Wisconsin students in 1988, the paper blends satire and comedy. *The Onion* grew exponentially as a newspaper distributed from college students in the Midwest to their friends around the country, and then as an online version. After the September 11 attacks, *The Onion* was among the first to break the moratorium on humor and not only led their comedic peers back to work, but also helped begin the long process of national healing. The headlines in the first *Onion* posting were as follows:

- "Not Knowing What Else To Do, Woman Bakes American-Flag Cake"
- "Hijackers Surprised To Find Selves In Hell"
- "U.S. Vows To Defeat Whoever It Is We're At War With"
- "American Life Turns Into Bad Jerry Bruckheimer Movie"
- "God Angrily Clarifies 'Don't Kill' Rule"
- "President Urges Calm, Restraint Among Nation's Ballad Singers"
- "Report: Gen X Irony, Cynicism May Be Permanently Obsolete"
- "Dinty Moore Breaks Long Silence On Terrorism With Full-Page Ad"
- "Bush Sr. Apologizes To Son For Funding Bin Laden In '80s"
- "Jerry Falwell: Is That Guy A Dick Or What?"
- "Hugging Up 76,000 Percent"
- "We Must Retaliate With Blind Rage vs. We Must Retaliate With Measured, Focused Rage"

Todd Hanson, the head writer of *The Onion* at this time, was interviewed by comedian Marc Maron about this satire, and he said that it was a difficult time that garnered varying responses:

> The story that people always talked about, about that issue was not on the front page, which was God angrily clarifies Don't Kill Rule. And he was saying, look I've been saying this for thousands of years. How much more can I explain it? You're pissing me off now. Quit it... And at the end of that story, you know, God actually—starts crying. And I was actually crying when I wrote that. I mean, it was—it was funny, cry, cry—more than funny, ha ha... Normally, *The Onion* loves to be irreverent... And we love to get hate mail. And we did get a lot of hate mail, right at the beginning of the day. But then throughout the day we started getting hundreds and hundreds more, eventually thousands of emails, and 90 percent of them were not only supportive, they were like—ecstatic. They were saying things like, God bless *The Onion*, you know (Hanson 2011).

This proved humor was still alive and powerful, and still able to conjure up a wide array of emotions. And soon, the late night comedy show hosts were back, the political cartoons aimed for humor over grief, and comedians tried new material. There were, of course, a few hitches in the giddy-ups along the way. Comedian Gilbert Gottfried was assailed for his tasteless remarks at a Friars Club Roast for Hugh Hefner, saying he couldn't catch a direct flight because "they said they have to stop off at the Empire State Building" (Gottfried 2011a). Bill Maher lost his show *Politically Incorrect* when he said, "We have been the cowards. Lobbing cruise missiles from two thousand miles away. That's cowardly. Staying in the airplane when it hits the building. Say what you want about it. Not cowardly. You're right" (Maher 2001). The country was not yet ready for that kind of political humor or criticism, and these comedians were punished for their remarks.

But back in New York, arguably the home of comedy, comedians were ready to address the horrors of 9/11. Comedian Marc Maron was interviewed on NPR by Brooke Gladstone about comedy immediately after September 11, and he responded:

> I mean, there was a period there where you couldn't even go below 14th Street, really, unless you live there. And as soon as

comedy clubs started functioning again, we were out doing it. And, you know, they haven't found most of the bodies, you can still smell the thing burning. Are we gonna stand up on stage and act like it's not happening down the street? So we weren't afforded that time (Maron 2011b).

The events of September 11 had a galvanizing effect on the nation, which went from declaring irony's death to a wealth of humor after the initial shock wore off. When the public recovered from the devastation of the attacks and stopped blindly following President Bush (43), political humor returned. President Bush and Vice President Cheney grew increasingly unpopular as politicians but increasingly popular as humor targets. Writers such as Molly Ivins honed funny and critical articles criticizing the president which were, for the first time, widely distributed thanks to the Internet. Flash-animated political cartoons and TV satire shows produced for webcasting were distributed everywhere. Thanks to technological innovation, there were soon many more homes for satire than ever could have been imagined. This happened at exactly the same time that the country grew disenchanted with their president, and satire flourishes of time of political dissatisfaction. Jon Stewart took the helm of *The Daily Show*, eventually *The Colbert Report* was launched, and there was ample satirical material in all forms that could be easily watched, read, and sent virally. Thanks to technology, we have become a nation drenched in satire. Said The Second City's Kelly Leonard:

[To] get attention is a whole other thing than it was back in 1995. Because of the *Onion*, *Colbert*, *Daily Show*, because of the Bush years and the subsequent Obama years, the focus on politics and satire and all of that is sort of hyper-realized. It was still sort of under the radar in the mid 90's and now it is obvious (Leonard 2010).

This explains how we have so much satire, but it does not to speak to its popularity. The popularity comes from our skepticism of our leaders, which grew directly from the years following the end of World War II. As Paul Lewis writes, when times are tough, we are "yearning for detachment from difficult problems" (Lewis 2006). Satire is one such mechanism for extrication because it's a fun way to criticize our leaders and laugh at the same time. The very nature of satire demands that it poke at the established order, which is the core of liberal political thought. That the satire of the late 1950s through the present day poked a disproportionate number of Republicans, however, does necessarily not lend itself to partisan bias. Some of the most strident satire was aimed squarely at LBJ during his presidency, and Clinton spawned a cottage industry of political humor all on his own. Instead, the more common satirical themes of the time were not partisan but ideological: a claim against the "establishment" whomever that happened to be. These were not conservative arguments against any one institution or administration, but instead a larger set of liberal arguments opposing the powers that be. One of the best arguments against an ideological bias in this time period stemmed from the commercial demands of the burgeoning entertainment industry. One of the "king makers" of the comedy world was indisputably Johnny Carson, host of *The Tonight Show*, who mandated the kind of material that could appear on his show. David Steinberg, who had caused trouble for the Smothers brothers with his sermonette on religion, appeared often on *The Tonight Show* and was told to steer clear of the overtly political material. Writes Richard Zoglin about Steinberg on *Tonight*:

> Steinberg was one of the first comedians to take on the subject [of Watergate]. 'I was very political at the time,' he says, 'I felt Nixon was a crook.' His Watergate material went over well in nightclubs. But on *The Tonight Show*, Johnny Carson told him to stay away from the subject; the country wasn't ready yet (Zoglin 2008).

This changed, of course, and the nation grew more accepting of material that challenged the political authority. Certainly the mood of the country had to be amenable for the satire to hit its mark, and so even, when satirical humor was at the forefront of opinion making, there had to be a receptive audience for it to actually work. That some of this satire as considered radical should not be surprising, given its tone and fury. Satire grew with the discontent, reflecting and echoing the sentiments of discord at the time. Satire helped to illustrate the greater public's unhappiness with government, and then moved on to our distrust of our leaders. It blossomed at a time when such disgruntlement was becoming increasingly acceptable. And once the permission to criticize is given, it is hard to take away.

Thus, as the media grew so too did political comedy, which had been around for all of American history but which found its voice during the twentieth century and grew exponentially after that. That this satire was liberal is indicative not of bias, but indicative of two more obvious explanations: the first is that satire has to reflect an antipathy toward the established order; the second is that satire will consistently epitomize the cultural and political mood of the time. Satire during the mid-twentieth century fulfilled both of these requirements. The massive growth of satire in the later part of the twentieth century could not, however, have occurred were it not for our indisputable history of political humor.

From the founding on to the present, we Americans have laughed at our leaders and at ourselves, finding humor within sharper commentary on the political culture. It has not been entirely consistent, and there have been historical periods when political satire has not been either accepted or prevalent. This is because the very nature of political humor asks the audience to be in on the joke, to mock the established order and the public who accepts it. Early American humor focused on the deconstruction of hierarchy, and later comedy examined the differentiation between groups and identities. As Arthur Dudden writes:

> With almanacs, newspapers, and comic showmen popping up everywhere in the nineteenth century, a widening variety of humorists focused their talents on the indigenous resources at hand to poke fun at foolish or knavish political figures...By the middle of the twentieth century, the gloves were removed, as political humorists regularly directed their wit—and their wrath—at more substantial matters of public policy and personality (Dudden 1985).

The founding, Reconstruction, and postwar eras were fertile periods for American satire, as these were times when the public was outspoken in their criticism of the political establishments. All of this helps to explain why modern political satire is so popular, since current culture is steeped with distrust, cynicism, and snark. Without the forefathers of satire, this work could never have happened. And without understanding satire's historical significance, we cannot accurately gauge how important contemporary satire is to our own political culture.

Two of the most essential elements of historical satire that remain true today are the satirists' commitment to reveal the transgressions of American politics, and their aim across the ideological spectrum to those whose offenses demand attention. In order to accomplish these tasks, it takes a special kind of person with unique talents. This is where the book now moves.

CHAPTER 4

Art and Profession

Adults love to ask children, "What do you want to be when you grow up?" Some kids know exactly what they want to be based on some inherent interest or skill learned from their surroundings or their parents. Some children have no idea, opting to shrug or give a standard superhero/princess response.[i] Most of those drawn to the dramatic arts admit to feeling something special the first time they performed, heard applause, or made someone laugh, and there has to be a very good reason for people to enter the profession since 99 percent of actors do not become Al Pacino (or even Al Yankovick). The poverty-paved road to thespianism is riddled with tricky potholes that serve as obstacles from continuing in a profession with wildly uneven work schedules and paychecks. The first people to mention the impracticality of the profession are the artists themselves, but they also speak of their commitment to the craft, oftentimes beginning their arts studies in college. The decision point of dream versus practicality is reflected in their major choice, which more often than not focused on drama, theater, or some other aesthetic. Tim Slagle told me:

> I started in film [At the University of Michigan]. I wanted to get into film, and then, and then I realized...the amount of unemployed film makers, so I switched to engineering and then I realized if I succeeded I would have to spend the majority of

---

[i] My 6-year-old daughter's goal: horse-riding hairdresser.

the rest of my life with engineers, and so I switched to physics and I realized that they are the same people as engineers only they smoke pot. And then I started doing open mic nights and I said: "Well, why finish college—I am going to be a star in five years?" (Slagle 2010).

Since most actors and comedians do not, in fact, becomes stars in five years, and the threat of unemployment is strong, there has to be something special that pulls people toward the performing arts, or else it does not seem very likely people would go into the profession at all. When it comes to comedy, this something special is often the ability to make people laugh, a "gift" it is said, that has a powerful force. So this attraction to humor seems to drive the train of professional comedians and satirists, and consequently, it is not surprising that even the most political of humorists say being funny is more important than being right (which is addressed further in Chapter 5). After all, the desire to entertain brought them into this line of work to begin with. This chapter examines the education, temperament, and politics of these comedians to show why their very nature may attract them to comedy *and* to the left at the same time. It also examines show business to explore the possibility of institutional bias and the financial imperatives that drive decision-making. But first, a look into the psyche of the satirist—his or her training, goals, and interests.

College, Majors, Interests, and Intellect

A college education is important for many professions, and it appears that political comedy is one of them. While advanced education is necessary to become a lawyer or a doctor, college is not mandatory for a satirist—but this education helps. Part of this may be the writing and analytical skills that a college education requires, and part may be the dramatic training that students can obtain from majors like performing arts and theater. I would not have thought to look to college education as a contributing factor in a humorists' political leaning but for the trends that emerged from my interview questions.

Let me back up here a moment and explain why I asked about education. As mentioned, I was a C-SPAN producer for five years and was able to watch a significant number of interviews conducted by Brian Lamb, the founder and CEO of the network. Lamb is renowned for his interviewing skills, and his conversations with policy makers are regarded as among the best in the business. He has a way of asking seemingly innocuous questions in between the more penetrating ones that allow a subject to feel comfortable and a viewer to gain tremendous insight into a subject or a person. One of the questions Lamb almost always asks an interviewee is, "Where did you go to college?" And so, armed with this example as my guide, I began all of my interviews asking the exact same thing. I found that with very, very few exceptions, all of my interview subjects did go to college, and even more interesting, the writers I interviewed studied the arts rather than politics. *None* were political science majors, which struck me as interesting since they were (to varying degrees) writing political material. Time after time I heard "theater" or "humanities" or "philosophy" as major choices, but no one mentioned my field. As a political science professor, I tried not to take umbrage,[ii] but it led me to the conclusion that instead of being political activists, or even being politically motivated, these humorists were educated theater nerds. And damn proud of it. And so this trend led me to think about college attendance and major choice as possible contributing factors to someone's political preference.

It is a common misconception, oft repeated and accepted as conventional wisdom, that all college students are liberal. Perhaps the majority of students at specific universities (such as UC Berkeley, UMass, Amherst, or NYU) trend left, but this is absolutely not universal. Take it from someone who teaches at a predominantly conservative public university, the idea that college students are uniformly liberal is absurd. Still, despite large numbers of conservative students at universities around the nation, many college kids are liberal which helps to perpetuate the stereotype. Voter data from the 2008 election shows that a plurality of citizens between ages 18 and 29 self-identified as Democrat (45 percent) compared to 29 percent who identified as Independent and 23 percent as Republican. The data also

------

[ii] It's a great major!

showed that of this age demographic, 63 percent with a college degree voted for President Obama and 33 percent voted for Senator John McCain (Staff 2008). So not all college students are liberal, but clearly the young have more of a predilection for liberal thought. After all, Winston Churchill once said, "Show me a young Conservative and I'll show you someone with no heart. Show me an old Liberal and I'll show you someone with no brains." It is likely that college students who are surrounded by student clubs and activities for like-minded folks have more opportunities (and more time) to be politically active than their brethren who leave high school and immediately enter the work force.

Census data from 2011 states that 28 percent of the American public has a college degree (Census 2011), but in the entertainment business, the percentage of those with college degrees rises significantly. There is a wide variety of comedy forms that demand varying degrees of education, and while it is not a hard-and-fast rule, it appears that most TV comedy writers have gone to college. It has been this way since the start of television: in 1956, *Time Magazine* featured research from an Ohio State University graduate student who interviewed 56 of the 250 TV comedy writers in the United States and found that they mostly fit a type:

> On their own vital statistics: the average TV comedy writer is 38.8 years old. Most of them are married, come from large cities, have had some college education, are Jewish and, before becoming writers, did everything from washing dishes to assisting veterinarians (Editors 1956).

In 1994, a writer named Robert Strauss wrote an article for the *Los Angeles Times* that was subtitled, "From the Halls of Ivy . . . to a Table at the Ivy," which stated, "Harvard, Yale and Co. are turning out more than just lawyers and bankers; prime time is filled with the work of their alumni. Once these writers feared being stigmatized by their classmates—but six figures later, they're having the last laugh" (Strauss 1994). When, inevitably, people wrote to the *Times* to complain about the article, most of them made the argument that the college *they* attended was not an Ivy League school, but they made it in Hollywood anyway.

Blogger Tim Slagle noted this difference in the education levels of comedians in the varying humor forms:

> I think you will find that more people who work on television shows do have the college degrees versus people who are in talk radio and stand up. A lot of us just did not finish the degree. And I think part of that is the procedure of going through college is similar to what you have to do when you are submitting a script or . . . the bureaucracy and structure that exists on television shows. It is more similar to college, whereas . . . in my realm it tends to be more entrepreneurial where you just get in the car, you get a cell phone, you get a web site and you get a stack of 8 × 10s and you start doing stand-up (Slagle 2010).

The Onion was founded by students from the University of Wisconsin, the *Harvard Lampoon* still spawns legions of humorists, and *Doonesbury* was begun at Yale, home to its first targets. Going to college appears to be one important first step toward a career in political comedy. The next step is picking a major.

It seems fairly obvious that arty people would be drawn to arty majors, and there are plenty of arty majors out there, from theater to performing arts to philosophy. While certain college majors specifically prepare you for a specific career, arty majors, encased within the liberal arts sphere of higher learning, prepare students more generally. Parents may get sticker shock at the price of college today and demand that their children pick majors that will definitively land them jobs upon graduation, but many students are drawn to majors within the liberal arts because of the type of people they are. This draw is going to affect their careers once they graduate, but they know this in advance and use their college years to study and learn the things that most interest them. Graduation day always seems far away until the alma mater plays and the mortarboards are tossed, and until that time, many undergrads just assume that they will land a job and all will be well. Most of the time, these students are correct in this assumption, but for those with arty majors, their career path may be far away from what they studied in college. Put simply, there are not enough jobs in the arts to sustain the people who graduate with arts majors. Said Second City's Andy Cobb, "Yes, I studied philosophy and music theory at the

College of Wooster... if ever there were a formula for unemployment right?" (Cobb 2010). Rob Riggle from *Saturday Night Live* and *The Daily Show* said something similar in an interview with comedian Marc Maron: "I was a theater and film major, so that means I was going to be a waiter upon graduation. Because you just don't graduate as a theater and film major and go become an actor. You can study acting. You can try to get gigs, you can try to get a job, but you're not going to get paid anything" (Riggle 2011).

An expert in the field of education economics conducted a study on the relationship between college majors, occupation upon graduation, and wage earning. John Robst from the Department of Mental Health Law and Policy at the Florida Mental Health Institute found that those who majored in liberal arts and visual/performing arts (among other similarly focused disciplines) had a high percentage of jobs without relation to their major. Robst argued that majors that teach more general skills more often led to graduates entering an occupation that differed from the degree field than occupation-specific majors. Accordingly, majors with specific foci such as business management, engineering, and health had a higher percentage of graduates actually working in that field. Adding insult to the injury of liberal arts majors, Robst found that those in "mismatched" occupations earned less money than those whose jobs "matched" their major (Robst 2007). So to recap, students drawn to the performing arts may gravitate toward a major that will probably land them a job outside their chosen field that will then not pay them very well.

Additionally, performing and liberal arts majors teach skills that focus on analysis and relativity, studying a multitude of points in order to determine a "truth."[iii] Moral relativism is not what one would call a conservative value, so maybe it makes sense that liberals would be drawn to these majors in the first place. If so, then the next logical step is clear: what you study in college can shape your belief system, and someone geared toward the arts might pick a major that reinforces their artistic

---

[iii] This is what made William F. Buckley so angry (at Yale in particular and at liberalism in general) in 1951.

side with the pedagogy of the discipline. According to Tim Slagle: "[Comedians/satirists] tend to be arts majors, or liberal arts majors, which might also be a reason that there is a bias. A lot of where your bias comes from, I believe, is what you know" (Slagle 2010). Conservatives at this point will argue that the academy is chock full of (politically) liberal professors pushing their agenda in a (nonpolitical) liberal arts education.[iv] Perhaps, but it is also possible that the (nonpolitical) liberal arts inherently demand attention to the ethereal and the philosophical—subjects that are by definition the opposite of concrete. I have been scolded by conservatives to not stereotype their philosophy as absolute, so allow me to provide evidence of the ideology's undeniable fundamentalism.

There are many types of conservatism, to include fiscal, social, and neoconservatism, and all have horses in the political race right now. In the Bush (43) administration, the neoconservatives had the reins of power, as evidenced in the Bush Doctrine of preventative war. No less a scholar than Normal Podhoretz, one of the fathers of the neocon movement, wrote an article on the Bush Doctrine in *Commentary*, the conservative magazine read by influential public intellectuals and policy makers alike. The Bush Doctrine was the philosophical foundation that explained the rationale for the preemptive invasion of Iraq. In his article, Podhoretz argued that the Bush Doctrine included "four pillars," which included support for Israel, holding other governments responsible for state-sponsored terrorism, the rejection of moral relativism, and the right to preemptively invade a nation that posed a threat to the United States (Podhortez 2002). Sounds pretty absolute to me. Some conservatives have questioned the significance of conservative power now that Obama is in office, arguing that Democrats control varying branches of government. While true, the debt ceiling crisis of summer 2011 (the example used in Chapter 2) helps to show how the truly absolute Tea Party coalition (undisputed conservatives they) could throw a monkey wrench into the Democrats' whole program. So I maintain conservatism has an absolutist quality to it, and I do not think this is stereotyping. To take a page from Dennis Miller's

---

[iv] See Horowitz, David.

views on profiling after the September 11 attacks, I think it is being merely observant.

Satire and political humor eschews this absolutism and lives in the grays. It takes a concept and plays around with it until the funny shines through. Similarly, liberalism is the ideology of exploration and relativism. Conservatism, conversely, roots itself in absolutes, where there are clear lines of right and wrong. *Conan* writer Brian Stack agrees:

> In general I think that a lot of humor is found in the gray areas of things, like being able to plant a seed, to be flexible and be able to see the absurdity in any particular point of view and I think that hard core liberals and hard core Republicans are some of the most humorless people I've ever met, you know, because they aren't willing to see any gray areas. It is all absolute with them and I personally don't think there is a lot of humor to be found in absolute (Stack 2010).

Said *SNL*'s Alex Baze:

> Conservatism, by definition, means that you don't want things to change, that you want to conserve the way things are. So, if you are not trying to change anything, then what possible commentary or criticism can you have? By saying that you are a conservative you are basically saying, I'm pretty much fine with the way things are (Baze 2010).

This adherence to the status quo is the antithesis of liberal arts training, which demands inquiry into a wide variety of viewpoints and a rejection of convention in pursuit of larger truths. The academic movements toward deconstruction[1] and postmodernism[2] are prime examples of this.

Said Second City's Kelly Leonard:

> I am sure if you break down elements of the conservative political ideology unattached to a current American Republican Party or a current American fringe unit like the Tea Party, you could probably find stuff in there that is as important to a minority living today as it would be to a white person or whatever, but no one is going to that level of critical thinking, and comedy has to be right away. It has to be quick and everyone has got to

understand what it is for it to be funny. It has got to have that quick element of surprise. We are not a deep enough country to go there (Leonard 2010).

Adam Felber described conservative's "high amount of reverence," arguably the exact opposite of comedy, and Ruth Rudnick argued that in her experience, conservatives are cautious by nature:

> People who are conservative tend to be very careful...It is like there is a carefulness about it. There is like not a bounce, bounce, jump, jump, jump. And, I think for some reason people who write for [satire] shows or do improv even there is, you need to have a kind of abandon about you. And, I think there is not as much abandon when you are conservative because that goes against being conservative...Stoic goes against satire because stoic is the opposite of satire. Stoic is: I am going to be really in control and that is against comedy...But if you have a room full of right-wing people and a room full of left-wing people, the left-wing people, I am sure, can come up with that embarrassing story a lot faster than they can (Rudnick 2010).

Which leads back to the liberal arts. While the interest in the liberal arts by theater-minded people does not necessitate mental agility, the skill set of a satirist certainly does. Accordingly, the talents of a satirist can be honed in a liberal arts education which similarly explores fluid content. Says comedian David Razowsky, "I think that satirists and artists both have their minds open to much stimulus... [and] whatever is out there in the atmosphere you are aware of it, you are holding on to it, you're open to it" (Razowsky 2010). Does this ability to juggle so many parts at once necessitate liberalism? Answers Razowsky, "I don't think a lot of conservatives are able to really put those pieces together" (Razowsky 2010). While it sounds like bait for conservative outrage, Razowsky's observation may lead to a larger point. Actor Keegan-Michael Key spoke with me at length about the ways we process information, arguing the inherent beliefs about tradition and adherence to norms drive our behavior: "Everyone of us thinks we are right...If you are designed this way or if you are 'nurtured' this way, then you are going to be nurtured to be an outside of the box person as opposed to an inside of the box person" (Key 2010). Key directed me to University of Virginia psychologist Jonathan Haidt, who has conducted a fair amount of research about the ways liberals and conservatives think and what they care most about. One study from 2009 tested what Haidt calls the "moral foundations theory" which examines moral intuitions:

> The authors developed several ways to measure people's use of 5 sets of moral intuitions: Harm/care, Fairness/reciprocity, Ingroup/loyalty, Authority/respect, and Purity/sanctity. Across 4 studies using multiple methods, liberals consistently showed greater endorsement and use of the Harm/care and Fairness/ reciprocity foundations compared to the other 3 foundations, whereas conservatives endorsed and used the 5 foundations more equally (Graham 2009).

This study found that liberals fashioned their moral classifications based mostly on issues of fairness and care while conservatives built their moral systems also focusing on loyalty, authority, and purity. The first two qualities are more fluid than the last three, which trend toward the concrete and absolute. Put another way, this is one reason that liberals can be moral relativists and conservatives reject this philosophy. Haidt's research shows that our political ideology is connected to the way we judge the world around us, and in this regard it makes sense that liberals would be interested in the liberal arts, which investigate the indefinite and the unknown.

This investigation is an important quality of comedy, and the ability to question everything is a crucial ingredient of satire. Comedian Will Durst told me:

> The word liberal, in the dictionary usage, is accepting of many viewpoints and I think that is what happens with comics. You've got to be fairly smart to be a comic. You've got to be able to juggle 18 different skills all at once, the memorization, improvisation, you have to be a good actor or you've got to be able to turn on the charm on stage like a light bulb (Durst 2010).

Comedian Jimmy Tingle concurred with Durst's assessment and contrasted it with the conservative temperament. Tingle told me, "The great thing about comedy is its unpredictability—and conservatism is predictable" (Tingle 2010). This, of course, does not mean that conservatives can't be smart, unpredictable, or funny, but it does show a connection between the skill set of a political humorist and the lessons taught in the liberal arts of universities. Writer David Razowsky agreed, and when asked if there was a special set of talents necessary to produce effective satire, he said:

> Oh my gosh, yeah. You've got to be aware of what is going on in the world and you've got to have your own opinion, and you have to be open for change, and you've got to hear as many different sides of the story as you can, and you've got to be able to surrender your beliefs, and you've got to be clear. You have to do all of this, and at the same time see that there is a prism necessary in order to look at something from different sides (Razowsky 2010).

And all of this together does not equate to liberals being more intellectually gifted than their conservative counterparts—it just shows that the same mechanisms that hard-wire our brains toward interests and career paths are the same mechanisms that drive our political beliefs.

Additionally, the choice of a non-political science major also adds evidence to the theory that these satirists are not particularly politically driven. The depth of the political engagement for most of those with whom I spoke was on par with the average interested American: they knew what they generally believed about American government, but in the main they certainly weren't focused on the system or the process. Their primary focus was on the art form rather than the political, and to this end (as Jon Stewart said on Fox News), their ideology informed their comedy. It did not consume it. Interestingly, when asked about their political leanings, a small minority of those I interviewed indicated a strong political sense. The nonconservatives were generally less adamant than their right-wing counterparts. Only a handful identified themselves as very liberal—the rest had a "yeah, I guess" attitude about their politics and many made the argument that both sides of the American political divide were defective. Conversely, all of the conservatives I interviewed were die-hards, seemingly in a defensive crouch about their ideals and positions in a professional world dominated by opposing thought. They reacted sharply to their position in the minority and felt powerfully that their political beliefs were rejected in their field. This stand was uniformly refuted by the non-conservative satirists who felt that *their* political stance was not the reason for their success, mostly because they didn't feel so strongly about their politics to begin with. This led to the possibility that the nonconservative satirists did not even realize they were all coming from the same political place. Writer Ned Rice made this contention and argued the result was a huge slant in the material:

> The liberal bias in the media in general is such that they don't realize that they are biased. That is how insidious it is. It is kind of amazing. You know, everyone thinks they are normal. Everyone thinks they are the middle. Everyone thinks they are moderate. Everyone thinks they are just about average, and it is just not true... They don't go out and say, "I am the liberal comic." They just say: "Hey, I am going to do some comedy." But if you listen to their jokes most of them are from a left of center perspective (Rice 2010).

Perhaps the prevalence of liberal thought negated a desire to debate or discuss. Actress Ruth Rudnick opined that maybe political leanings were so uniform as to be assumed:

> I think it is understood what they want to do. They might not articulate it to each other even, about like: "We've got to get Bush out of office or we've got to make the Democrats win." Let's say that is their agenda, I don't think they even have to talk about it. Do you even have to talk about it if that is what you want? You know, if I want to drive safely, I don't have to say to you: "I'm going to get in the car and drive safely now." I will say what kind of car I want... do I want to clean my car, do I want to get leather seats? But it is a given that I am going to drive safely (Rudnick 2010).

This is a great point. Most people do not spark political conversation based on agreement. Normally, people talk about the things they disagree with, and even then, if everyone is agreeable to the disagreement then the conversation is uninteresting.

It is also possible that because the topic of politics was not the driving force of the humor, it was similarly not the driving force behind the conversation among the writers. Kevin Dorff said that because of this common belief set, politics was rarely discussed at *Conan*, even when there was time to do so:

> There are a lot of times in the day where we do have two hours, three hours, where you are frozen. You know, you are waiting to hear something or you are waiting to get down to edit. You are waiting in the spotlight to get in there and edit a piece or you are waiting, you are dressing in some costume sitting in a room waiting to rehearse. So, there is lots of down time. I mean we shoot the breeze but yeah, it definitely seems like most of the writers, most of everybody, don't seem too far apart on their politics, but the topic never came up much (Dorff 2010).

Another point that occurred to me as I traveled from south-central Pennsylvania to New York City, Chicago, and then Los Angeles to interview writers and comedians was that all three of these cities, the homes for the entertainment and comedy industry in America today, are really liberal. Given this, it makes sense that conservatives in the business feel defensive about their political positions because even away from work, they are surrounded by people who disagree with them. As one of a handful of Democrats who live in an entirely conservative area, I can tell you firsthand that this is enough to make one defensive. Bringing this back to education, if you look at living situations on college campuses then, it makes sense that students will gravitate toward like-minded colleagues and not opt to hang with those who disagree with them. On college campuses, this means living in certain areas, taking up certain activities, and choosing certain majors. Consequently, if a conservative student is interested in the arts he or she may ignore these interests if he or she thinks those clubs and majors are full of lefties. No training or exposure, no movement beyond college into a career.

There is something to the training that is important for political humor to work. Not only is the focus of the material essential, but so is timing and an ability to look at things from varying perspectives. As a result, a liberal arts education may be perfect for a comedian's training, but this is where political attitudes can also be solidified. Most satirists made the argument that of course satire is supposed to have a view point—that is par for the course for the art form. As cartoonist Garry Trudeau said in an interview on NPR, "I'm a cartoonist so I'm by definition unfair, I mean, that's what satire is" (Trudeau 2011). But even with a clear viewpoint, the nonconservative satirists argued that the viewpoint did not necessarily have to be liberal. *Wait, Wait*'s Peter Sagal told me:

> There are people who do satire from a liberal perspective it seems, but nobody says, "Well I'm out there and I am interested in doing satire from a liberal perspective." Nobody says that because nobody is beginning with an ideological bent. I mean even somebody like Garry Trudeau doesn't sit down and say: "What can I do to advance the liberal cause?" I am going to make fun of what I think is funny. You have to start there. I think the reason that P. J. O'Rourke is successful is not because he is a conservative satirist but because he is really funny. It just so happens that his sensibility is such that the things that he thinks are funny tend to be associated with liberal causes (Sagal 2010).

Someone's politics will drive what they think is funny, and to that end, the viewpoint is important to direct a joke. This is where the multifaceted approach of the liberal arts may support the satirist in his or her task. A political humorist can find the funny in a multitude of targets, while an activist has one focus. Cenk Uygur of *The Young Turks* agreed, stressing the importance of approaching humor with a viewpoint but without a specific agenda. A real activist plays for a team, something Uygur says he does not do:

> On our show we are not afraid to tackle any issue. It doesn't matter liberal/conservative. Of course, people view us as very liberal, but they reality is on many, many instances I will go in the other direction because I am not on any team...I would never spike a story or not do a story because, oh, no that will make liberals look bad or that will, you know, that doesn't conform with my ideology. On a political level, if Charlie Rangel's got four different apartments that he calls primary residences that he is there or not, well then why do I want a Democrat stealing my money as opposed to a Republican? (Uygur 2010).

The ability to examine an issue from a multitude of viewpoints can facilitate the crafting of a joke that is unexpected or remarkably cutting. Additionally, the ability to pivot and shoot at a variety of targets broadens a satirist's range. All of this put together means that those drawn to the performing arts may be trained with a skill set in college that will augment their abilities as a humorist. The temperament of the satirist and the training he or she receives can help explain the political beliefs of the professionals. If this is true, and liberals are drawn first toward artsy majors and then toward arty careers, then by virtue of this, the arts will be chock-full of them, which also might dissuade conservatives (especially social conservatives) from entering the profession. Social conservatives may find it uncomfortable to work with people in the theater arts who are, as *SNL*'s Alex Baze says, "cartoonishly liberal." In other words, if the impression is that the profession is stacked with lefties, maybe right-wingers would avoid such an environment.

Very few comedians work nine to five, and even TV comedy writers work unusual hours and have atypical schedules—not exactly the most traditional of job conditions. Additionally, with the exceptions of the most successful humorists, the work is not consistent nor a necessarily reliable form of income. One former writer for *Colbert* told me that the year before she started at *The Report*, she filed her income tax returns with almost a dozen W-2 forms. All put together, the profession itself may attract a certain type of individual: someone with a predilection for free thought, a desire to explore a variety of viewpoints, and a willingness to work odd hours with unpredictable schedules alongside people whose lifestyles Pat Robertson thinks were the real reason for the September 11 attacks. Performers and writers are used to the unpredictability of their careers while others in different professions are not. Take it from someone who covets her tenure, predictability is important to certain types of people, and less so for others.

When I made the connection between interest, college major, subject study, and ideology with conservatives, they reacted pretty forcefully against the theory.[v] They also took the stand that the argument gave credit to liberals for being more open

---

[v] Really, really forcefully.

minded and smarter than their conservative equivalents. Said Tim Slagle sarcastically:

> Of course Liberals are predominant in college, Liberals are more intelligent. Of course they're predominant in the arts, they're more talented. Of course they're predominant in Journalism, they're more unbiased. I think you see what I'm getting at. That kind of thinking is so pervasive, that it is taken as conventional wisdom. If a young job applicant makes the mistake of claiming conservative politics, he's considered unintelligent, untalented, and biased, and he's not hired. That bias has effectively politically homogenized a lot of the major institutions today (Slagle 2010).

Perhaps. But for the record, the argument is not that liberals are smarter, but that they might be drawn to certain things and conservatives to others. I take Slagle's point, however, and realize that a bit of confirmation bias of my own may be at play here.

What began as an interviewing technique, then, led to some possible conclusions. College education is important in order to enter the field of political humor, major choice plays a role, and the nature of the profession serves to winnow the field to a small cadre of writers and humorists. Thousands are trying to break into this field, submitting jokes to *SNL*, vying for interviews at *Colbert*, and sending writing samples to *The Onion*. The education and training of all of these potential satirists is probably pretty impressive. It is not fixed that these people are liberals, but given their education and training, it is likely that they are.

Hollywood Bias

Conservative humorists at this point will call foul and argue that they would be thrilled to enter the comedy profession, but the deck is stacked against them because of the liberal bias of the entertainment industry. Time and again I heard from conservatives that the doors were shut to them, and they could not succeed through the regular channels. Writer Ned Rice made the point that this liberal bias has forged new media ground for conservatives as a result:

> Conservative talk radio and Fox News became very successful because conservatives, who are roughly half of the population,

were not hearing their perspective reflected in any of the mainstream media—not on the evening TV news, not on public broadcasting, not in newspapers, not in magazines, not in popular entertainment, nowhere. In other words, there was an unmet need in the marketplace. So when talk radio and Fox came along conservatives flocked to them. This is also why liberal or progressive talk radio like Air America Radio has been a failure: progressives can hear their perspective throughout the mainstream media every day, any time they want to so there's no unmet need there (Rice 2010).

As mentioned in Chapter 1, the issue of bias in the entertainment industry has been addressed elsewhere, and for a more comprehensive examination, I urge readers to seek this out. But because the conservatives I interviewed felt so strongly about bias in the entertainment industry, this topic demands a bit of exploration here. The complicated relationship between the government and the artistic community (writers, actors, and artists) during the Red Scares of the 1950s calmed in time for an even more complicated relationship to develop between the government, the major corporations that own the entertainment media, and those who work within the industry. One thorough examination of Hollywood bias was published in 1993 by political scientist Herbert Gans. Gans argued that due to the financial goals of the entertainment industry, those who produced its products had to be more cognizant of audience wishes than of their own political ideologies. He drew the distinction between the ideological leanings of those in Hollywood and the commercial product produced by the Hollywood entertainment industry. Gans further distinguished between the potential creative input of various industry players (differentiating among actors, producers, directors, technicians, etc.), and determined that even if there was a preponderance of liberalism within the artistic community, this did not translate to a biased entertainment product. This was because artists have little input on production, and the producers of the entertainment were more focused on the bottom line. Thus, Gans concluded his study finding that Hollywood films and television programs were not, in fact, liberal in content (Gans 1993). More recently, in 2011, Steven Ross wrote *Hollywood Left and Right: How Movie Stars Shaped*

American Politics and argued that, in the words of the *Los Angeles Times* book review, "the movie industry has been as quietly conservative as publicly liberal. After all, where did Ronald Reagan come from?" (Kellogg 2011).

These scholarly conclusions do not stop conservatives from arguing that bias in Hollywood exists, and there is a mixture of scholarship, evidence, and long-held conventional wisdom that aims to prove it. Writer John Eberhard argues that those in Hollywood are so liberal that they "are not representative of the population of America" (Eberhard 2004). Author Dave Thomas studied the 2009 Emmy Award speeches and determined a bias against conservatives (Thomas 2009). Dale Berryhill wrote a book simply called *The Media Hates Conservatives* in 1994 and Tim Grossclose wrote a similar tome in 2011 called *Left Turn: How Liberal Media Bias Distorts the American Mind*. Conservative pundits argue that the Hollywood establishment is so liberal as to be exclusive and discriminatory against conservatives. Writers such as Michelle Malkin (2009) and Ann Coulter (2007) rail against the so-called "liberal media elite," and conservative humorists argued to me that this was the sole explanation for their scarcity in numbers.

Liberals, however, disagree with this contention and maintain that there are no obstacles for conservatives to enter the industry, they are just not successful. In 2003, a comedy group called The Right Stuff was launched in an effort to bring conservative humor to America. This was a time when, with President Bush's approvals still high, conservative humor might have worked especially well, but it did not:

> The group traveled to New York City during [2004's] Republican National Convention. It performed eight nights at the Times Square Laugh Factory. But other than that week, it struggled to find gigs and petered out by the end of the election (Libit 2009).

Said Julia Gorin, one of the comedians in the group, "For all the whining the conservatives did [about the lack of comedy], they didn't do much to represent... Between liberals and conservatives, liberals always support the arts more. I found that out very personally" (Libit 2009). All of this said, several pieces of evidence do support the contention that Hollywood is dominated by those on the left. First, the most vocal political figures in Hollywood are liberal activists, and those vocal actors are big names. In math terms, Sean Penn plus Matt Damon plus Susan Sarandon plus the entire cast of *Glee* does not equal Chuck Norris plus Kelsey Grammar. It is easy to see high-profile celebrities speaking out and connecting this to left-wing entertainment domination. Additionally, according to the Center for Responsive Politics, which tracks campaign finance for all federal elections, in 2008 the "TV/Movie/Music" industry gave $9.2 million to then-candidate Barack Obama and $3.45 million to then-candidate Hillary Clinton, but only $1.2 to then-candidate John McCain (Center for Responsive Politics 2009). This evidence points to a preponderance of liberalism in Hollywood, at least among the celebrities and very wealthy power players there. Conservative satirists also maintain long-held beliefs about who runs the show based on personal experience and anecdotal evidence. Said Tim Slagle: "Hollywood is so one-sided politically that they assume the rest of the nation is . . . they see what they see . . . in their social circle and they don't realize that the country itself is 50/50" (Slagle 2010). Evan Sayet agreed, and said that liberals were the "gatekeepers" of the entertainment industry. He said that when he brought his conservative satire show to the Showtime cable network, it was rejected because of these gatekeepers: "I was told point blank when I brought *Right to Laugh* to Showtime they said this will probably be the most successful television show we've ever had, we can't do it. It would hurt are brand" (Sayet 2010). Several conservative satirists told me about the Friends of Abe group, a clandestine Republican organization that meets in secret to avoid ideological persecution. The fact that this group even exists shows that the perception of bias is fairly well entrenched. An article from the *Washington Times* about the Kennedy Center's Mark Twain Prize made the argument that "conservative humorists need not apply" and noted that Bill Cosby was the only thing close to a conservative to win the award:

> Practically every other recipient of the Twain Prize—a list including Whoopi Goldberg, Carl Reiner, Tina Fey, and Lilly Tomlin—has been an outspoken lefty of one stripe or another. In 2004, Lorne Michaels even won the thing, for goodness sake,

meaning it's easier for a Canadian to be named America's top humorist than it is for a conservative born in the U.S.A. (Stevens 2011).

Across the board, conservatives argue that Hollywood is so biased against them they cannot make it in the industry with their political beliefs announced. Even more, conservative comedians are certain that their ideological leanings harms their careers. Evan Sayet told me, "There are no more gigs to be gotten because you are a conservative. Many, many gigs to be lost because you are conservative" (Sayet 2010). And Tim Slagle concurred: "[Being conservative] can wreck your career...Because the, the liberal bias is so ingrained throughout Hollywood that, that people will not want to deal with you if you are a conservative" (Slagle 2010).

On the other hand, liberal writers expressed a similar frustration to me about their inability to pitch truly leftist material. The idea that liberals controlled the industry was, according to several satirists, completely ludicrous. Comedian Marc Maron made the distinction between feeling socially isolated and professionally shunned and addressed the conservative accusation of being shut out:

> That may be at dinner parties, but it's certainly not in getting work. If [a conservative comedian] has a hard time getting work as a comedian, because his big angle is "I want to be an angry right wing comedian," because God knows those people don't have a voice in this country. That's such horse shit (Maron 2011b).

Other comedians argued that the conservatives were in the ultimate power positions within society and the dominance of the right held control over the entertainment industry. From Second City's Kelly Leonard: "Right now, the conservative movement in America is representative of the power in America: White, paternal, wealthy and that is the object of satire, so...what are you fighting against? What are you being satiric of? This idea that they are not the powerful is crap" (Leonard 2010). *The Young Turks'* Cenk Uygur made the important distinction between political party and ideology and argued that even when the Democrats are in control, the liberals are not:

> Growing up I remember thinking that there were funny political satire guys who were conservative and because, liberals used to have more power, so you can make fun of Ted Kennedy because Ted Kennedy had a lot of power and he, at times, misused it right and it was a good point to point that out. Now, of course, conventional wisdom will beg: "What is this guy talking about? The Democrats have the House, the Senate, the White House, they couldn't be more in power." Bullshit, they're not liberals, they are not progressives, they're corporatists, so even the Democrats are incredibly conservative now... For them to pick on liberals, who are they going to pick on? Dennis Kucinich? Is that really funny? I mean, the little thing that Dennis provides is good fodder for them, but it is not like he is you are ripping down a powerful guy. You know, you are picking on a guy who is barely hanging in there (Uygur 2010).

It is possible that blatantly left-leaning material is just as difficult to pitch as right-leaning material because it is going to bother half an audience. Second City's Andy Cobb concurred, and told me about his arrival in Los Angeles:

> When I first got out here [to L.A.] a guy was asking me for a couple of pitches. And I gave him some ideas... He very patiently, much like a father explaining to a child, said that there are people in charge of the studios and networks and even though actors and even agents or things like that might be more sympathetic to a political cause that people of a right wing persuasion tend to be the people who actually pull the strings. So, that is why no left wing programming gets on the air... I always knew that but I didn't expect anyone to come and say that to me... While we do live in sort of an ideological bubble in LA and New York, I certainly don't think that anyone every got rich by saying, oh, I am going to do leftist material. It just doesn't happen that way (Cobb 2010).

But conservatives (obviously) disagreed and after the evidence of bias is posed, the argument goes that the liberals will reject conservative talent no matter what. From Nick DiPaolo, the argument is that the left in the entertainment field will beget more lefties: "Liberals hire liberals" (DiPaolo 2011). He went on to argue that the perception of bias might be enough to discourage conservatives from going into the business in the first place: "Well why would you go into a business if you're conservative if you know it slants left. You're gonna meet a dead end half way up the ladder... that's why. You know what I mean? They obviously know who runs the business. And that's why they don't go into it... [Or] maybe they do and they only get so far" (DiPaolo 2011).

Both sets of contentions include attitudes hard to refute because in some cases they are valid, and they often rest on conventional wisdom that has been affirmed and reaffirmed over many years. These entrenched beliefs emerge from decades of patterns that have been set, arguments held on to, and stereotypes that have been developed. Both Nick DiPaolo and Tim Slagle made the point that historical precedent in the past 40 years has led to the left simply dominating satire. First, from DiPaolo:

> Because it's been the other way for so long, you're not going to see a real big conservative comic in our lifetime. I really believe it. Because the stone has been set... Because the people have been exposed for the last 40 years to *ABC, CBS, NBC* and it was liberal and... Political correctness comes from the left in my opinion. Evangelists—they never got people fired. It's Al Sharpton and women's groups. They put... you know speech codes on campuses? That shit doesn't come from conservatives. We've created this environment for the last 40 years (DiPaolo 2011).

The previous chapter provides evidence that DiPaolo is right in that the history of political satire reflects an essentially leftist slant. Certainly, the patterns set during the revolutionary periods of the late twentieth century reaffirm humor's place in an antiestablishmentarian political culture. Tim Slagle agreed, noting that the historical trend left pushed the change too and this led to conservatives being the constant butt of the jokes while those on the left were given a free pass: "The left is just unaccustomed to being treated the same way they have been treating the right" (Slagle 2010). Comedian David Razowsky concurred and argued that the "best audiences were conservative" because they could take the joke. The worst audiences? The liberal ones:

> The worst audiences at *Second City* were liberal and Democratic, especially the ones from Chicago's North Shore, which consisted of suburban Jews, because they took it all personally. Say there was a show bought out by Temple Shalom or something, we would call it the "Jews Against Comedy Show." They just didn't get it (Razowsky 2010).

According to Slagle, this imbalance has had a two-pronged effect: liberals have had a harder time being made fun of, and conservatives have adjusted too well to mockery:

> They're used to it . . . Here is a great example, let's look at the history of the Presidents through *Saturday Night Live*. Okay, first president, President Ford played by Chevy Chase, remarkably with no makeup or voices. And, how was he played? Well, a guy that did prat falls, a guy that was clumsy and stupid and oafish. The next President, Jimmy Carter, played by Dan Akroyd. How was he played? As a guy so intelligent that he didn't realize that people were making fun of him (Slagle 2010).

A problem that has arisen from these set patterns is the difficulty in making jokes that challenge existing impressions. This goes back to the idea that the jokes that are funniest are those that are most accessible to the most people. This means that jokes resting on stereotypes will be more readily accepted than those that challenge them. Thus, the humor that rests on the hackneyed political party labels or the impressions of the political ideologies of the last 40 years serve to reinforce these existing stereotypes. So if the prevailing impression is that liberals are bleeding-hearted hippies and Republicans are monocle-bedecked, vest-wearing gazillionaires, these jokes will be made more often than others. Several conservative satirists argued that any joke they made that went against the existing conventional wisdom was immediately rejected. Ned Rice gave an example:

> The premise of a joke . . . you know, the thing you bounce the punch line off of . . . has to be something that's generally perceived to be true, whether it is or not. Dean Martin wasn't really

drunk all the time on stage, but since most people believed that he was Dean did a lot of jokes about being drunk on stage. Anyway, certain conservative beliefs are not shared by the general population, like the idea that having a strong military can actually prevent war, or the idea that some anti-poverty programs have actually made the problem worse. This makes it hard to get laughs from jokes that are written from a conservative perspective. Unless your entire audience is very partisan conservatives! (Rice 2010).

When comedians make political jokes, they often fall back on preexisting ideas which can mandate for satirists to find very specific audiences. Someone who wants to do political material also has to expect that if they take sides they automatically lose half of their audience the second they advocate a position. Tim Slagle described doing stand-up at comedy clubs where the audience "just wanted penis jokes," and political material was eschewed:

> Part of the reason why I started going away from satire was because the clubs weren't comfortable with it in general...I don't think the nation has ever been more polarized or more evenly split than it has been. That happened around [the year] 2000...the 2000 election polarized everybody. So it, it has been that way for 10 years now, so that anytime you make a political joke it is, you know, half of the audience is going to disagree with it (Slagle 2010).

Even if someone only dabbles in the political, they would assume this would be very much on their mind. Marc Maron argued that club owners are hesitant to book political comedians for exactly this reason:

> If you've got a club owner who doesn't give a shit who's in week to week, they just want to sell tickets. If you're a political comic you'd better be coming with your own draw...There [are] really not that many political comics and it's not because people don't have the courage to do it. It's because most people think its tedious, and most people don't do it very well (Maron 2011b).

Radio host and stand-up comedian Pete Dominick argued that when comics pick sides, they have to find niche audiences that like their material—especially right-wing comics: "'Conservative' comedians aren't very successful. They don't find an audience, they find niche audiences" (Dominick 2010). Boston College professor Paul Lewis, author of *Cracking Up: American Humor in a Time of Conflict*, made the point in an interview with Politico that this niche quality supports right-wing political humor: "Conservative humor has never been dead and has never lost its voice... Just don't look for it in the comedy club" (Libit 2009).

The polarization of the political material can be off-putting for both the comedian and those who employ him. Tim Slagle told me that this drives decision-making on the part of comedy club bookers who select performers for their shows. He made the argument that the ideological makeup of the audience further drives the type of political comedians who are booked. How so? Because, says Slagle, the liberals are the ones who complain. Talking about these club managers, Slagle wrote in an email:

> I mentioned that a lot of [club owners] are hesitant, because when a political joke is made, there is a good chance that half of the audience will be on the side getting attacked by the joke. What I didn't get around to, is that clubs who DO take the chance with booking a satirist, they quickly learn that it's always the Left Wing people who complain to management. (Left Wing people are the kind who like to write letters.) So club owners will be more hesitant to book a Right Wing act. Some owners might not even look at it politically, they'll just say: "I always get a lot of complaints when I book that guy, so I won't" (Slagle 2010).

It is possible that liberals complain more often than conservatives, but complaints of any stripe are discouragement from booking any political comedians at all. Will Durst made the point that it's all about money. If you can bring in an audience, then the club bookers will hire you, period:

> There are some very conservative comics but they are smart enough to hide their opinions because it is not the grease and shoot to the big time, I'm telling you. [They say] they won't get booked because all the club owners are liberal. That is bullshit. The club owners, all they care about is the bottom line... Paul Mooney is a political comic and he is [conservative], but he sells

tickets and he is way out there and he takes a lot of chances and he gets away with it. He has built up a following and his people will buy drinks (Durst 2010).

Political humor is a specific type of humor, and when an audience knows a comedian specializes in politics, they are ready for the subject matter. When political humorists have a following, they can be as political as they want without risking very much. Ask anyone in the coveted 18-to-24 demographic about *The Daily Show*, and chances are they'll know who Jon Stewart is. Will Durst is a stand-up comedian, but his column is syndicated in newspapers around the country and so he has enormous name recognition. Tim Slagle is a blogger for one of Andrew Breitbart's sites and so visitors there know what to expect from his postings. These preexisting understandings of a satirist can constrain or compel the amount of political material a comedian uses. Says Durst:

> When I do my little one-man show in a theater and they come to see it on purpose, then I know that they are there for a reason and they want to hear what I am saying. But, if I am just in a comedy club and they just wandered out to a comedy club sometimes they just want to hear dick jokes, you know. Oh, no it is fine, and fair and right in genre because unfortunately due to the booking policies of the clubs that is what they have come to see and that is what gets successful and that is who gets re-booked and so you are propagating that audience. You are salting that audience...when they know who you are and they know what you do, your audience will skew that way (Durst 2010).

For those who are less well-known or are just starting out, this makes using political material more risky. Marc Maron argued that using political material detrimentally limits a comedian's career:

> Once you get pigeon-holed as a comic, it becomes divisive automatically just be how you are labeling yourself. So when you are a political comic that really means that when you enter a work situation or before anyone even hears what you have to say, half of your audience has already decided who you are (Maron 2011b).

And once you get a reputation as a specifically flavored political humorist and develop a following, you'd better not change your mind too much lest you lose your following. Ask Dennis Miller about that.

Even within these niche audiences and even for those with a dedicated following, conservatives argue that the political climate is such that they cannot make conservative jokes for fear that even a like-minded audience will be uncomfortable with their material. Conservatives in general love to rail against political correctness, but we can disregard this attack and see that specific topics such as race, gender, and ethnicity garner a tremendous amount of discomfort. Conservatives argue, therefore, that in what one satirist called our "hyper-sensitive culture," their jokes are not amenable to conservative satire.

This naturally leads to the question of, what is funny? But we'll forgo that temporarily and address the issue of political-correctness-stymieing humor. Nick DiPaolo spoke forcefully about how, as a white, straight man he was limited in the jokes he wanted to do about race, gender, and sexuality. He gave me an example of a joke he told on Sean Hannity's Fox News show and explained the effect of political correctness on joke reception:

> Hannity is such a straight laced guy...We were talking...it was right after the stimulus bill and he was asking why there was so much pork in it, and I go: "Maybe Obama left so much pork in it because he's trying to prove he's not a Muslim." Which is actually a great line. It's a great joke. Hannity turned, like, white. You see what I'm saying? And he's on my side politically, but that's too "anti" a thing to say...I mean, even if the audience is mostly Republican they're afraid to laugh out loud because of this politically correct environment that's been created over the last 40 years...You see what I'm up against? And you're gonna tell me that Jon Stewart or left-leaning comic has these conversations when they want to rip Senator Craig or whatever? And like I said, even people who have the same politics as me, they get uncomfortable sometimes if I do something that's really off-color in a club, because they might be construed as racist or misogynist, for laughing at it out loud (DiPaolo 2011).

The obvious response to this line of argument is that some humor isn't funny or that even satire that is supposed to be a poke in the eye to the established culture must operate within social norms. But this is a topic debated often among comedians and satirists, and the question of off-color material divides along the "comedy is supposed to be challenging" and "put a sock in it" lines. Marc Maron spoke quite eloquently about this argument on his podcast, WTF, when interviewing comedian Gallagher:

> There's this idea around doing certain jokes that are clearly bullying, that are clearly minimizing, whether the jokes are about gays or blacks or whatever...and there's a way to do that stuff and there are people who have license to do it. Does everyone have the license to do it? Of course. Is there a price to pay for it? Sometimes. Can you please everybody? No. Can you entertain everybody? No. Ultimately it's going to be what's in your heart—how do you treat other people? Do some of those jokes reveal hypocrisy? Absolutely. But there's this argument...that what you do as a comic is release aggression, you ease aggression, you disarm things. And I think that's true. But I think there's a deeper level to it too, that you also reveal hypocrisy, that you satirize extremes in order to make a point about society, about our culture, how we see the world. I agree with that. But at some point, if you're doing jokes that hurt people...well, OK, fine. You can say, "They're babies. They can't take a joke." Well maybe they've been taking that joke their entire fucking life and all they hear it as is pain and attack (Maron 2011a).

But even when comedians temper their tongues or when their humor is satirically mocking racism or homophobia, there is still ample room for misunderstanding. When an audience doesn't get that a joke is really a joke, the satire can fall flat. *Conan*'s Brian Stack told me about a character he created for *Late Night*:

> He was kind of a big bossy type crooner from the 30's who was incredibly, misogynistic, racist, like he'd talk about cooperating with the Nazi's but he sang about it in a very you know, Bing Crosby type voice, and I always thought it was so over the top...But I was often shocked like how people had read into that, [saying] "I can't believe you are talking about women that way or talking about minorities or the poor." He would talk about how the poor should set up with gladiator bikes. Like things like that that were just, you know, I considered so cartoonishly over the top but even then, you'd have people would

write in and say: "As a woman, I am deeply offended." I even sang songs about the Irish being, getting fucked before they were born and I am Irish. So, I was singing songs about my own people and making fun of them and people would write in and say: "As an Irish person I am deeply offended" (Stack 2010).

Maybe it is this overly sensitive political climate that limits the types of jokes conservative satirists can make, or perhaps it is that conservatives find different things funny than liberals do. Certainly the targets are going to vary. Liberals will pick on conservatives (although because they are liberals they will also pick on themselves—see Chapter 5), and conservatives will pick on liberals. But things get complicated when conservatives allege that political correctness hinders their humor when their targets are not white, straight, Christian men—because let's face it, many liberals are none of the above. One terrific example of this is found in President Obama who is, with an African father and a white American mother, the very definition of African American. Writer Jimi Izrael went so far as to describe the president thusly: "When you look at him you see he's black. I mean it's not like he's Vin Diesel and we're all scratching our heads" (Izrael 2011). The issue of the president's race has surfaced for comedians who are sensitive to accusations of racism, and a confounding problem has been discussing a president who came into office so widely adored by the left.[vi] The combination of this, according to conservatives, has been a comedic free pass for a president they don't like very much. Tim Slagle said that liberal satirists "have a hard time seeing anything funny about him," but that mocking the most powerful man in the world was an important function of a satirist, no matter who was in office:

> It is probably a myth but it is a myth I adore that the, that the jester was kept on the court of the king because he was the only one that told the king that he was an idiot and the reason why good kings would always have a jester, it was because there would be at least one person whose job it was to remind them that they were human (Slagle 2010).

[vi] A standing the president managed to change within a year.

Other conservatives argued that there was much to make fun of, but race sometimes got in the way. Even liberals agreed that it could be tricky when doing racial material about Obama, even if the joke was clearly not racist. I asked Will Durst why it was so hard to mock Obama, and he told me this:

> Well, for one thing it is hard to mock hope. Hope is a very fragile thing and if you are kicking it, it is like kicking a small, furry whimpering thing with big eyes...Also, the racial thing it has a lot to do with it. It is hard to take on Obama and not mention his race and once you have mentioned his race audiences...don't want to be seen as laughing at something that might be racist. If they don't know it is racist, if it is just racial they think that it kind of bleeds into racism, so you have that problem. For instance, I do a joke, you know, the Tea Party movement apparently there are a lot of people in this country that never get used to the fact that we are now being governed by a black guy living in public housing. I get laughs sometimes and sometimes, you know, the audience goes ohhhh... [Another joke:] We can elect an African American President but first why don't we try out a half black guy, you know, like a starter negro, you know, a hybrid, baby steps and we work our way up to Ving Rhames (Durst 2010).

When the jokes are more focused on policy or politics, rather than the personal, then race shouldn't come into the equation at all. But even then, President Obama is a confounding figure for many satirists and comedians to mock, simply because he does not have many obvious physical ticks that humorists like to lampoon. Said Keegan-Michael Key:

> It has been very difficult for us, for any of us, to find a way to chip away at the veneer. You know, when you do a sketch about him it is never satirical it is always putting him in a position, in a comedic position. There is no comedic engine...The only thing I have found is a couple of mobile signatures and, but they don't lead us to anything satirical so it falls back into the land of parody (Key 2010).

This line of argument makes conservative satirists pretty angry, and they maintain that there are many things to make fun of about Obama but liberals pull the punch. One joke from Nick

DiPaolo aimed at Obama's status as a left-wing darling: "I say you liberals think he's a messiah. You really think he's a messiah. And you may be right, because the minute he was elected I was pointing at my TV going 'Jesus Christ!'" (DiPaolo 2011). But as President Obama's time in office has extended, so too has the number of jokes aimed at him. Nonconservative satirists argue that they make plenty of jokes about the president, and happily so. Many agreed with Tim Slagle's earlier point that making fun of the president is the point of their job.

It is the satirists' duty to make fun of those in power, but their politics will drive what they think is wrong, outrageous, and funny. Perhaps we do have a hypersensitive political culture today, but sensitivity (like humor) is in the eye of the beholder. Arguably, if material is offensive, then both liberal and conservative audiences will reject it automatically, but liberals and conservatives have varying ideas about what is offensive. Several of the conservative satirists with whom I spoke argued that generally liberals found too much offense in innocent material which was problematic for them. Liberals would argue that offensive jokes should not be made in the first place, and so the circle continues.

The market demands of humor mandate jokes that are funny to many people. Just because a satirist has the freedom to make an argument doesn't mean he or she will be able to do so. One sticking point that many of the satirists spoke about was the financial viability of doing political humor: it is not everyone's cup of tea, and as a result, in order to hit the big time, more often than not satirists have to combine their material with other, less specific material or tone down their act to accommodate less political audiences. This means that while a satirist may have all the freedom in the world to practice his or her craft, he or she may not be able to afford to do so. Additionally, this "free market of ideas" theory is put into place when the consumers drive the market and demand that offensive material be removed. Here I turn to Jello Biafra, lead singer of the punk group The Dead Kennedys, who was interviewed by Paul Provenza about this topic:

> America has a far *less* free press than many other countries. You can write anything you want to, but who's going to publish it? Sure, you can put anything you want to on the Internet until somebody

complains and MySpace, Facebook, or Google take it down. You can say anything you want to—as long as nobody gets to read it or hear it (Provenza 2010).

The market demands for material would seemingly be greater in the age of the Internet, but what has happened instead is that in order to be heard above everyone else, material has to be edgy enough to warrant attention or be commercially appealing. Thus, it is up to the public to accept or reject material—hence Biafra's complaint.

Conclusions

All taken together, these questions about humor are important to distinguish from the satirists themselves. The kind of person who wants to go into political humor is the kind of person who wants to be a creative artist. The kind of training such a person needs to become successful in the field is the kind of training found in the liberal arts. This together creates a type and environment that attracts more liberals to the field. Certainly the milieu of comedy and the business of entertainment have a preponderance of lefties in their ranks. This is a problematic explanation for conservatives who argue that this prevalence conspires to keep them out of the business at all. Another explanation for the paucity of conservative satirists, beyond the education and profession of the art, concerns the nature of satire itself, which is addressed next.

CHAPTER 5

Being Funny and Being Right, Being Left and Being Right

There is something about satire, the art form that combines comedy with criticism, that may attract more liberals than conservatives to its ranks. Satire is an outsider art, the weapon of the underdog who uses humor to criticize those in power. Every mode of criticism consists of varying qualities, and thus different critical forms play to the strengths of certain kinds of people. For example, talk radio is predominantly a conservative venue and liberal attempts to tap into the AM outrage have generally failed.[i] Does this mean liberals cannot do talk radio? Probably not, but it does mean that liberals are more receptive to a different vehicle for criticism. So there are several qualities of satire that make it a fecund field for liberalism: its antiestablishmentarianism, its desire to take on hypocrisy as a target, and its position as the vehicle of the little guy. This chapter explores satire as an art form, examining its qualities and its necessities to distinguish it from other types of criticism. It also explores political humor to show that the driving force of this breed of criticism is humor, making the point that being funny is more important than being "right." This helps to distinguish the satirist from the advocate, the comedian from the activist.

---

[i] See *Air America*.

Qualities of Satire

When I spoke with satirists and comedy writers, everyone agreed that the best targets were those in power and the best foils were those who abused their power. Marc Maron put it succinctly: "The voice of the victim is much funnier than the voice of the oppressor" (Maron 2011c). This antiestablishmentarian viewpoint drove most of the comedic lines, and distrust of power was pervasive. As shown throughout history, when a politician is in power who is beloved by many (it happens), or when the nation is united in a feeling of patriotic contentment (unfortunately rare), or there is a perceptible national fear (sadly common), then being against "the man" is tough to pull off. But in times of political dissatisfaction, there is a greater hunger for political humor that rails against politicians and those in power positions. This helps to explain the rise of satire during the first decades of the twenty-first century. President Bush began his tenure in office with historically high approval ratings following the terrorist attacks on September 11, but even though he was reelected in 2004, Bush's star began to fall dramatically in public opinion after the shock of the attacks wore off. The Gallup polling company tracked his approvals throughout his eight years in office: President Bush began his administration just above the 50 percent mark, spiked to a 90 percent high point in 2001 after the attacks, and steadily declined from there. His first term average was 62 percent. His second term average was 37 percent (Gallup 2009). If satire's popularity grows with political dissatisfaction, then this might explain its success targeting Republicans during the time of Bush's popularity decline.

Criticism against those in power is funnier than humor that comes from the political or social elites themselves. Said *SNL*'s Alex Baze:

> You can look at the world as establishments and anti-establishment, or at the very least establishment and everybody else. You can't say all comedy, all political satire, political criticism, is aimed at the establishment. But if you are a member of the establishment there is A) nothing for you to mock, and B) Everything you mock is something you control so who are you complaining to? (Baze 2010).

This is an excellent point: when people in power use humor, they tend to make fun of themselves or other people in power. Mocking people who are economically, politically, or socially beneath you is fairly well verboten—it feels mean spirited and it isn't very funny.

Satirist Andy Cobb agrees with this assessment and made the point that funny cannot be found by making fun of the little guy:

> A lot of times a lot of comedy comes from an anti-authoritarian point of view, and if you are going to ref for the man your bets better be pretty high because otherwise, there just isn't a real big comedic factor to be had for showing for BP, you know, or any of the other things that I feel like I see on *Fox News* (Cobb 2010).

Because of this antiestablishment quality, satire works best when it originates from those being mistreated. It is sort of a comedic standard—the complaints of abuse, rejection, or "no respect." When applied to politics, this means it is more difficult for those in power positions to make fun of those whom they represent. Thus, satire has become the weapon of the underdog, mocking those in power and those with a clear advantage. To this end, the late political writer Molly Ivins once said, "Satire is traditionally the weapon of the powerless against the powerful. I only aim at the powerful. When satire is aimed at the powerless, it is not only cruel—it's vulgar" (J. Lewis). In modern America, there is much hue and cry about difference between the elites and the rest of us (the 99 percent as it were), and those with the gigantic 401K plans are keenly aware of this.

Of course this is not new. Comedian Lewis Black used the historical example of humor brought about by the immigrant experience to illustrate the underdog quality of comedy:

> I do think that there is some correlation between that immigrant experience and trying to transition and be treated like shit . . . poor people survive through humor or, I mean, if they do survive, they survive through humor. You know, that is the big thing. That is how you can deal with life, in looking at a disparity in this you can either be emasculated by that or enabled. Humor is an enabler (Black 2010).

This idea feeds into the old saws that humor is the best medicine and the one about bravery consisting of laughter in the face of danger. Satirist and talk show host Matthew Filipowicz put a stronger point on it: "Generally it is not funny if you are attacking those who are powerless . . . I mean like, hey a homeless guy came up on the street and I told him, hey get a job, ba dum dum—It's not funny" (Filipowicz 2010). Former MSNBC host Cenk Uygur argues that in the end

> it is easier to make fun of things that are in power. Like if you are picking on your weaker, younger brother or you are picking on a little old grandma, it is not funny. You are being a dick. But if you are picking on the powerful or the establishment, that is, of course, funny. Right? (Uygur 2010).

No less a liberal than Franklin Delano Roosevelt outlined this leftist dedication to the powerless in his second Inaugural Address: "The test of our progress is not whether we add more to the abundance of those who have much, it is whether we provide enough for those who have too little" (1937). This conception of liberalism helping the weak has remained consistent throughout modern times; Marc Maron described liberalism as "the big tent, which is [where] everyone deserves a voice" (Maron 2011c). This voice, sometimes, comes in the form of political humor, speaking truth to power and fighting for those who are not in positions of influence.

This then brings up an important point about who holds the reins of power, which gets us back to ideology since much of where you stand depends on where you sit. Cenk Uygur argued that "the conservatives are overwhelmingly in power" (2010) which may best be explained by his left-leaning ideology, but his argument about conservative power-holders is a widely accepted. Conversely, conservatives argue that when Democrats control the White House and pass mandatory healthcare legislation through Congress, then conservatives are not the ones in command. They make a good point. However, in early twenty-first-century America, while both political parties have power and rotate in and out of positions of leadership, the primary political ideologies are unequally represented by those elected. Simply put, the nation has moved rightward in the last half-century and even as Democrats are in power positions, liberals are not dominant in Washington. Many Republicans will reject this assessment and call the Democratic leadership socialist, but just ask the Democrat's progressive base and you'll fund far more stinging condemnations of the party's moderation. This battling makes sense, because it is a political imperative to acquire power and the political party not in charge always complains that they are being trod upon. If one spends time in Washington, DC, it is fairly obvious that power is achieved simply by virtue of being elected, regardless of party affiliation, but control over Congress or of the executive branch does provide more influence. Thus, when one party is dominant, the minority party cries "victim." But regardless of which party is in control of the government, a few of the qualities of American ideology and partisanship do lend themselves toward ideas of power: liberals tend to side with the poor and the powerless, and this is one important characteristic of their philosophy. At the same time, while conservatives certainly do not spit on the poor, their political philosophy leans more toward self-determination. This manifests itself in liberal policies supporting welfare and conservative efforts to roll back government assistance. As a result, the left oftentimes is associated with the struggling while the right is associated with the powerful. Add to that the nation's shift rightward in the past four decades and the culmination is a larger collection of conservatives in power, fewer liberals elected to office, and an overwhelming sense of betrayal at those who seem to "sell out" to those in the center.

Regardless, conservative comedian Evan Sayet argued that the very notion of conservatives or Republicans being powerful is a misconception: "Okay, you are engaging in a leftist canard which is that somehow the Democrats are the party of the powerless, the Republicans are the party of the powerful. That is simply not true" (Sayet 2010). Sayet's point is prescient at a time where party power waxes and wanes fairly regularly, and liberals argue that the Democrats are not doing enough for the defenseless.[ii] But there is something about the ideas of conservative power that sticks; Ned Rice expanded on this a bit more:

> If you just glance at the newspaper headlines, if you just listen to the news with one ear and...just sort of dabble in it, liberal ideology probably will appeal to you more, because it seems— and I am making huge, giant air quotes here—it is nicer. Okay, it seems nicer. We are going to take care of people, we are going

---

[ii] Although I doubt this is was Sayet was arguing.

to do this, we are going to take care of poor people, we are going to take care of this and that. You don't have to worry about anything. We will take care. And we are all for peace. We don't want anyone to get hurt. We don't war, guns are bad, we shouldn't hurt animals. So, that is all appealing...because most people want to be nice (Rice 2010).

The cartoon image of Republicans as having vested suits, monocles, and money bags has permeated our culture, and this caricature persists. The GOP mascot is an elephant, for heaven's sake. Because this impression endures, it is easy to make a joke predicated on this assumption. Said comedian Peter Grosz:

I think it is because jokes and satire is about ease and relaxation and laughter...and conservatism is like a guy in a stuffy suit. Everything they do says "don't laugh at me" and "don't make fun of me." All that makes you want to do is make fun of them...I think there is something specific about that actual conservative character that sort of begs to be made fun of, especially with young audiences...That conservative image of power is more like ripe for taking down (Grosz 2010).

And let's be honest: it may be easier for a camel to go through the eye of a needle than for a rich man to enter the Kingdom of God,[iii] but it is a heck of a lot easier to make fun of a rich man than it is a poor camel.

Many of those whom I interviewed referenced the jester speaking truth to the king, and remember who was in the power position there. Ned Rice noted the definition of satire as deconstructive: "It tends to be David versus Goliath. In other words, the butts of the jokes tend to be the man, right, the government, the king, the boss, the little guy makes jokes at the expense of the guy who has got his foot on the little guys neck, right?" (Rice 2010). This aim at the powerful is well within the liberal wheelhouse. After all, liberals want to change the political system for the purpose of social justice. Additionally, going back to the root of conservatism being to conserve, there is something to be said for mocking those who want to preserve

---

[iii] Matthew 19:24.

the status quo. Comedian Jimmy Tingle said that he saw his humor as just this type of deconstruction:

> I saw it as almost a battle between myself and the way things are; the status quo and the way I saw the world in terms of what it could be or what it might be. So, I think conservatism by its nature is preserving the status quo. I mean, conservatives would [now] argue [that] they want to change 'the status quo' but traditionally, I think liberalism is trying to improve the society or improve the world in terms of justice (Tingle 2010).

The humorists I interviewed felt strongly that if one principal goal of satire was to speak truth to power, then another goal was to illustrate the difference between what is and what should be. This distinction also comes from the liberal toolbox, since the constant exploration for change is not part of the conservative ethos. Abraham Lincoln said, "What is conservatism? Is it not adherence to the old and tried against the new and untried?" Former *Colbert* writer Allison Silverman spoke about the questioning nature of satire:

> My father is a scientist and actually one of the things that I do find interesting is that like the three big people I have written for, Conan [O'Brien] and Stephen [Colbert] and Jon [Stewart], all three of them have fathers who were scientists...And, I think that there is something to that, the idea of being questioning and I think there is something anti-authority about being a scientist...I think that there is a sense of like, yeah, of taking down structures or showing up authority that is pretty key. I don't really know why that is, but I totally think it is the spirit (Silverman 2010).

The liberal commitment to change is exemplified by satirist Ambrose Bierce in *The Devil's Dictionary*, which was first published in 1906: "Conservatism, n: A statesman who is enamored of existing evils, as distinguished from the Liberal who wishes to replace them with others" (Bierce 2011). This desire for change is often rooted in a fight against the established order, and two humorists from Second City spoke of their theater's commitment to "fighting the man." First, from Kelly Leonard: "We're the island of misfit toys, you know, this is a place where being different is celebrated. And, traditionally the world of theater is one that tends to be of a more liberal mind set" (Leonard 2010). And from *Conan*'s Kevin Dorff who worked at Second City on one of their most heralded productions, called *Paradigm Lost*:

> Some of the theses of the show being: don't believe what you hear. You know, do question what you are getting out there and don't despair necessarily of that. Just because you are being lied to doesn't mean you can't do anything about it...I mean, it was no new thing to say, "Hey, the world is not on the up and up," but it was a neat and timely way to remind everybody of that message. I think that is when *Second City* is at its best...It asks that question, never really gives you a lot of answers, but it asks a lot of funny questions. I remember Sheldon Patinkon, an Emeritus presence at *Second City* for years reminding us that *Second City* works best when it asks questions like "Who do you trust, who do you love?" (Dorff 2010).

More often than not, this trust for the comedian is not found within the establishment. Trust is more often found in the questions that disarm the power structure, which is why the status-quo quality of conservatism is often not very funny. If comedy is a humorous protest and a vote for change, then conservatives will not be ripe for this pursuit. Along these lines, changing the status quo begins with a grumble and becomes an objection. Said *SNL*'s Alex Baze:

> You know, the other thing comedy almost always is some form of complaint...If you are fine and there are no complaints, then there is no comedy. That is why *Fox News* comedy didn't work. They were complaining about the people who weren't as powerful as them. It is like: Well, if someone is not as powerful as you, then there is nothing to complain about, you have won. Stop hitting me. You know, it just doesn't work that way. So, I think, people are liberals or lefties or leftists, or whatever, because they have some change they want to see. One way to do it is to complain in a hilarious fashion about the way things are (Baze 2010).

No matter one's party affiliation, picking on those in power is always funny because they're the ones with the muscle. Our ability to speak out against authority is one of the greatest strengths of American democracy, and the real reason for the First Amendment, which guarantees that we can express out opinions without fear of retribution. When Democrats, arguably members of the political party more closely aligned with liberalism, are in power, political jokes should (and do) fly at them as well.

Speaking truth to power is one crucial component of satire, which is why there are those who argue that satire does not necessarily have to be funny to work. But since most satire is supposed to be funny, it is helpful to find a consistent source of laughs. And what is funnier than falseness? Hypocrisy is one of the biggest instigations of political satire and humor, because breaking down insincerity and duplicity is the most effective way to criticize our elected officials. The vast majority of politicians run for office on a platform that inherently includes their contention of excellence, so when they fall far short of this quality then big laughter ensures. This extends across the partisan divide, since politicians of all ideologies are susceptible to hypocrisy, but because conservatives oftentimes wrap themselves in a moralistic blanket, they seem to be the targets of this type of satire more often than liberals. Allison Silverman concurred with this assessment:

> There are certain things that shows like the *Daily Show* and the *Colbert Report*...have a jump on it, and that can sort of cross party lines. Number one is hypocrisy...It was really important to me that we take a critical eye with the left as well. However, I will say that I do think conservatives are a lot more fun to make fun of for a few reasons. They are way better at declaring things and declaring things gives you something to work against (Silverman 2010).

This makes sense: when an openly gay politician is caught being gay, there is no hypocrisy there, and the same thing goes for politicians who advocated gay rights policies. However, there is more to make fun of if a politician takes to the bully pulpit to condemn homosexuality and is caught in a gay scandal,[iv] or if you are a married "devout" evangelical Christian caught in an extramarital affair with your staffer's wife,[v] or a governor who uses his devoted family and his faith as a campaign prop only to be caught in

---

[iv] Sen. Larry Craig (R-ID)
[v] Sen. John Ensign (R-NV)

Argentina with his mistress over Father's Day weekend.[vi] But the same principal applies for politicians who run on platforms of "family values" and then get ensnared with a mistress,[vii] who wear the badge of dogged reformer and then get caught with a hooker,[viii] or who uses his wife as a campaign prop and then tweets pictures of his penis to unsuspecting women.[ix] See? It stretches across party lines! Hypocrisy is a fertile field for a comedian to sow. Says former *Colbert Report* writer Peter Grosz:

> When political satire was about like, Bill Clinton, that was really juicy because he just lied so blatantly to everybody and pointing out the truth in that was just as satisfying, I think, to people as something like finding out that an anti-gay preacher or politician is actually gay. It's like, *come on*, you know. They are making easy targets of themselves (Grosz 2010).

Pete Dominick agrees: "If a guy is railing against, you know, for these 'family values' and then he gets caught with a hooker, it's, that's great, well there you go. That's comedy to everybody" (Dominick 2010). And while this certainly includes Democrats and Republicans, conservatives tend to bang that morality gong a bit louder, which means they will be brought down harder when they are caught.

To a person, regardless of his or her political leanings, every comic I interviewed agreed that hypocrisy was always great joke material. Cenk Uygur used an example to prove this point:

> When one of the leading Christian right bachelors in the country was caught going on vacation with a rent boy...I mean, how's that not funny? And, then when people are caught doing something wrong that is always great too because one you get to expose them and two they are always going to come up with some hilarious excuse. You know, like, in the rent boy story, oh, I got him to carry my luggage...Who in their right mind would believe that? (Uygur 2010).

[vi] Gov. Mark Sanford (R-SC)
[vii] Sen. John Edwards (D-NC)
[viii] Gov. Eliot Spitzer (D-NY)
[ix] Rep. Anthony Wiener (D-NY)

Inherent in the revelation of hypocrisy is the selfishness involved, the implicit argument that someone's own needs are more important than their words or that of the greater good. Conservative satirist Tim Slagle used a different example of hypocrisy which he felt showed how funny it could be: "I like hypocrisy ... [when] vegetarians will expect you to prepare them a special dish when you come over there, you know, when they come over to your house to eat. But, never will they do that for you" (Slagle 2010). No matter what, hypocrisy is fun to mock—it is an obvious flaw, easily understood and highly relatable. Writer Ned Rice pointed out that Jon Stewart is especially good when he is exposing hypocrisy:

> He is good at scouring hypocrisy and, you know, double standards. That is a great deal of what a satirist does is point out hypocrisy and to point out double standards and Jon has done that well. He doesn't do it every day, he can't, but when he has done it recently it has been good (Rice 2010).

Breaking down the artifice that undoubtedly comes with hypocrisy is the juicy stuff of the ultimate "gotcha" moment laced with a touch of "I told you so." It feeds into the dominant idea that politicians are liars, easily corruptible and inherently flawed. It is also very easy to understand, and the jokes will land successfully because of this.

Criticizing those in power and exposing hypocrisy are two dominant forms of satire, but these forms would be useless without one crucial component: anger. Comedic aggression can be focused anywhere, but anger tends to be motivated by a situation that is wrong or a politician who is off beam. Humor is one mechanism by which anger can be constructively processed. There are different breeds of anger, some of which can be channeled into humor and some of which cannot. For example, revenge isn't particularly funny, but righteous indignation is. Making anger funny is a tricky thing to do; not all anger can be treated the same. The kind of anger that is hostile, personal, or cruel is rarely funny, so when jokes emanate from this place, they probably will not be very successful. Several writers mentioned that this angry starting place, which leads to ad hominem attacks and antagonism, weakened any humor to be found in joke material. Speaking about political ideologies, *Real Time with Bill Maher* writer Adam Felber noted this difference:

> Conservatives can be very aggressive, you know, perhaps more aggressive than liberals...I think there is a difference between hostile aggression and just Type A personalities. Comedy is full of very Type A personalities. Whether you are, you know, the meanest, most dastardly old-timey, you know, standup comic, or you're the most cooperative, friendly, suave comic: You are Type A...I don't think that is the same sort of aggression as anger (Felber 2010).

More often than not, a satirist starts with some sense of outrage or anger. Milquetoast humor is best left to nonpolitical humorists striving for popularity, steering clear of the topics that can alienate an audience. This means that even with a political comedian's aspiration for success, there has to be some sense of outrage. Many humorists hone this anger to an art, and others mask it within a kinder tone, but all political humor contains some sense of anger at a situation. This is fairly logical, because the events that spark outrage tend also to be the ones that are prominent in the zeitgeist. We tend to have a short attention span in this country, which is why, when something piques our interest, it dies out fairly quickly. When something is close to our heart, we tend to have a passionate response about it, which is where satirists find their material and an audience finds either laughs or offense. Said satirist and talk show host Matt Filiopwicz:

> I think the stuff that gets you maddest, the stuff that gets you angriest, are the things that you should be talking about the most because those are probably the most important topics out there and they are probably the things that [need] keeping the most attention to (Filipowicz 2010).

Events that don't make you mad are impossible to make fun of because it is the inconsistency and oddity of life that we pass judgment on. Once we have accepted a situation as "normal," there is nothing to mock. When life deviates from the normal, it is a natural response to look for the cause of the problem, which then leads to taking sides. Said Keegan-Michael Key: "You can't write effective satire unless you take a side" (Key 2010).

Second City founder Bernie Sahlins said that the side to pick was always against the power structure, because "it points out that it is the way things are and the way things ought to be" (Sahlins 2011). But because this can be abrasive, one effective way to make this point is by couching it within softer material. One former Second City writer gave credit to Sahlins for crafting Second City shows with a running order that obscured the criticism and made it palatable for an audience: "A 90 minute show, 45 minutes first act, 35 minutes second act, and hear ideally a series of unconnected sketches: . . . dick joke, dick joke, dick joke, indictment of the audience's lifestyle, dick joke, dick joke, dick joke, so it is kind of like when you are not looking—here is the thing." So the best satire has a point of view, starts with some anger, but is couched in a way that can make an audience laugh. Take Stephen Colbert for example. His "Stephen Colbert" character is a comedic construct but, as David Razowsky says, he is also very real. The character is a bombastic blowhard who speaks before he thinks and reacts with knee-jerk pomposity to any confrontation. The real Stephen Colbert is the guy who created the character. Razowsky compared Colbert's character construction to the epitome of satire, Jonathan Swift's *Modest Proposal*: "[Colbert] does have a point of view, a very, very strong point of view . . . But that is what satirists do, you know. How do we control population? Eat the kids" (Razowsky 2010).

While anger can be processed into humor, when it stays simmering in vitriol, it just ends up pissy and not very amusing. When a comedian is so angry they are unable to distance themselves from their emotions, aggression can slide into somber. Additionally, when a comedian takes personal shots against someone it ceases to be funny. Observed Andy Cobb:

> If somebody that is allowing it to cloud their judgment and drive them to just sort of having a little ad homonym like "liberals are stupid," then that, that certainly detracts from the comedy. Perhaps similar to the way that our demons always drive us or destroy us, if it is clouding your judgment as a comic that is an issue. But if it is inspiring you to work than I think that is probably a good thing. But, you know, I think that is what is great about *Saturday Night Live* over the years,

it comes from all sort of ideological ranges and I believe they have some conservatives writing on their show[x] (Cobb 2010).

Cobb's point is a good one: the same type of emotion that can encourage funny material can also make it profoundly unfunny. Aware of this, satirists occasionally avoid the most passionate of topics, holding instead to the more mainstream material. The comedians were split when I asked if they would use material they felt extremely strongly about to make a joke. Some said "absolutely," and others said "no way," but all maintained that a certain kind of rage was crucial for satire to find its groove. What may temper the anger of satire is the idea that something better does exist, even if it is not being achieved at the moment. As far back as 1940, the anger of satire (and satire's root in goodness) was noted in scholarship that examined the composition of this specific breed of humor. From Louis Bredvold, who wrote in the *Journal of English Literary History*:

> We often speak, too, of the anger and malice of the satirist. But we must distinguish between the simple and instinctive forms of these feelings and their very limited and specialized character when they become associated with indignation. The anger of the cheated horse-trader who vows revenge is one thing; the anger of a just God is another, and more likely to help us understand the nature of indignation...The judgment at the core of the feeling of indignation involves a conviction regarding righteousness; indignation is the emotional realization of righteousness and all great satirists, as has always been observed, have been moralists. Though their picture of mankind has been anything but cheerful, they have not yielded to the ultimate cynicism, the derision which is directed against the very concept of the good (Bredvold 1940).

If satire is the process of turning anger into joy, then there has to be some sense of joy within it. Satirists, as deeply cynical as they might be, have not yet "yielded to the ultimate cynicism."

Satirists may be cynical about the world around them but most are even more skeptical and disparaging about themselves.

---

[x] They do.

Most of the comedians I interviewed acknowledged (occasionally massive) insecurities on their part. The combination of comedic anger with insecurity leads to self-deprecation, which can be quite funny, and this ultimately allows other humor to grow. Self-deprecating humor seems to be the gateway to peripheral mockery—once you make fun of yourself, then everyone else around you is fair game. Said Andy Cobb, "I guess that is a lot of what comedy is. You have to first make fun of yourself to make fun of anything effectively or accept that you can be the butt of the joke like anyone else" (Cobb 2010). If something is too important to you, it is unlikely to be funny, and if you take yourself too seriously, you probably are not self-deprecating. This is why those on both extremes of the ideological spectrum are not very good comedians. Put another way, if you are a member of PETA,[xi] you are less likely to find humor in the absurdities of PETA's lobbying tactics, which are actually pretty outrageous.[xii] Along these lines, if you are devoutly religious, you are less likely to find humor in atheistic comedy or in comedy that openly mocks religion. There is something similar between the absoluteness of politics and religion, which may be why political activists have a hard time finding the humor in their beliefs, and those who are devoutly religious cannot find humor in jokes that question their beliefs. According to Keegan-Michael Key, this absoluteness leads to the same kind of rejection of relativism which is where humor can originate. He pointed out that those in fundamentalist circles will say, "Look folks, I didn't write the Bible. I don't like it either, but that is what it says so that is what we are going to do" (Key 2010). This serves to separate comedians who are clearly unreligious and will mock religion from those who are devout and scoff at those who question their beliefs. Organized religion is such an important quality of American society that satirists often like to use it as a foil. Key warns that finding humor in religion can

---

[xi] People for the Ethical Treatment of Animals, a fringe animal-rights group.

[xii] Examples include (but are not limited to) staging a nude model protest, displaying a topless pregnant woman in a cage, declaring animals have Thirteenth Amendment citizenship rights.

be tricky, especially if the person making the joke misjudges the target:

> I think, most of the people that I work with had had some kind of negative experience with Catholicism, [and they'll say] "let's write a scene about the negative experience that I had with Catholicism." And they are going: "Now that is religious satire." Actually, it is just you making fun of a church. That is all it is. There is no satire there at all really, you are just mad at some priest (Key 2010).

This is why simple anger is not enough to make a joke, and the reason people with especially strong beliefs, either about politics or religion, are seldom comical about their passions. The comedic graveyards are filled with the carcasses of unfunny jokes whose aim was askew, or whose end point was not accessible enough for an audience. This gets back to the origination point of a political joke or satirical argument which must be, to some degree, aimed at being funny.

Being Funny and Being Right

Time and again satirists argued that the genesis of a joke may have been politically motivated, but the punch line had to be funny, which meant the laugh line was more important than the message. Many satirists mentioned the term "clapture"[xiii] to signify when an audience agrees with your point but doesn't think you are being funny as you are making it. Clapture is by all accounts, to be avoided at all costs. In fact, a good number of interviewees mentioned clapture in the same tone of voice as one would mention syphilis.[xiv] The idea of telling a nonfunny political joke that made a point without humor seemed repellent to most. Former *Colbert Report* writer Allison Silverman defined clapture as such:

> A lot of time audiences when they sort of agree with your point, will clap instead of laugh, and it is almost even worse than if there

---

[xiii] Pronounced "clap-tur," the term has been credited to Tina Fey, Amy Poehler, and Seth Meyers. I am not certain who originated the term, but it has become ubiquitous in comedic circles. I heard about it often.

[xiv] Quietly, gravely, with an implied denouncement of the affliction.

was silence. It feels easy and heavy-handed and . . . I don't feel like it is a big achievement to make people clap, which essentially means to get them to admit that they agree with you (Silverman 2010).

Another former *Colbert* writer, Peter Grosz, agreed and added: "There was a phrase that Peter Gwinn said at work, one of our writers said it was a joke-like noise, like you would write a joke, but it really isn't a joke" (Grosz 2010). *The Daily Show's* Kevin Bleyer said that the point of the *Daily Show's* writing was to craft a joke that was timely and funny: "We are something that makes them laugh—hopefully—at something that they should be paying attention to. So, do we feel an obligation to cover the big stories? We do. Do we feel an obligation to be funny? We do" (Bleyer 2010). Finding the funny in politics is tough, since much of the material is not accessible to a general audience. Even more difficult is trying not to pander to an existing understanding or relying on a hackneyed argument. Being fresh and original, therefore, is also important. Relying on existing material or indulging an audience belies the whole point. Said Silverman:

> I kind of think that there are jokes that follow and jokes that lead in their inception and you can sort of decide that, okay I think my audience thinks this so I am going to write a joke that reaffirms that my audience thinks this. And, that to me is frustrating. Another one you can do is like, well I think this and I am hoping my audience will think it too . . . In my mind, to write what you think your audience already believes is a drag. I think it is not only like kind of morale-sapping but it is just usually not as good because if you don't really think it then you don't have really anything insightful of it (Silverman 2010).

The consistent and immense pushback against clapture was evidence that the "funny" trumped the "right." While material could be edgy or uncomfortable, when it became motivating or preachy, it ceased to be humor. Lewis Black was blunt about a joke being a joke and not a "message":

> You can ask every comic working who does anything like that. All you worry about is if they laugh. Everything else is meaningless. Otherwise you shouldn't fucking be up there . . . You learn

that early on, these people don't come here to listen to you fuck-
ing bullshit...Go on the lecture circuit. They came here to be
entertained and that is the deal (Black 2010).

This funny imperative was so widespread among those whom I
interviewed that it extended across ideological lines and throughout varying comedic forms. *Conan* writer Brian Stack argued
that the funny imperative trumped all questions of ideology or
politics on his show—all that mattered was the laugh:

> I think we didn't feel like there was a left-leaning or right-leaning
> agenda at our show. I think it was if we find a way to do some-
> thing funny about Cheney or we find a funny way to do some-
> thing about Obama or we find, just basically we go with what's
> funny. Even though I think a lot of the shows have a reputation
> as being leaning to the left, and I think that is probably accurate
> in general. When it comes down to it, we are really just trying to
> write something funny...In comedy you can't really afford to
> grind a political ax if you are not being funny, you know. Who
> wants to be hit with a sledge hammer? (Stack 2010).

Stack went on to quote comedy writer Mike Nichols, who argued
that the point of all comedy—even political comedy, ostensibly—is the humor. According to Stack, Nichols said something along the lines of, "The unspoken question the audience
always has is: 'why are you telling us this?' And if the answer
isn't: 'Because it's funny,' there better be a damn good other
answer" (Stack 2010). David Razowsky put a finer point on this:
"Oh, God, making a point is so boring. Funny trumps logic"
(Razowsky 2010). But making a point is par for the course, and
since comedy is a business, many have to balance their humor
with their criticism. According to Second City's Kelly Leonard,
being funny and being on point are equally important:

> For ticket sales it is more important to be funny. For legacy it is
> more important to make a point. Both are very important to me.
> And ideally, this is just true with the format, the cabaret review
> format allows for all of that. You have plenty of room to be silly
> and smart. You have room to be interactive and presentational.
> You have room to have great solo moments of performance and
> true ensemble moments. It is a big tent art form (Leonard 2010).

Making a point is not the same as agitating and this brings up an even bigger conundrum: how do you make a point without killing people with it? Said Ned Rice, "Nobody wants to be lectured. When you go to a comedy show you don't want to be lectured. That is something I wish people would remember and they sometimes don't" (Rice 2010). When comedians do not remember to temper their opinions, they run the risk of becoming hostile, personal, and (most importantly) unfunny. To illustrate this point, *Wait, Wait*'s Peter Sagal talked about Will Ferrell's depiction of president George W. Bush versus the illustrations of Bush from cartoonist Ted Rall. He referenced one particular scene from Ferrell's one-man Broadway show about Bush called *You're Welcome America*:

> There was that great moment in the middle where all of a sudden it was like [Bush] had this terrible moment of doubt…like "What if I mess this up?" And he is haunted by the thought of the soldiers that were killed. And in a weird way, that thing makes the rest of it possible. There is this moment where Will Ferrell actually humanizes it. You know…Will Ferrell in a real way kind of likes him. Will Ferrell's George Bush is dumb and does stupid things, is oblivious, but he is a decent guy which is why you watch him. You contrast that with, say, Ted Rall who pictured Bush as literally a bloodthirsty monster with fangs and blood dripping down his fangs. That is not funny. I mean, that is just literally hateful in that he hates him and it is literally repulsive. I am repulsed by it and I do not wish to look at it any longer (Sagal 2010).

Political comedians, especially those who feel strongly about their politics, may be tempted to proselytize, but most of those I interviewed warned against this. One former Second City cast member told me that if a comedian tried to make an argument, then the joke becomes preachy—and no one wants to be preached at. Comedian Will Durst agreed, going even further into defining his job description:

> My job is not to proselytize; my job is not to change the way anybody is going to think. As a political comic you can't change the way people think. You can play feeds and make them possibly more inclusive and willing to listen to other arguments, but

you can't change the way people think. My job is to make people laugh out loud, on purpose, against their will, so that is what I attempt to do (Durst 2010).

This makes for rough going when an audience so clearly rejects your own beliefs as rooted in your comedy, as Durst described in an appearance in New Mexico: "I started doing my Sarah Palin material and the audience went dead. They were laughing at Bush jokes, they were laughing at Obama jokes, they were laughing at pretty much everything and I hit Sarah and it was like an oil slick. And, I just moved on, you know, I didn't beat them over the head with it" (Durst 2010). But even when you "die" in front of an audience, it's better (according to the comedians and writers) to die rather than to preach.

Of course there is preaching in satire—it appears to be an occupational hazard. Conservatives argue that, inherent in their material, liberals preach their politics and are therefore biased. On the other hand, several liberal satirists argued that conservatives were more concerned with being "right" than their liberal counterparts and thus conservatives were more preachy. Both sides went on to reason that a concern with being "right" lessened the humor of the joke, since politics could inform material but being funny was the ultimate goal. Neither side copped to being preachy. This is because when it comes to politics, those who are interested enough to specialize in the topic always think that they are right. I try to tell my students that there is a difference between truth with a capital "T" (i.e., there are three branches of government) and truth with a small "t" (i.e., the federal government can be a solution to social problems). The first cannot be debated. The second cannot be conclusively proven. But even though everyone's small "t" truth is different, political humor must be rooted in some sort of widely accepted reality (the big "T" truth) or else the joke will not land. This is how many audiences view material: they see the differences between satirists being honest and those trying to be "right." I asked writers how they balanced their opinions and beliefs within their humor, and many told me that anything funny had to be rooted in an accepted truth.

Facts (as opposed to opinion) went a long way in establishing this truth. Said *SNL*'s Alex Baze:

> It doesn't get you anywhere comedically to put beliefs in. If someone doesn't share your belief then they've got nothing to laugh at. But, of course your beliefs are based on a set of things you know to be true...I've observed the world and I have decided that left is the way to go, and other people have observed the world and decided that right is the way to go...But, it doesn't do me any good to try to push a belief into a joke...There has to be a truth about it, which is why both sides are fair game. Whatever is in the zeitgeist whatever people know the truth to be at the moment is all you can play with (Baze 2010).

The reason observational comedy is so successful is because these comedians comment on things their audience can relate to. There is an element of truth in the joke. When politics is added to comedy, these truths had better be uniformly understood because when a punch line hinges on opinion, there is more at stake. This kind of comedy, predicated on opinion and not fact, is not going to work for a mass audience. *SNL* writer Doug Abeles said:

> If it ends up just being strident, it is not going to be funny and what resonates if that you have somehow, hopefully, been able to articulate or reveal some truth, universal "truth" that an audience connects to. You know, that is what will make the joke succeed...not that people agree with your politics...We'd rather, at least on 'Update,' sort of earn the laugh based on the funny rather than the audience agreeing politically...We're really just going for the funny, so regardless of the target it has got to, it's gotta have something more than just, you know, a political point of view (Abeles 2010).

Which brings us back to the "truth." What may end up dividing satire along ideological lines is the fact that in today's political climate the "truth" is seemingly flexible. Stephen Colbert coined the term "truthiness" to help illustrate how even the big "T" truths are debated as if there was wiggle room in fact. From the *Merriam-Webster Dictionary*, the 2006 Word of the Year: truthiness.

> 1. truthiness (noun)
> 1: "truth that comes from the gut, not books" (Stephen Colbert, Comedy Central's *The Colbert Report*, October 2005)
> 2: "the quality of preferring concepts or facts one wishes to be true, rather than concepts or facts known to be true" (American Dialect Society, January 2006) (*Dictionary* 2006)

When one can easily hop online and find evidence of untruths, it can feel like the big "T" truth is, indeed, gone. This makes it especially tough for political comedians searching for humor that is factually based and widely accepted. For example, satirist and talk show host Matthew Filipowicz said that anything humorous had to be rooted in the truth, and he gave this example:

> If something is going to be funny it has to have some kind of basis in reality and truth...Victoria Jackson will go in front of a right wing crowd and say "Obama is a Nazi" and the crowd will go, "Ahhh!" and they will laugh, because to them that is a reality even though he is not a Nazi, he is not a Socialist, he is not a Communist, he is not a Marxist, Fascist, Stalinist, Maoist, Taoist, or whatever they want to call him, you know, or Muslim from wherever. He is not any of that (Filipowicz 2010).

I happen to agree with Filipowicz that Obama cannot be characterized as any of the above classifications, and I can look to political science literature to back up my assertion with evidence. But just as easily, there are those who will look to "Obamacare" as *their* evidence of socialism and reject my truth wholeheartedly. So in political debate in general, the truth is a bit up for grabs. In political comedy, this means that in order to garner the biggest audience, a satirist has to remain pure to his or her craft and take shots across the board. This magnanimity can take two forms: either making sure the jokes are totally balanced between ideological targets or making sure they aim at the same kinds of hypocrisies, inconsistencies, and failures no matter the party affiliation of the target. In other words, as Jimmy Tingle said: "Good satire goes after more than just one political party" (Tingle 2010). When asked about balancing jokes between politicians on both sides of the aisle, most satirists stated they cared about a "fair hit" more than balance.

Asking about the fair hit meant a few things. First, the question could be asked: was it a reasonable joke aimed at a politician who had made an obvious mistake? *SNL*'s Alex Baze gave the example of mocking Obama too soon after his election: "Jokes about Obama not being very effective three or four months after the election, not a fair hit yet. He hasn't had time" (Baze 2010). While this idea of the fair hit is easily agreed upon, sometimes a fair hit will seem obvious to some and not to others. For example, *SNL*'s Doug Abeles spoke about a joke that the NBC officials noted because they did not think the hit was fair:

> After "Sully" Sollenberger's heroic landing in the Hudson we did a feature on "Update" where it was Andy Samberg coming out dressed in a goose outfit and being very angry that no one was talking about the geese that perished . . . and NBC had a note for us which was "too soon for that." We were like too soon? . . . Too soon? It was called the "Miracle on the Hudson," not the "Tragedy on the Hudson." It had a happy ending. It is okay to make light of an incident that had a happy ending. I understand, sometimes you have to be sensitive when things don't have a happy ending, but when a story has a happy ending there is no such thing as "too soon." (Abeles 2010).

In the end, most of the time it is the audience that really determines the fairness of the hit. According to Baze: "If something is not a fair hit, they just won't respond, so there is no point in throwing something out there if it is not a fair hit" (Baze 2010). And this brings us back to ideology: what seems like a fair hit to liberals (fighting the power) may not feel fair to conservatives (shrinking the government to the size where it can be drowned in a bathtub) and vice versa.

All humor has to start from somewhere, and this is where the "bias" accusation comes from. We are one polarized little nation right now, and we are spending very little time talking to one another, and more time talking past one another. Loudly. So here come the satirists, making fun of the political environs. They aim their guns at the obviously funny (political sex scandals) or the outrageous (a vice president shooting someone in the face) or the generally accepted (Al Gore is stiff; George W. Bush is inarticulate). This means that something widely discussed in the media is not only fair game, but obvious fodder and so political jokes begin there. An example from the 2012 presidential campaign came from Texas governor Rick Perry, who was running for the Republican nomination. Perry flubbed a debate answer so badly that even his opponents on the debate stage could be overhead disparaging Perry as he floundered. Perry opened a statement by saying that if elected president he would shut down three cabinet agencies, and then forgot which ones he would shutter. Fifty-three *very* long seconds later, Perry finished his disastrous statement by saying, "Oops." Everyone (really—*everyone*) teed off on this. Across the media, humorists began from the same starting point, which was (essentially) that Perry was a dummy. Was this biased or was it accurate reporting? I vote accurate: who sets up his own statement and forgets the hook? Even Perry knew that he looked ridiculous, and went on Letterman to make fun of himself in an attempt to prove affability. So the mocking was universal; Jon Stewart explained this on his show:

> Many of the Republican faithful thought Rick Perry would be the answer to their prayers. Turns out, he was the answer to ours. You know, a comedian can spend his whole life digging through the comedy mines for sound bites he can use to sustain his family. Sometimes a fella can lose hope. But then, Rick Perry gives you 53 seconds that can change a man's life. Oh Lordy, I give you this thing I found: The Dope Diamond...Are you not entertained? There is so much meat on that bone and it is all breast meat. (Stewart 2011).

Calling the gaffe the *"ABC Wide World of Sports* agony of defeat–worthy brain turd," Stewart hammered home the point that a mistake like Perry's was comedic gold, and this had nothing to do with ideology or bias. This leads to another point, that humor amplifies the existing political discussion. If there was not a national narrative about Perry's "oops" moment, the jokes would not be particularly funny. With this amplification comes a price: political discussion is becoming louder and louder.

The arguments being made in comedy are similar to arguments being made in earnest. Satire and political humor add to the existing political cacophony where a large number of voices vie to be heard. The mood of the country is especially angry, and this mood is fueled by the ubiquity of 24-hour cable pundits, talk radio shock jocks, and bloggers hurling personal invectives at politicians and political actors. Satirical critique is more easily accepted when it is embedded within a softer frame because of the tone of political discussion today, but it often becomes part of the larger political discussion and sometimes loses its uniqueness as a comedic form. When all of these political voices blend together, it is easy to see how commentators can allege politicking on the part of the comedian. *Wait, Wait*'s Peter Sagal wholeheartedly rejected the allegation of activism and talked about his vision for his show:

> We are not interested in advancing an agenda...I actually have gotten somewhat sanctimonious about it of late because I am really distressed, as a lot of people are, about the degradation of the discourse. The fact that not only is there a constant war going on in the media but the battlefield is expanding to include everything and I find that really tiresome. People are yelling at everybody. People are screaming at everybody. You've got either conservatives screaming about liberals, liberals screaming about conservatives or the middle [which] means that you have both conservatives and liberals screaming at each other. That makes me sad, actually sad. So, what I like to think of our show is as a respite. That is why I really don't want to take any sides because there is enough of that (Sagal 2010).

Sagal's argument that we are a nation of polarized yellers is right on the mark. We are having a hard time engaging in debate or hearing opposing thought, so entrenched are we in our own beliefs that we cannot see the validity of someone else's. This brings up an important point, which is that most of the satirists I interviewed did not see themselves as biased because they felt their targets were all, by virtue of their political positions, fair game. The late Christopher Hitchens wrote in the *Atlantic* that the liberal rejection of their own biases helps to reject their own claims of impartiality:

> Baudelaire wrote that the devil's greatest achievement was to have persuaded so many people that he doesn't exist: liberal platitudinousness must be a bit like that to those who suffer from it without quite acknowledging that there is such a syndrome to begin with (Hitchens 2009).

Perhaps this is true. It is plausible that if we only hear arguments that reaffirm our own positions and reject those that challenge us, we have lost the ability to see our own biases as anything other than our own conceptions of fact. But the allegations of partiality have become rather skewed from reality when comedians are taken to task for mocking people who deserve mocking. Back to Sagal:

> We make fun of Sarah Palin on our show a lot. People write in and they say, you liberal bastards, you are showing a liberal bias. My response is: "What does thinking or joking about Sarah Palin being an idiot have anything to do with my policy preferences? What does that mean about my views in the role of government in the economy, what does that mean about my views about anything?" ... It is just that people, usually conservatives, have decided that if you don't like Sarah Palin, you are a liberal (Sagal 2010).

This is likely because in our ideological incubation, the politically attentive public squats in a defensive crouch about their beliefs, ready for a fight when provoked. The further out on to the ideological spectrum, the more defensive the position, probably because the feelings are stronger out there. Second City's Kelly Leonard made the distinction between conservatives within the GOP arguing that the more hard-line conservatives had a harder time laughing at themselves than establishment Republicans did. But then again, so too did the hard-line liberals. He told me about the crowds at Second City and the temperament of the audience:

> My personal experience is that Republicans who are not tea party members or fringe, so your everyday standard Republicans ... probably [have] a better sense of humor than the Democrats I meet. That has been my experience. They are smart, they get satire, they don't mind being poked fun at. They

also tend to be less high and mighty liberal do-gooder. A lot of liberals like to be offended on behalf of other people and that gets in the way of having a good time. However, there is a fringe element that appears to be gaining in voice, thank you Twitter, and those folks have no sense of humor. The minute you committed yourself to writing vitriolic statements on billboards, it is really hard. Having a sense of humor about yourself goes out the window because that requires vulnerability, and vulnerability requires understanding and empathy and appreciation for gray areas. So going to black and white, there is no home for satire. There is home for screaming (Leonard 2010).

In our polarized political environment, any slight or commentary opposing our beliefs can be treated as antagonistic instead of amusing. This means that a joke is almost never a joke, but is instead seen as an attack perpetuated by an aggressor. Most of the satirists I spoke with were emphatic about the humor imperative above all, but the more politicized they were, the less likely they would see the value in opposing thought. Hitchens's accusation essentially asks, can these satirists accurately gauge their own partiality? I will hazard a guess that most readers are already shaking their heads no. Political humorists cannot accurately evaluate their own biases because they are too deep within them. Confirmation bias, as noted in Chapter 1, is the phenomenon described by economics professor Daniel B. Klein as, "People embracing statements that make defending their positions simpler" (Klein 2011). Klein has termed this the "my side bias" because people are prone to believe things that reinforce their existing opinions. One consequence of "my side bias" in this research will lead conservatives to believe that the field of political humor is closed to them because of the evidence of ideological bias in the entertainment industry. Concomitantly, liberals will reject this claim, opting instead to affirm their own understandings of the business and the nature of comedy.

A second and equally important consequence of confirmation bias concerns the audience: it would make sense that political humor is going to be funnier if the audience agrees with the political point being made by the comedian. Accordingly, an audience that agrees with a political joke will find it funnier than one that disagrees. So does an audience have to be comprised of politically like-minded people? Certainly, when it comes to political material, the "my side bias" is going to play a role. But does this confirmation bias lead to something deeper—a more profound separation between partisans that drives humor reception? In other words, will conservatives find some things funny and liberals find other things funny? I became stuck in this question of being able to find the humor in political material with which I disagreed, mostly because were that the case then Dennis Miller was going to eventually lose his charm for me. I asked actor Keegan-Michael Key about this, and he rephrased the question nicely before answering it:

> Is it possible that I, as a liberal, couldn't find [conservative jokes] funny? Or is there another explanation was to maybe my sense just didn't grab into the humor? So, with that said, what do you think is funny in terms of political humor and it could be satire or just parody, and can you, can you hear a joke or see a performance that is enigmatic to your world view either be that spiritually or politically and find it funny? I think to the latter question I think yes I can...I feel like I can analyze a joke and say, that joke, that is well wrought. It may not have been well executed, but it is well wrought. I thought it was very interesting (Key 2010).

So here is one possibility: that the art of comedy allows for comedians and audiences to appreciate the humor of a joke even if they disagree with the political sentiment. Key went on to give the example of the Ricky Gervais film *The Invention of Lying*, which is a satirical criticism of all organized religion. Key is religious, but still found the film to be smart and funny: "I didn't like the point that the movie was making because I disagree with the point, but it was made brilliantly because I thought that the way they got into the point is what attracts me" (Key 2010). So humor is a sense, and some people find certain things funny, and some do not. This is going to color the reception of any joke, as is the audience's political leaning. But if we can separate our knee-jerk political responses from joke reception, then maybe the humor element outweighs everything else. I was able to interview several conservative comedians and found much of their material to be very funny, even when I disagreed with the sentiment. I watched a Dennis Miller HBO special with bated breath and ended up laughing quite a bit. But sometimes the jokes simply fell flat, which led me to the question, Is this even funny? And then I landed right smack in the middle of the confirmation bias question again.

There are some jokes we can all agree on—some things that are universally funny. Fabio being hit in the face by a flying pigeon while riding a roller coaster, for example, is unambiguously hilarious. And even in the political realm, there are things we can generally agree on, but more often than not, there are more complicated issues, hypocrisies, and situations that are very debatable. That said, even when situations are complicated or contentious, satirists dive right in because that's what they do. David Razowsky told me about a Second City show that he directed immediately following the September 11 attacks:

> I directed a show called "No Seriously We Are All Gonna Die"...And, I thought, oh my God, people have died and I am making fun of it. But then I thought, no this is a great title and it took me a while but I really wrapped my head around it. First I thought: we shouldn't be making fun of it. But then I realized that this was the time to do it. That it was the time to pull back and go: You know what? Life goes on...What it does is it pinpoints the fear that we are all living in, and we can't live in that fear and live our lives fully at the same time (Razowsky 2010).

One would expect that many people would be offended by this show, but we can also expect that it was a cathartic experience for others. What some people find distasteful, others will think of as ordinary. There are, of course, some things that can never be made funny, and there are sensitive periods when jokes fall flat (see Chapter 3), but many comedians see it as a particular challenge to bring humor during trying times. It is risky to attempt humor in the wake of tragedy, even when laughter is sought as a release from anxiety. When comedians and satirists take such risks, they jeopardize their careers and run the risk of failure. For example, in 2011 a tsunami hit Japan, killing thousands of people. Back in the United States, comedian Gilbert

Gottfried went on Twitter and tweeted a series of tasteless jokes that focused on the disaster. Here are three examples:

- I just split up with my girlfriend, but like the Japanese say: "They'll be another one floating by any minute now."
- My Japanese doctor advised me to stay healthy I needed 50 million gallons of water a day.
- I was talking to my Japanese real estate agent. I said "is there a school in this area." She said "not now but just wait" (Gottfried 2011a).

After these jokes went out on Twitter, Gottfried was fired as the voice of the Aflac duck, a presumably lucrative television voiceover job for which he was well-known. He was interviewed in *Salon* by Kerry Lauerman who asked him about his ability to spark controversy. Lauerman asked about the September 11 jokes that first got Gottfried into trouble a decade before,[1] which then led to a discussion about the Japan tsunami. Asked Lauerman, "You had to know the World Trade Center joke was going to be risky," and Gottfried responded:

Yeah. I definitely wanted a reaction. There was the case of people walking around putting flags on their cars and flags on their lapel like, "Look, I'm doing something," just like the red ribbon that cured AIDS. Scientists saw those red ribbons and suddenly realized they had to cure AIDS. And what I remember, too, about that time, they were thinking of canceling the Emmys, and then they decided to run the Emmys because there's just too much money in the Emmys not to run, but people would be dressing down. So Pam Anderson showed up and she was not showing as much cleavage—that makes the people who died in the World Trade Center feel that much better... I put up on Twitter a line from George Carlin. He said it's the duty of a comedian to find where the line is and cross it. And I thought that put it much better than I ever could (Gottfried 2011b).

So if satirists aim to find the line and cross it, they risk a great deal. But *Conan*'s Kevin Dorff argues that risking failure is an inevitable job hazard: "You know, successful comedy sketches, that is not something you are supposed to be able to bat, you know 800 or 900, when you are supposed to be batting about 100 or 200. If you bat 300 you are a real genius" (Dorff 2010). Political humorists generally don't care if they offend because they see that as in their job description. But when they don't care, they open themselves up to allegations of bias which they, in turn, generally don't care about.

But if political humor has the influence that scholars contend, then the appearance of bias is going to be significant, and in the disharmonious political media noise, it is hard to distinguish comedy from activism. Add to that the boundaries-pushing nature of comedy, and you have a recipe for calls of bias, activism, and heresy. And so political comedians have to find material that suits their audiences well enough for those audiences to get the joke, think it is funny, and appreciate the humor, even if it defies their own political beliefs. In today's political climate, this is going to be a Sisyphean task. It is even more difficult when one believes that people with different ideological beliefs will also have different senses of humor.

Conservatives and Liberals Have Different Ideas about Funny

If there are differences between the humor that conservatives and liberals enjoy, it is because there are differences in their temperaments. According to many of the satirists I interviewed, these differences manifests in the way an audience can accept a joke, and the way a comedian can make one. *The Young Turks'* Cenk Uygur said about his colleagues on the right:

> I think the main thing is they are not kidding. To do comedy you have to be kidding. They, so for example, if I make a politically incorrect joke, which I do all the time, the audience is perfectly aware that I am kidding. I don't think that all fill-in-the-blank are fill-in-the-blank. That would be ridiculous. But, when Rush Limbaugh makes a "joke" about that, is he kidding? We don't think he is kidding, so it is not funny (2010).

So *are* these conservative comedians or humorists actually kidding? A slight problem when trying to answer this is that when a conservative does the "all fill-in-the-blank" joke, it sounds too much like the standard conservative fare. Many of the set conservative platforms are centered on sweeping generalizations about social groups. Liberal comedy does a similar generalizing, but it tends to include criticism of itself in the process. Actor Keegan-Michael Key argued that these generalizations on the part of conservatives can lead to some very smart humor, and argued that Rush Limbaugh in particular can be funny, even if the joke is practically indistinguishable from the rest of Limbaugh's more serious material. In fact, Key made the argument that Rush Limbaugh was a conservative satirist whose humor sometimes goes undetected for the exact reason that it blended in with his nonhumorous dialogue:

> For Rush Limbaugh to be able to put spins on things the way he does shows that he certainly has the capacity for satire. When he says, "If you see a guy laying on the street just move him closer to the first address sign that you see that is spray painted on the curb. Just make that his address. We are good to go. Let's eat." You can't be stupid and say that (Key 2010).

This is a perfect example of conservative humor because it makes an argument using laughter, but what is interesting is the fact that you cannot really tell if Limbaugh thinks it is genuinely a good idea or not. Confusing the audience is not something limited to the right—Stephen Colbert does it constantly according to the Ohio State University study—but audience confusion is problematic. One important element of political humor is being able to see the punch line when it lands.

Another argument made about the different styles of political humor goes back to the point about being impolite. Most comedians ramp up their material in order to make it offensive, because shock brings the kind of cathartic laughter that is really popular.[2] When you add politics to this, the resulting material can be pretty provocative. *Bill Maher* writer Adam Felber told me about what happens when a whole bunch of satirists get into a room together:

> Everything is allowed in the writer's room which is another reason, maybe, why it is hard for conservatives... The room is a hostile environment where there are, there is just no sacred cow. When I say a hostile environment, I mean it is hostile to reverence... You go into that room and you are just going to be laughing about everything. You have to be... In every writer's

room I've ever been in you, you'll joke about homeless people, you will joke about AIDS, you will joke about anything that has to do with human sexuality. There is nothing serious. Nothing that you won't joke about. And, in fact, if there is stuff that disturbs you, that is not a good place for you (Felber 2010).

If this is true, then it also means that the humor that comes out of these writers' rooms will not appeal to conservative audiences, because most of the easily accessible material is pretty indecent. For example, mocking political scandal is de rigueur in political comedy because hypocritical infidelity is comedic gold, but to a social conservative, infidelity is not funny: it's just wrong. The difference between the liberal outlook of moral relativism and the certainty of conservatism manifests itself in these kinds of political fights, which bleed into the types of jokes told by political humorists. This is something that conservative humorist Evan Sayet says is occasionally a challenge:

I just the other day was talking about so many jokes that I have that I can't do. A lot of them, just stuff that has to do with sex, stuff that has to do with drugs, in general, that has nothing to do with politics. I am not talking about the politics of sex, the politics of drugs. I've got funny sex jokes, I've got funny drug jokes (Sayet 2010).

When I asked why he could not do these in his shows, he told me that his conservative audience had come to expect something different from him—they expected clean shows that did not include that kind of bawdy material: "It's not what my audience has come to see and it is not what I promised them. You know, it is kind of like Bruce Springsteen having written a classical song and why can't he do it. I guess he could every once in a while, but how many of those would he insert into his concert?" (Sayet 2010). The promise that many conservative comedians make to their audience comes, according to Sayet, from the fact that the kind of comedy found in clubs simply does not appeal to these audiences:

They don't want to pay $20.00 or whatever else it costs to watch some 18-year-old spoiled brat or 25-year-old spoiled brat who has never matured say shallow and hateful things about Christianity, shallow and hateful things about the United State military, shallow and hateful things about America in general...The political take from the [comedic] communities—meaning the mainstream comedy seen in clubs or on late night TV—that I have spent time with in the past and have spent time with over the years is shallow and anti-good (Sayet 2010).

While I disagree with Sayet's blanket condemnation about club comedians, he does have a point, that conservatives eschew the kind of ribald language that often comes with modern comedy. To recap: a huge challenge facing political humorists is the fact that most audiences don't care enough about politics to seek out this type of humor. A challenge facing conservative satirists is that their conservative audiences are specific about the kind of language they want to hear and the topics they want addressed. And a third challenge may be that conservative audiences may not even see the value in the humor. Keegan-Michael Key made the point that conservatism places values on conservation, loyalty, and hard work, which flies in the face of comedy. He told me about his best friend in Detroit, who is a firefighter and "not a big fan" of President Obama:

He is like: I am sorry dudes. All I did is what I was told to do, which was work my butt off, so that is what I did. I worked my butt off. I made my money so why should I have to give my money to those people who didn't work their butt off?...So that person, that conservative is going to say, I don't understand, look I don't get the satire thing, I don't get it. Why are we even doing it? Or, I should say, why are *you* even doing it, elitist liberals? Why don't you work?...I believe the conservatives find satire frivolous. They find it frivolous. So, when we, when we do see conservative satirist...the reason liberals say they are mean is because their satire, the nature of the satire is also black and white (Key 2010).

The spirit of conservatism may not avail itself to political satire, but conservatives make themselves targets of it, which adds another problem to the mix. This is where Evan Sayat's conception that comedians are "anti-good" probably comes from. But liberals are targets, too, if only by virtue of their sheer liberalness. I asked satirist Will Durst what was funny about the left:

They are never willing to compromise because you can't compromise the truth so they will fight to the death for an inch of law and, you know, they are willing to eat their own. It is not just me, I mean, wasn't it Robert Frost who, 100 years ago or even more, said sometimes it is hard to get a liberal to take his own side in an argument? (Durst 2010).

The libertarian disposition is one well suited for satire, according to a number of satirists. This is probably because the antiestablishmentarianism of satire fits in nicely with the antiestablishmentarianism of libertarianism. One television writer wondered why there are not more libertarian satirists, and he noted that many times political satire is an outsider kind of caution. But the problem with being a libertarian comedian is similar to that of being a libertarian politician: it is a pretty specific club to be in. Writer Tim Slagle noted that his own libertarian tendencies become self-selecting:

> I've been Libertarian for a real long time and I got so solidly Libertarian that I got to the point where only Libertarians found me funny. Everyone else thought that I was going out of my mind and I realized maybe I had to back off the Libertarianism for a while...I tried to be more generic and that didn't seem to work either. And, in the meantime the whole Tea Party thing kind of erupted and I said: "Whoa, I might as well go back to my old market." I guess that would be where, where I am now (Slagle 2010).

This is a cautionary tale, a warning shot about niche audiences and a comedian being too narrowly defined. Slagle told me about a conversation he had with the late Bill Bradford, the former publisher of the libertarian *Liberty Magazine*:

> He came up to me after a show and he said: "You've got to stop calling yourself a Libertarian comedian" and I said: why? He said: "Well usually when you put Libertarian in front of something it is meant as an apology. It is like, well, we couldn't find a real musician so we go a Libertarian musician."...I laughed, but I recognized that he was right. It is that, a lot of time, you know, with Libertarians, is that guys that can't make it in, you know, other areas, have, you know, gone for that angle, gone for the select demographic and, I think that is the problem with the conservative satire that you see (2010).

Going for this specific demographic can keep you going with select groups, but it will not expose you to a wider audience.

And we are indeed moving toward this type of niche programming, where we watch, read, and discuss only the things with which we agree.

Moving Toward Niche Audiences/ Leading with Politics

In an age with 24-hour television, iPods, satellite radio, and split-second Internet access to everything, it makes sense that we are moving toward programming that is so specific, it seems at time to be tailor-made for each one of us. Much has been written about the effect the ubiquity, speed, and constancy of the mass media has affected our lives and our politics,[3] and as we inch toward a personalized media climate, there is a likelihood that our entertainment will become individually exclusive. Building upon the accusation that the entertainment business is run by liberals and the resulting product is biased, there has been a conservative effort to craft entertainment programming exclusively for conservative viewers. The Right Network was funded in part by actor Kelsey Grammar and was launched online in 2010. It features original programming such as Evan Sayet's *The Right 2 Laugh* comedy show and a show from "Joe the Plummer" called *Waddaya Know Joe?* The website posts its mission as such:

> We are proud Americans.
> And we're inspired by the many Americans before us who've stepped forward to help move us all forward. So now we're stepping forward. We're creating a platform where people can join the national conversation. A place where they can be inspired, entertained, laugh together, or just sit back and enjoy being part of a vibrant community with a similar perspective—a right-minded perspective that includes an entire spectrum of opinion from thoughtful and reserved to bold and brash...
> We seek to present the values and beliefs that America was built upon. We aim to be straight shooters and will always come to the party with a potent point-of-view. But we will not dominate the conversation...we'll stimulate it. And we will listen happily as the many voices of the Right combine. We'll always encourage debate and we will not shrink from the fight, if it's a fight worth having (Right Network n.d.).

While it does not appear that The Right Network has exactly flourished, its existence supports the idea that not only are we dividing ourselves politically because of our ideological beliefs, but we are also now going to divide our entertainment, too. This means that when it comes to comedy, there will be an increasing divide along political, topical, and demographic lines. As we move away from general humor, we also move away from that common entertainment experience of yesterday. When we had three TV channels, everyone essentially watched the same thing, but no longer. In fact, the media research organization Experian Simmons did a study in 2011 and showed that liberals and conservatives had wildly differing entertainment interests. According to the study, which examined where conservative Republicans and liberal Democrats found their TV entertainment, the lists of the top 25 shows for each political demographic did not overlap *at all*. Not one show was on both lists. The top five shows on the left were:

1. *The Daily Show with Jon Stewart*
2. *The Colbert Report*
3. *Masterpiece*
4. *30 Rock*
5. *Parks and Recreation*

Meanwhile, at the other end of the spectrum:

1. *Barrett-Jackson Collector Car Auction*
2. *This Old House*
3. *The 700 Club*
4. *Swamp Loggers*
5. *Top Shot*

Central to my own research, the comedy shows *Late Show with David Letterman, Late Late Show with Craig Ferguson, Saturday Night Live,* and *Conan* were all on the liberal list. Only *The Tonight Show with Jay Leno* was on the conservative list[4] (deMoraes 2011). The study was done, by the way, to inform politicians where to best spend their TV advertising dollars based on constituent viewing habits. This means that liberal viewers watching *30 Rock* will be exposed to Democratic politicians far more than Republican ones, which will lead to even more political isolation.

While this may seem divisive and exclusionary, *The Young Turks'* Cenk Uygur thinks that most people bounce around the dial a bit to get a wider variety of programming:

> Everything is a spectrum, right. So, there will be 20–30% of the country certainly on the right wing side and probably a slightly smaller percentage, but some percentage of the left wing side who won't listen to anything, because their identity is invested in that ideology. So, if you challenge that ideology you are challenging their identity, they take great offense to that and so they will shut it out no matter what, okay. So, I get that. But I still think there is a chunk in the middle that could be as large as 60% that will sometimes check out Rush Limbaugh, sometimes check out Jon Stewart, sometimes check out our show, sometimes check out CNN, sometimes check out *New York Times*, sometimes check out the *Onion*, get a slathering of all this and then in their own way come to a conclusion and say: "Okay on that issue or on the ideology or on that election I got swayed to this side." I don't think that 60% is going to say, oh, I am never going to watch *The Young Turks*, I am never going to watch Rush Limbaugh. I just don't believe it...I am much more hopeful than that (Uygur 2010).

Comedian Andy Cobb agreed, arguing that this allows more voices to be heard, which is positive thing. He began talking about the people who self-select their media choices to reflect their politics:

> [In] general one can to choose that route about stuff and I am sure people do, but part of me thinks an intellectually curious person in an on-line world is checking out stuff that doesn't necessarily agree with you...I know a lot of progressives who will watch Glenn Beck to learn what that fucker is up to and to get a little riled up and to get that emotion of watching somebody who is saying things that are really angry...You know, the internet can really offer it up and we've got to search it out...I think what is great is that there used to be a time when you were in competition for three networks to get our opinions on. They had to appeal to the broadest spectrum possible, the point of view in comedy, and what is great now is that we have this proliferation of viewpoints that allows point of view comedy and aside from the exclusion of anybody else. My being on U-Tube doesn't exclude Evan [Sayet] from being on U-Tube as well or any conservative. They can do wherever they want to do (Cobb 2010).

As I fear for the hyperspecialization of entertainment and comedy, the truth of the matter is that audience demand will drive programming and with so many available media outlets, we are probably destined for this isolation. This will have a two-pronged effect for comedians: on the one hand, a comedian will want the largest audience possible, but on the other hand, a political comedian with a niche audience may find specialized success, but then must continue to feed that particular beast. I do think that the abundance of entertainment is a positive thing, where many more voices can be heard. But the increasing political seclusion we will all feel when we wrap ourselves too tightly in niche programming is bound to have some important consequences for political discourse.

Speaking of niche audiences, I was eager to ask writers and comedians about the Fox News Channel's effort to combat *The Daily Show*: a program called the *Half Hour News Hour* which aired 15 episodes in 2007. It made complete sense to me that if Fox News had a lock on the conservative television viewer, a conservative satire show would be an automatic smash hit. They had the audience prepositioned—what could go wrong? Apparently, quite a bit, because as it turns out, you can't do comedy on a news channel.

You Can't Do Comedy on a News Channel

I asked for people's impressions of the *Half Hour News Hour* (*HHNH*), and the answers ranged from "absolutely horrible and brutally so" to "really not good," and they never got better than that—even from the conservatives. One theory was that, when the political argument trumped the funny, the end result was never very enjoyable. *Conan* writer Kevin Dorff said the political impetus smooshed the humor, and compared the *HHNH* to the anti–Michael Moore film *An American Carol*:

> The problem with the *Half Hour News Hour* is that they were so determined to make it conservative rather than satire that it actually failed, same thing with *An American Carol*. I mean . . . it would have been really funny 15 minute film . . . But there was so much [of] an attempt to make it a conservative satire that they forgot about the actual satire, and I think examples like that are the reason why it does have a tendency to fail (Dorff 2010).

Writer Andy Cobb agreed, and since the *HHNH* was supposed to be the conservative answer to *TDS*, he went back to that show to explain why *HHNH* was not as funny: "I don't think *The Daily Show* would be nearly as funny if it were the *Progressive Daily Show* or *Now the Left* or *The Liberal Media Hour*" (Cobb 2010). By emphasizing the political over the humor, the joke is lost in transition. Another problem with putting politics first is that when the politics leads, the need for an actual joke lessens. It's as if the partisanship carries the show. Said *SNL*'s Alex Baze:

> It was mostly just loud and complainy with not a whole lot of basis in fact or reality.... They did a lot of word play because if you don't know how comedy works that is where you start: You make puns, you notice that this word sounds a lot like this word... Protest signs and tea party signs are good examples usually. They noticed very early on that Obama sounds like Osama, and so they did a lot of jokes about this. And it was like, okay those words sound the same or similar, but that doesn't mean anything. There is no underlying fact... you are making the joke without the foundation. I guess they had a little audience that laughed, but it is not the same (Baze 2010).

When the jokes do not have a solid foundation to begin with, they probably are not very funny, and this leads to the question of why the joke was made to begin with. Along these lines, Marc Maron said about Fox News: "They're the most humorless bunch of bullies in the world" (Maron 2011c). This leads pretty quickly to the assessment made by comedian Peter Grosz, who said about the *HHNH*:

> There was something about it that was... mean. They would make jokes at the expense of liberals and it was like: this isn't a satire show, it is an ideological show... I think on that show it was like they thought: Oh we will just do an answer to what we think is liberal satire and all they did was just barely read the headlines and didn't get any of the meat of it. All they got was thinking that satire is making jokes about liberals. Then it was mean things about Nancy Pelosi... that show was just mean (Grosz 2010).

So to begin with, the humor of the *HHNH* was, perhaps, lacking. But another problem was that the program's structure was not conducive to making it funny either. I spoke with Ned Rice, who was a writer for *The Half Hour News Hour*, and he told me about his time working on the show:

> It's hard enough to do satire to begin with, much less satire from a conservative perspective. Also, the *Fox News Channel* is not an entertainment channel so it was very difficult to get them to understand what we were trying to do. Almost without exception the best material we wrote was rejected by the network because it was considered too controversial... having to do with things like the Iraq war, race relations, gay rights... the show was supposed to be a right-of-center version of *The Daily Show*, but it ended up being very different than that (Rice 2010).

One can see how trying to wedge comedy onto a news channel would be structurally challenging, since the host network simply is not geared for that type of entertainment. In addition to the over-emphasis on ideology and the structure of the show, one final element of the *HHNH* helped to kill it: it was on a news channel. My initial thought that a self-selecting conservative audience would be ripe for satire seems to be completely negated by the fact that Fox News is not some place people go to for laughs.[xv] Fox News has been a cultural game-changer in extending the popularity of punditry, and in doing so, has solidified its image and mission in the eyes of its viewers. Throwing a comedy show into the mix of partisan opinion and hard news does not necessarily work. It is important to remember two key points: *TDS* and *Colbert* are both on Comedy Central, and other news network comedy attempts have flopped, including the *Dennis Miller* show on CNBC and the CNN program *DL Hughley Breaks the News*. Even in the era of soft news, perhaps this total blend of entertainment and information is too much to absorb. *TDS*'s Kevin Bleyer wrote for Dennis Miller and said that his CNBC show was cancelled for exactly that reason: "It was on CNBC which people don't necessarily presume is the place to go for talk shows of that sort" (Bleyer 2010). Comedian Nick DiPaolo summed up the *Half Hour News Hour* thusly, "It was kind of a half-assed attempt, you know? But that's my point... they were restrained in what they could say. Even on *Fox*... you can't do comedy on a news channel" (DiPaolo 2011).

[xv] Insert Steve Doocy joke here.

Conclusions

The very nature of satire demands it to be an outsider art: it mocks those in power, takes aim at hypocrisy, and demands justice through humor. The definition of satire is that it differentiates between what exists and what should be, and in doing so, criticizes those who are not doing enough to strive for the ideal. There is, rooted within political humor, a weird idealism that sometimes gets lost within the cynicism. If a humorist were so cynical he or she could not be funny, then nor would he or she try to illustrate the wrongs of society in the hope of getting it right. Since the more important motivation of modern political satire is the humor and not the politics, the liberalism of the satire—that antiestablishmentarian idealism—is more than tempered by the pursuit of the funny over the desire to make a point. Consequently, the humor that ceases to be humorous has a pretty short shelf-life, and the satirist who is enraged without being funny is not tremendously successful. At a time when we are so polarized and frustrated, Americans may think we want entertainment that mirrors our angst, but truthfully, we look to satire and humor as an escape, a cathartic laugh to release our pain. The good satirists know this.

Research points to satire's influence on our political behavior, news programs are taking jokes and comedians seriously, and the opinions and beliefs of funny people are being blended into the mix of political commentary in our increasingly polarized world. No wonder critics are calling "bias." Regardless of these calls, however, there is an important point to be made: comedians and satirists do not follow the same rules as activists, politicos, or news journalists. And I hate to sound stodgy, but these are essential rules for us to understand. As *Conan*'s Kevin Dorff said, "By trying to make the news of the world around us a more entertaining place to be . . . I think we've only succeeded in making it almost a much more confusing place than it was" (Dorff 2010). Having satire on news programs blurs the line between what is a joke and what is serious. It also legitimizes and gives new meaning to jokes, and so it increases the call of bias and allegations of partiality because people are taking this more seriously than the writers intend. Back to Dorff, who gave an example of why news channels were terrible places for satire, because the missions of satire and news are so totally and completely different:

> Not long ago I was watching CNN and they were talking about a sketch that had appeared on *SNL*. And, I just don't remember what the sketch was about, but the CNN anchor said: "Very funny, a very funny sketch and I really enjoyed it and when we come back after this message we are going to fact check that sketch to see if it was accurate," and then they went away to commercial. I turned the TV off and I honestly said to myself... you've got to be kidding. You are going to fact check a comedy sketch? You completely missed the point... When you apply the journalistic concept like fact checking to a comedy sketch you really are now using the wrong tool for the wrong job. You are trying to fix a sink with a saw, you know, you are just using the wrong tool for the job (Dorff 2010).

As shows like *SNL* and *TDS* and *Colbert* maintain their ratings strength, there will be concern that they are unduly influencing their audience. Perhaps the example of the *HHNH* is a good one in showing that putting politics over humor—in fact acting as an advocate or an activist—cannot work in the field of modern political satire. When *Wait, Wait* tells its jokes, it aims for the laughs, just as *The Onion* does in its online news programming. But critics will allege bias, and in our politically divided culture, these accusation will stick.

The final chapter explores why this may be a bad thing.

CHAPTER 6

Conclusions

When people claim partiality in political satire, it is essentially the same thing as calling bias in an opinion piece—bias is sort of the point. Satire is a form of political criticism and political humor of all stripes aims its guns at politicians who are seen as inadequate. Satire must have a point of view or else the joke isn't satire, which means there must be some bias inherent in the material. But critics of modern political humorists who call bias really are not worried about this in itself. They are, perhaps, more concerned that the satirists have left behind their primary entertaining function in order to advocate. When critics call bias, they are really charging "activism" because an activist is not trying for laughs—he is trying to change people's minds. There is trepidation that a popular and easy-to-understand form of political commentary does double duty as crusading.

Even though the vast majority of political humor emphasizes the humor over the political, every now and then the advocacy occurs. *The Daily Show* aims to amuse, and host Jon Stewart argues vociferously that entertainment is his only goal, but the show has veered into activism when the topic seemed important enough. One example of this occurred in 2010 when a bill was stuck in Congress that would provide September 11 responders federal funding for healthcare. *TDS* dedicated a show to the legislation in an effort to combat what Stewart called "an outrageous abdication of our responsibility to those who were most heroic on 9/11" (Carter 2010). In a *New York Times* article about the show, Syracuse University Professor Robert

Thompson compared this kind of advocacy to the journalism of Edward R. Murrow and Walter Cronkite, and New York City Mayor Bloomberg said about the episode:

> Success always has a thousand fathers, but Jon shining such a big, bright spotlight on Washington's potentially tragic failure to put aside differences and get this done for America was, without a doubt, one of the biggest factors that led to the final agreement (Carter 2010).

Congress passed the legislation, and much credit was given to Stewart's focus on the issue for the bill's final success. But from this legislative success also came the concern that the show shifted from reflecting reality to shaping perceptions, which is something that Stewart says he does not do. It is something that all of those whom I interviewed said was not their mission. This is one reason why the shortage of conservative political humorists concerns those on the right: there is not the balance of advocacy when advocacy occurs.

Another reason for concern is that political humor is becoming increasingly present in our culture which is steeped in media content. In 2012, the Pew Research Center for the People and the Press produced an updated study that examined where the American public gets its campaign news, just in time for the upcoming elections. The study's data showed that 15 percent of those polled who were aged 18 to 29 "regularly learn[ed] something about [the] campaign" from late night comedy shows. This number was compared to 12 percent who learned about the campaign from the nightly network news and 11 percent who learned from a local newspaper (Pew Research Center 2012). This gives late night comedy an impressive platform, and the dearth of conservatives in comedy may be concerning as more individuals look to this entertainment for information as well. This leads to the third area of unease when discussing a messaging form that is ill-suited to represent the real issues at stake. The brevity necessary for the comedic structure means that humor cannot inform, even if it wanted to. Serious demands depth, but funny tends to hit quickly. This contrasts notably with the seriousness of real news dissemination which *should* delve deeper into the issues and spend more time examining problems, and it also contrasts with the very workings of government itself. The policy-making process is purposely slow, and the lack of speed is a tradeoff for democracy. The more voices that are heard, the longer policy making is going to take and the harder it is going to be to describe. But this is the price of pluralism, our democratic system which is responsible to many citizens. Comedy, especially the modern forms of political humor, is not so labored. As comedian Marc Maron put it:

> You have a populace that loves the immediacy of technology...they want closure, they want it quick, they want to get hit hard and quickly and they want a lot of it. And the pace at which government works couldn't be more opposite. The comings and goings of the democratic machine are plodding, slow, they're tied up in a lot of language and they're constantly being debated and things just take a long time. So all of this political comedy and political talk shows, they make it seem like things are immediate...and it doesn't work like that. There's a fundamental disconnect between how people take in information and the actual process of political change (Maron 2011c).

The political messages conveyed by comedy may be smart and nuanced, but they are not lengthy or deep. If all of this quick political comedy is only representing one side of a political argument, then even the brief attention to political questions cannot lead to adequate debate, or to even representation. Conservatives fear their side of the debate is not represented at all.

These reasons are sufficient to understand the concern of those on the right about the dearth of conservative political funnymen, but the arguments bump up against those in support of political humor's effectiveness. To begin with, the entirety of American history is riddled with satirical criticism where skilled comedians have taken aim at the powerful, drawn attention to a social ill, and made the people laugh at the same time. It is part of our culture, part of who we are as a nation. The First Amendment came first because the founders felt strongly about our right to speak out against the powerful, and from the time of the founding there has been political humor that has been influential and informative. Satire has always mirrored the political climate, amplifying a complaint through humor while reflecting the existing criticism. Satire has historically been a parallel protest using laughter to underscore the nation's social wrongs. It has never worked particularly well in times of national sorrow, but it works beautifully when it focuses on the power hierarchy and serves as a check on the establishment. Satire has also enjoyed the historic expansion and technological development of the media, taking advantage of new media forms to spread the humor. When the printing press got big, so did political cartoons. When television became ubiquitous, *The Smothers Brothers* led to *Saturday Night Live*, which gave rise to Comedy Central which brought us *The Daily Show*. Historically, satire has been a weapon of the underdog, and it always has been used against the dominant. It will continue to play an important role in American culture because once you give permission to mock the power structure, this permission is impossible to take away. And once the technology becomes available to spread the mocking quickly, cheaply, and effectively, its popularity is inevitable.

Another reason to applaud satire's success, and to allay fears of activism, is that generally comedy stays within its own lane. It is the satirist's job to shed light on the mess of politics, but it is not his or her job to go any further than that. So when *TDS* had a show about the 9/11 responder bill, arguably it shone that light. The show did not extend its coverage to recommend any other solutions than for Congress to continue the action is was already taking. It did go so far as to encourage legislative completion, but it was not *The Daily Show*'s bill in question: it was a bipartisan effort that gave aid to locals of New York City. Arguably, since the show is taped in New York and Jon Stewart lives in the city, the push was not partisan but geographic in its impulse. Interest groups and genuine activist groups have been known to craft legislation themselves in their lobbying efforts, but in this case the urgency was not to create something new but finish what was already begun. When political cartoons use metaphor to symbolize an injustice or when The Capitol Steps parodies songs to make a bigger point, the group is not going any further than to suggest something is amiss. Anything more than that exceeds the purpose of satire. It is this character of comedy that not only attracts certain creative people to its ranks, but also demands a specific form. Accordingly, the obligation to actually be funny is going to drive the material creation more than any force to advocate. Jon Stewart may have one show with a serious message, but it is doubtful that he would have many more, especially given that he broadcasts *The Daily Show* on

Comedy Central. The whole reason for satire's triumph is that it couches criticism in laughter, so when the laughter is taken away, its chances for success diminish considerably.

The honesty that comedians are allowed in their material makes for some of the most trenchant and insightful commentary available. *The Daily Show* example of the 9/11 responder bill is one good illustration of how a comedy show can bring more attention to a political issue, which can encourage progress. Another example is found time and again in Stephen Colbert's insistence on using his character's lofty ambition as a mechanism to illuminate political problems. Colbert has testified in front of Congress (in character) about immigration and about campaign finance reform. In doing so, Colbert brought even more light and attention to these important topics while he entertained his audience (and made lawmakers extremely uncomfortable). But Colbert has gone much further in his criticism than his congressional testimony, and since 2011 has used his platform to blast the campaign finance system. In order to show how types of campaign structures were easily corruptible, Colbert created a 501(c)4 organization, which is a nonprofit that is able to take anonymous donations and politically advocate. Colbert also created a Super PAC, which is an independent expenditure group that can pay unlimited funds for political ads, provided there is no coordination between the Super PAC and a candidate's campaign organization. [1] These two constructions have been amazing archetypes Colbert has used to explain difficult campaign finance law to a novice audience.

The Colbert Super PAC, invented to illustrate the absurdity of this type of fundraising group, was so effective that it lost its treasurer to the real presidential campaign of Texas governor Rick Perry. Colbert's Super PAC shenanigans were so fundamental in the argument about campaign finance reform that the mainstream media began to devote real attention (and real air time) to Colbert and his campaigning activities. He set up an exploratory committee that allowed him to contemplate a run for the "President of the United States of South Carolina" and he took his show on the road. In short order, Colbert went from creating the Super PAC (called "Americans for a Better Tomorrow Tomorrow") to running ads in Iowa before the 2012 Republican primary, to turning over the Super PAC's financial control to Jon Stewart in order to highlight the weaknesses of the coordination rules that applied. All of these efforts were satirical shots to show how ridiculous the campaign finance system was. In several sketches on *The Colbert Report*, former FEC Chairman Trevor Potter[2] discussed the rules that apply to Super PACs, 501(c) groups, and coordination with presidential campaigns. These dialogues and send-ups illustrated the lackadaisical nature of Super PAC regulation without preaching, making the argument more effectively through humor than a ream of editorials ever could. Beyond the set, Colbert went to South Carolina where he tried to enter the Republican primary election even though he was unable to run as a write-in candidate on the ballot. To compensate for this, Colbert organized his campaign alongside former GOP presidential candidate Herman Cain. Since Cain had dropped out of the presidential race but was on the South Carolina ballot and could not be removed, Colbert stepped in and told the voters to vote for Herman Cain as a vote for Colbert. His argument was that South Carolina voters should vote for the ultimate outsider—someone not even running for president anymore. In a speech at the College of Charleston, where Colbert appeared with Cain, Colbert spoke about Super PACs and his own political activity:

> The pundits have asked is this all some joke? And I say if...being allowed to form a Super PAC and collecting unlimited and untraceable amounts of money from individuals, unions and corporations and spend that money on political ads and for personal enrichment...If that is a joke then they are saying our entire campaign finance system is a joke. And I don't know about you, but I have been paid to be offended by that (McMenamin 2012).

All of Colbert's satiric creations, from the Super PAC to the 501(c)4 group to the South Carolina presidential campaign, were the perfect forms for the argument against themselves. Critics made the well-honed argument that Colbert's involvement in the presidential race was more distracting to the political process than instructive, and that it made a mockery of the entire system. But this last point was precisely the point, as evidenced when Colbert asked a *New York Times* reporter about his campaign actions: "What's the difference between that and money laundering?" (McGrath 2012). By assuming the mantle of political candidate and going through the machinations of fundraising, Colbert and Stewart hammered home the argument that the system was flawed. Did this spark cynicism? Perhaps—but no more so than the actual campaign finance rules themselves. Amidst immense hue and cry about campaign finance, *Citizens United*, and Super PACs, no argument so clearly and effectually explained the problems. When the laughter died down, the problems were underscored and Colbert's audience was more aware of the issues and the political climate as a result. This example is one of many where satire can illustrate political problems and educate the public along the way. It may not have been a profound exploration of *Citizens United*, but it was an effective form of criticism.

If conservatives discount the work of popular satirists out of hand because they are biased, then the good work of these satirists will be lost. Popular political humor can highlight and bring attention to some of the most important issues facing us today. To discount the entire critical form as biased is sort of like throwing the baby out with the bathwater. If satire is dismissed by half of the voting public, then its critical value is never fully realized. Satire can help to illuminate the wrongdoings of government and also distinguish between the way things are from the way things should be, demanding critical thinking on the part of the satirist and critical viewing or reading on the part of the audience. In other media venues, we are not so challenged, and material is often so simplistic that intelligent consideration is unnecessary. In political media, this simplicity often turns into crude arguments over winners and losers, which negates an audience's need to analyze. And while political humor does not strive for depth, it does often demand attention and questioning. This lack of analysis on our part, the preponderance of "right and wrong" narratives that weakens consideration and shortens debate, also serves to further divide us instead of bringing us together to solve problems as a whole. That sounds pretty idealistic, and it is unrealistic to expect everyone in Congress to gather together to share, but since lawmakers represent all of us, it might be a good idea for them to work together. The more divided we are, the worse things get. Abraham Lincoln, who knew a little something about divisions in American politics, famously stated, "A house divided against itself cannot stand," and today we are drowning in our divisions. Partisan indictments and denunciations may make for good entertainment, but they are lousy for governing. This brings us back to the satirists, who take aim at the whole political system in order to show how ridiculous it is when things cannot get done. The fact that all politicians are fair game means that the laughter can temper our discord as the jokes are spread around. Satire has the possibility to unite if we let it.

There are clear explanations for the lack of conservative political humorists in modern satire, to include the nature of the business and the essence of political humor, and these issues have already been explored. But there is one more possibility for the scarcity of conservatives in the field that should serve as a caution as well: if critics of satire eschew the art form as liberally biased, it might dissuade conservatives from joining the ranks. And conservative comedy is not only possible, but also its proliferation might add to the political conversation. The argument that Hollywood is closed to conservatives loses some of its strength in an era with Internet, cable, and podcasts. If conservative political humorists want to shine a light on issues or problems, they can easily craft their own comedic critiques of the political system from a perspective they find more appealing. This has been done online by a wide variety of partisans on both the left and the right: the Women's Media Center created a satirical news program to criticize the misogyny of the mainstream news; the Media Research Center created the webcast "Newsbusted" to call out left-wing media bias in a style that imitated *Saturday Night Live*; Fox News's show *Red Eye* has a channel on YouTube that is the go-to outlet for a significant number of political comedians. The very same 2012 Pew Research Center study that showed so many 18-to-29-year-olds getting their news from late night television also revealed an increasing number of voters that age going to YouTube or online-only entities for information as well (5 percent and 13 percent respectively) (Pew Research Center 2012). If you want conservative humor, you do not have to look too hard to get it, and if more conservatives join the profession, it will be increasingly easier. It is not impossible for conservatives to mock the powerful, and in today's heavily mediated environment, there are channels available. Calling attention to the imbalance is instructive, but using it as a reason for conservatives to avoid political humor is not only counterproductive but also self-defeating.

The allegations of ideological bias in political satire have serious implications within the larger discussion of our political discourse today. If those on the right conclude modern political satire and political humor excludes them, then this discourages deliberation and debate, even within arguments that are rooted in irony or humor. When one side of the political divide closes its ears to criticism in modern politics, reasoned discussion is impossible. The number of Americans who are putting on earmuffs to avoid hearing opposing thought is increasing, and so too is the lack of political compromise or rational debate. Our entire political system is predicated on compromise, so when the two sides walk away from the table, the entire system comes grinding to a halt. This is an increasingly significant problem, and the heightened partisan rhetoric that widely casts aspersions, calls names, and turns up the anger does not help.

There are political satire television and radio programs around the world, from the United Kingdom to Israel to Iraq, because laughter is a universal reaction and because politics is such a fruitful source of humor. In the United States, satire is becoming so ubiquitous in our vast media landscape it is blending in with all of the other bits of information available to us. In 2011, *The Onion* ran a story about Planned Parenthood building an $8 billion "Abortion-plex"; this enraged Facebook users who believed it to be true. Months later, a Republican congressman from Louisiana fell for the joke and, in an outrage posted about it on his Facebook page, said the group was offering "abortion by wholesale" (Horowitz 2012). After the congressman was embarrassed by the entire episode, *The Onion* editor Joe Randozzo said that he was "delighted to hear that Rep. Fleming is a regular reader of America's Finest News Source and doesn't bother himself with *The New York Times*, *Washington Post*, the mediums of television and radio, or any other lesser journalism outlets" (Horowitz 2012). Satire is awfully hard to escape today; we are awash in political comedy. Comedians are running for office, sometimes as a joke, but more often in order to make a point. Comedian Steve Berke ran for mayor of Miami Beach. Will Rogers, Pat Paulsen, Dick Gregory, and Doug Stanhope have all run for president (as did Stephen Colbert—twice). These campaigns were used as comedic arrangements to show the craziness of politics, but when comedians actually want to do something, they have to abandon humor all together. Al Franken, formerly of *Saturday Night Live*, ran for the US Senate quite seriously in 2008 and made it. He is the junior senator from Minnesota now, and while his fundraising letters are pretty funny, Franken is a very serious legislator. At some point, he realized that preaching about politics was not entertaining, and that comedians were not tasked with changing the nation's politics, so he changed his profession. As so many of those interviewed said, no one wants to be lectured by a comedian and no matter how influential Stewart and Colbert are, they are unable to do much more than make jokes.

We increasingly seek out comedic material to temper the bad news of the day. We look for the humor in our politics because times are tough, and also because we can find funny without trying too hard. But at the same time that we seek out political comedy for entertainment reasons, we also can find perceptive reflections on our politics and society. It is up to the voters not to conflate the purposes of comedy and news, it is up to the public to know a joke when they see one, and it is similarly important for partisans not to assign harm where there is none. As politicians and the voting public determine how to take these comedians seriously, they will also continue to debate their points of view. In other words, we should let political comedy be edifying and fun, and not force it to go any further.

Elections are fights for political dominance, and policy debates are fights for courses of action that will affect nations. But political humor is not supposed to be a fight, serving instead as a refuge from all the yelling. With this, I return to Dennis Miller:

> Laughter is one of the great beacons in life because we don't defract it by gunning it through our intellectual prism. What makes us laugh is a mystery—an involuntary response...The point is, people who are threatened by jokes are the same people who tend to refer to actors on the soap operas by their character's name. Listen, there's a real world, and then there's the joke world, okay. The joke world we can get tough—wear a cup (D. Miller n.d.).

Political satire will continue to play an important role in our political messaging. Some of the humor will be insightful and some of it will be dreadful, but it is evident that humor is a crucial component of our political process, and debate without it is a loathsome proposition. Keeping it as part of the debate—and not a substitute for it—is crucial. The laughter that brings the nation joy in troubled times is, after all, the satirist's highest purpose. Our republic is stronger because of this.

Notes

1 Who Brings the Funny?

1. Obscenity, incitement to violence, and threatening the life of the president are several examples of restrictions on expression.
2. There have been several cases of threats against political cartoonists and comedians made by Islamic extremists who felt their religion was being mocked. These examples include (but are not limited to) the Danish political cartoonist who drew a depiction of the Prophet Mohammed, the creators of South Park who pretended to, and David Letterman who mocked Al Qaida.

3 Mirroring the Political Climate: Satire in History

1. I urge readers to review K. J. Dover's (1974) and Jeffrey Henderson's (1980) work on Aristophanes, and see Peter Green (1974) and Susanna Morton Braund (2004). Other work on Juvenal includes texts by Gilbert Highet (1960) and J. P. Sullivan (1963). I have also been directed by very smart people to Ralph M. Rosen, *Making Mockery: The Poetics of Ancient* Satire, (New York: Oxford University Press, 2007).
2. Apparently, the "definitive" Pope prose is found in the volume edited by Ault and Cowler (Oxford: Blackwell, 1936–1986), and the "definitive" text for Gay's poetry is edited by Dearing (Oxford: Clarendon, 1974).
3. The best collection from Swift comes from Cambridge Press: *English Political Writings 1711–1714*, edited by Goldgar (2008). Thanks to Dr. Sharon Harrow for her assistance in finding this authoritative resource.
4. The most authoritative biographies of Franklin are from Isaacson (2003) and Brands (2002), and I recommend readers look to these two authors for more information on one of the most fascinating of our founding fathers.

5. Mary Alice Wyman wrote a book on Seba Smith and Elizabeth Oakes Smith called *Two Pioneers* (Whitefish, MT: Kessinger Press, 2006) that contains more information about the author of "Major Jack Downing" and his wife, a poet.

6. John Adler has written a well-respected book about Nast and Tweed called *Doomed by Cartoon*. (New York: Morgan James, 2008)

7. Twain's writings *On the Damned Human Race* have been edited by Janet Smith and published by Hill and Wang, New York (1962), Ron Powers wrote a definitive biography, *Mark Twain*: A Life (New York: The Free Press, 2006) and Mr. Twain released his own auto-biography decades after his death: *Volume I*. Berkeley: University of California Press, 2010. Garry Wills wrote an authoritative biography of Henry Adams called *Henry Adams and the Making of America* (New York: Mariner Books, 2007) and Adams, too, wrote an auto-biography, which was released while he was still alive: *The Education of Henry Adams*; it was re-released by the Massachusetts Historical Society, Boston, in 2008.

8. The biography of Will Rogers was published by University of Oklahoma Press (2000) and a book about his political life, written by Richard White, was published by Texas Tech in 2011. Additionally, several collections of his witticisms and sayings have been published recently.

9. Terry Teachout has published a biography of Mencken titled *The Skeptic: A Life of H.L. Mencken*, (New York: Harper Perennial, 2003), and Mencken himself worked with Alisatire Cooke to pub-lish a collection of his writings (New York: Vintage Books, 1990).

10. Andres Schiffrin's *Dr. Seuss & Co. Go to War: The World War II Editorial Cartoons of America's Leading Comic Artists* addresses this as well (New York: New Press, 2009).

11. Zoglin has written a book about stand-up in the 1970s called *Comedy at the Edge*. New York: Bloomsbury, 2008; I highly recommend read-ers with a greater interest in this area to read this book.

12. David Simmons wrote a book titled *The Anti-Hero in the American Novel* which more deeply explores the connection between literature and the counterculture of the 1960s (New York: Palgrave, 2008).

13. The most definitive work on *The Smothers Brothers Comedy Hour* is a book written by David Bianculli titled *Dangerously Funny*. New York: Simon & Schuster, 2009.

4 Art and Profession

1. From J. A. Cuddon, *A Dictionary of Literary Terms and Literary Theory*, 3rd ed. London: Blackwell, 1991: "The term denotes a par-ticular kind of practice in reading and, thereby, a method of criti-cism and mode of analytical inquiry."

2. From the *Stanford Encyclopedia of Philosophy*: "A set of critical, strategic and rhetorical practices employing concepts such as difference, repetition, the trace, the simulacrum, and hyperreality to destabilize other concepts such as presence, identity, historical progress, epistemic certainty, and the univocity of meaning."

5   Being Funny and Being Right, Being Left and Being Right

1. Discussed in Chapter 3.
2. Se *The Aristocrats*, a film described as, "One hundred superstar comedians tell the same very, VERY dirty, filthy joke," as evidence of this.
3. There are some authoritative works on this topic, to include books from Markus Prior (2007), Cass Sunstein (2009), and Matthew Hindman (2009).
4. This reaffirms the findings from the Center for Media and Public Affairs addressed in Chapter 2.

6   Conclusions

1. 501(c) groups have been used in political campaigns for years, but increasingly so since 2008.

   The Supreme Court case *Citizens United v. Federal Elections Commission* gave rise to Super PACs in 2010, and since then these independent expenditure groups have been under fire from all sides, the argument being that this kind of campaign finance allowance is a corruption of American politics.
2. Potter is currently a member of the law firm Caplin & Drysdale where he works as an expert in election law. He was general counsel to John McCain's 2008 presidential campaign.

Bibliography

Abeles, D. (2010, June 9). *Saturday Night Live.* (A. Dagnes, Interviewer)

Abrams, N. (2003). "From Madness to Dysentery: MAD's Other New York Intellectuals." *Journal of American Studies, 37,* 435–451.

Allie, E. (2011). "Little Shop of Horrors," from cagle.com: http://www.cagle.com/author/eric-allie/page/18/.

Altschuler, B. (2009, November 20). "Presidents as Theatrical Anti-Heroes." Paper presented at the Northeastern Political Science Association Conference. Philadelphia, PA.

Arnez, N. L. (1968). "Contemporary Negro Humor as Social Satire." *Phylon,* 339–346.

Alterman, E. (2003). *What Liberal Media? The Truth About Bias and the News.* New York: Basic Books.

Bakalar, N. (1997). American Satire: An Anthology of Writings From Colonial Times to the Present. New York: Penguin Books.

Baram, M. (2011, March 7). "Sarah Palin 'Not Afraid' Of Jon Stewart, Says Aide." From *Huffington Post:* http://www.huffingtonpost.com/2011/03/07/sarah-palin-jon-stewart-conservatives_n_832001.html.

Baum, M. (2005). "Talking The Vote: What Happens When Presidential Politics Hits the Talk Show Circuit?" *American Journal of Political Science* 49(April): 213–234.

Baumgartner, J. (2007). "Humor on the Next Frontier: Online Political Humor and Its Effects on Youth." *Social Science Computer Review* 29, 319–338.

Baumgartner, J. (2008). "Editorial Cartoons 2.0: The Effects of Digital Political Satire on Presidential Candidate Evaluations." *Presidential Studies Quarterly,* 38, 735–758.

Baumgartner, J., and J. S. Morris. (2006). "The 'Daily Show Effect': Candidate Evaluations, Efficacy, and the American Youth." *American Politics Research,* 34, 341–367.

Baumgartner, J., and Morris, J. (2008). *Laughing Matters: Humor and American Politics in the Media Age.* New York: Routledge.

Baym, G. (2005). "The Daily Show: Discursive Integration and the Reinvention of Political Journalism." *Political Communication*, *22*(3), 259–276.

Baze, A. (2010, June 10). *Saturday Night Live*. (A. Dagnes, Interviewer)

Bianculli, D. (2009). *Dangerously Funny: The Uncensored Story of* The Smothers Brothers Comedy Hour. New York: Simon & Schuster.

Bierce, A. (2011). *The Devil's Dictionary*. New York: Library of America.

Binelli, M. (2011, June 7). "Politics: Keith Olbermann on Why He Left MSNBC—and How He Plans to Get Even." From *Rolling Stone*: http://www.rollingstone.com/politics/news/keith-olbermann-on-why-he-left-msnbc-and-how-he-plans-to-get-even-20110607.

Black, L. (2010, June 15). Comedian. (A. Dagnes, Interviewer)

Bleyer, K. (2010, September 2). Writer, *The Daily Show*. (A. Dagnes, Interviewer)

Blumer, J. G., and Gurevitch. M. (2000). "Rethinking the Study of Political Communication." In J. Curran and Gurevitch (eds.), *Mass Media and Society*, 3rd ed. New York: Oxford University Press.

Bonsteel, E. (2011). "No Debt Limit Here!" Retrieved July 25, 2011, from Anti-Anti-Underground: http://antiantiunderground.com/?m=201107.

Borowitz, A. (2011, July 10). "A Letter From Rupert Murdoch." *Borowitz Report*.

Bredvold, L. (1940). "A Note in Defense of Satire." *English Literary History*, 253–264.

Buchwald, A. (1974, July 30). "Richard M. Nixon Will You Please Go Now!" From *The Washington Post*: http://www.washingtonpost.com/wp-dyn/content/article/2006/04/19/AR2006041901099.html.

Carr, S. A. (1992, Summer). "On The Edge of Tastelessness: CBS, The Smothers Brothers and the Struggle for Control. *Cinema Journal, 31*(4), 3–24.

Carter, B. A. (2010, December 26). "In 'Daily Show' Role on 9/11 Bill, Echoes of Murrow." Retrieved December 30, 2011, from the *New York Times*: http://www.nytimes.com/2010/12/27/business/media/27stewart.html?scp=1&sq=Jon%20Stewart%20and%20Murrow&st=cse.

Census, US. (2011). *The 2011 Statistical Abstract*. Washington, DC: US Census.

Center for Responsive Politics. (2009). "TV/ Movie/ Music." From Opensecrets.org: http://www.opensecrets.org/industries/indus.php?ind=B02.

Cha, A. E. (2011, April 18). "What's the Debt Ceiling, and Why is Everyone in Washington Talking about It?" From *The Washington Post*: http://www.washingtonpost.com/business/economy/whats-the-debt-ceiling-and-why-is-everyone-in-washington-talking-about-it/2011/04/15/AFSS4R1D_story.html.

Cobb, A. (2010, July 31). Writer, Comedian. (A. Dagnes, Interviewer)

Colbert, S. (2006, April 29). "Humaphors: The Top 10 Metaphors of Stephen Colbert." Retrieved September 2, 2011, from About.com: http://grammar.about.com/od/rhetoricstyle/a/ColbertMetaphors.htm.

Colbert, S. (2011, June 24). Comedian. (T. Gross, Interviewer)

Colbert, S. (2012, January 12). "Indecision 2012 – Colbert Super PAC – Coordination Resolution with Jon Stewart." Retrieved January 26, 2012, from *The Colbert Report*: http://www.colbertnation.com/the-colbert-report-videos/405889/january-12–2012/indecision-2012 – -colbert-super-pac – -coordination-resolution-with-jon-stewart.

Cornfield, M. (2005). " 'The Daily Show' Revolution." *Campaigns & Elections 26*(8), 34.

Critchley, S. (2002). *On Humour.* New York: Routledge.

Dagnes, A. (2010). *Politics on Demand: The Effects of 24-Hour News on American Politics.* Santa Barbara, CA: Praeger.

Deggans, E. (2006, October 6). "Where Have You Gone, Dennis Miller?" *St. Petersburg Times*, 1E.

deMoraes, L. (2011, December 6). "Research Firm Breaks Down Politics of TV." From *The Washington Post*: http://www.washingtonpost.com/lifestyle/style/research-firm-breaks-down-politics-of-tv-this-old-house-vs-the-daily-show/2011/12/06/gIQAQPSkaO_story.html.

Dewey, D. (2007). *The Art of Ill Will.* New York: New York University Press.

Dictionary, M.-W. (2006). "Word of the Year 2006." Retrieved November 15, 2011, from Merriam-Webster Dictionary: http://www.merriam-webster.com/info/06words.htm.

DiegoUK. (2011, June 20). "FULL VIDEO & TRANSCRIPT: Jon Stewart Fox News Sunday Interview." Retrieved July 9, 2011, from Daily Kos: http://www.dailykos.com/story/2011/06/20/986919/-FULL-VIDEOTRANSCRIPT:-Jon-Stewart-Fox-News-Sunday-Interview.

DiPaolo, N. (2011, February 3). Comedian. (A. Dagnes, Interviewer)

Dominick, P. (2010, July 12). Host, Stand Up. (A. Dagnes, Interviewer)

Dorff, K. (2010, July 29). Writer, *Conan*. (A. Dagnes, Interviewer)

Dowd, M. (1998, August 23). Monica Gets Her Man. *The New York Times*. From Pulitzer.org: http://www.pulitzer.org/archives/6217.

Draper, R. (2011, August 3). Author. (T. Gross, Interviewer)

Drutman, L. (2009, April 20). "The Truthiness of The Colbert Report." Retrieved September 8, 2011, from Miller-McCune: http://www.miller-mccune.com/media/the-truthiness-of-the-colbert-report-3788/.

Dudden, A. P. (1985). "The Record of Political Humor." *American Quarterly*, 50–70.

Durst, W. (2010, September 16). Writer, Comedian. (A. Dagnes, Interviewer)

Durst, W. (2011, July 10). "Pity the Rich." Retrieved from http://terrortrials.blogspot.com/2011/07/pity-rich.html.

Eberhard, J. (6 July 2004). "Liberal Bias in Hollywood." From intellectualconservative.com: http://www.intellectualconservative.com/article3576.html.

Editors. (1956, July 16). "Radio & TV Comedy Writers." From *Time Magazine*: http://www.time.com/time/magazine/article/0,9171,936706,00.html.

Feiffer, J. (2003, Jan 23). Cartoonist. (T. Smith, Interviewer)

Felber, A. (2010, July 26).Writer. (A. Dagnes, Interviewer)

Filipowicz, M. (2010, July 27). Writer, Comedian. (A. Dagnes, Interviewer)

Fisher, R. (1996). Those Damned Pictures: Explorations in American Cartoon Art. North Haven, CT: Archon.

Freud, S. (1928). "Humour." International Journal of Psychoanalysis, 1–6.

Gallup. (2009, January). "Presidential Approval Ratings – George W. Bush." Retrieved October 31, 2011, from Gallup.com: http://www.gallup.com /poll/116500/presidential-approval-ratings-george-bush.aspx.

Gans, H. J. (1993). "Hollywood Entertainment: Commerce or Ideology?" *Social Science Quarterly, 74*(1), 150–153.

Gardner, G. (1994). *Campaign Comedy: Political Humor from Clinton to Kennedy.* Detroit: Wayne State University Press.

Gertz v. Robert Welch, Inc., 418 (U.S. 323 1974).

Goldberg, B., (2003). *Bias: A CBS Insider Exposes How the Media Distort the News.* New York: Harper.

Goolsby, A. (2011). "Economist Plays Not My Job." From NPR.org: http:// www.npr.org/2011/09/03/140132048/economist-austan-goolsbee-plays-not-my-job.

Gottfried, G. (2011a, March 14). "Gilbert Gottfried's Long History of Tasteless Humor." From *The Hollywood Reporter*: http://www.hollywoodreporter.com /news/gilbert-gottfrieds-long-history-tasteless-167547.

Gottfried, G. (2011b, April 24). Comedian. (K. Lauerman, Interviewer)

Graham, J. H. (2009). "Liberals and Conservatives Rely on Different Sets of Moral Foundations." *Journal of Personality and Social Psychology*, 1029–1046.

Granlund, D. (2011). "Debt Ceiling." From MrDelozier.com: http:// mrdelozier.wordpress.com/2011/07/.

Grimes, A. (1956). "The Pragmatic Course of Liberalism." *Western Political Quarterly* IX(3).

Grofman, B. (1989). "Richard Nixon as Pinocchio, Richard II, and Santa Claus." *Journal of Politics*, 165–173.

Grossman, S. (2010, July 27). Writer, Actress. (A. Dagnes, Interviewer)

Grosz, P. (2010, June 15). Writer. (A. Dagnes, Interviewer)

Hanson, T. (2011, July 7). Lead Writer, *The Onion*. (M. Maron, Interviewer)

Hariman, R. (2008). "Political Parody and Public Culture." *Quarterly Journal of Speech*, 247–272.

Hart, R. P., and E. J. Hartelius (2007). "The Political Sins of Jon Stewart." *Critical Studies in Media Communication, 24*(3), 263–272.

Hayes, D. (2009). "Has Television Personalized Voting Behavior?" *Political Behavior 31*(2): 231–260.

Hitchens, C. (2009, October). "Cheap Laughs: The Smug Satire of Liberal Humorists Debases Our Comedy—and our national conversation." *The Atlantic*, 102.

Hobert, R. L. (2005, November). "A Typology for the Study of Entertainment Television and Politics." *American Behavioral Scientist, 49*(3), 436–453.

Horowitz, A. (2012, February 6). "John Fleming, Republican Congressman, Falls for Onion Planned Parenthood Joke." From *The Huffington Post*

http://www.huffingtonpost.com/2012/02/06/john-fleming-onion
-planned-parenthood_n_1257763.html.

Horowitz, D. (2009). *One-Party Classroom: How Radical Professors at America's Top Colleges Indoctrinate Students and Undermine Our Democracy*. New York: Crown.

Imus, D. (1996, March 21). 1996 Radio/TV Correspondents Association Annual Dinner. Washington, DC.

Iyengar, S., and Peters, K. (1982). "Experimental Demonstrations of the 'Not-so-Minimal' Consequences of Television News Programs." *American Political Science Review*, 848–858.

Izrael, J. (2011, August 26). Writer. (M. Martin, Interviewer)

Jamieson, K. H., and Cappella, J. (2008). *Echo Chamber: Rush Limbaugh and the Conservative Media Establishment*. Oxford: Oxford University Press.

Jones, J. P. (2007). "'Fake'" News Versus 'Real' News as Sources of Political Information: The Daily Show and Postmodern Political Reality." In Kristina Riegert (ed.), *Politicotainment*. New York: Peter Lang.

Kadetsky, E. (1992, November). "Quayle Bashing for Fun and Profit: 'The Quayle Quarterly.'" *Technology Publications*, 1–3.

Katz, H. L. (2001, November). "*Herblock's History*." Retrieved April 3, 2010, from loc.com: http://www.loc.gov/rr/print/swann/herblock/about.html

Kaufman, W. (2007). "What's so Funny about Richard Nixon? Vonnegut's Jailbird and the Limits of Comedy." *Journal of American Studies*, 623–639.

Kellogg, C. (2011, November 6). "Book Review: 'Hollywood Left and Right: How Movie Stars Shaped American Politics' by Steven J. Ross." From *Los Angeles Times*: http://articles.latimes.com/2011/nov/06/entertainment/la-ca -steven-ross-20111106.

Kercher, S. E. (2006). *Revel With A Cause: Liberal Satire in Postwar America*. Chicago: University of Chicago Press.

Key, K. M. (2010, August 3). Writer, Actor. (A. Dagnes, Interviewer)

Klein, D. (2011, November 25). Economics Professor. (B. Gladstone, Interviewer)

Kornheiser, T. (1994a, March 13). "No More Puns on Whitewater. Oar Else." *The Washington Post*, F1.

Kornheiser, T. (1994b, March 17). "Scandal is Hard to Handle." From *The Washington Post*: http://news.google.com/newspapers?nid=1955&dat=199 40317&id=IPghAAAAIBAJ&sjid=DaIFAAAAIBAJ&pg=1427,327547.

Krauthammer, C. (2011, July 28). "The Debt-Ceiling Divide." From *National Review Online*: http://www.nationalreview.com/articles/273017 /debt-ceiling-divide-charles-krauthammer.

LaMarre, H., Landreville, K., and Beam, M. (2009). "The Irony of Satire: Political Ideology and the Motivation to See What You Want To See." *International Journal of Press/ Politics*, 212–231.

Lamb, C. (2001). "Save the Cartoonist." *The Masthead*, 25.

Lamb, C. (2004). Drawn to Extremes: The Use and Abuse of Editorial Cartoons. New York: Columbia University Press.

Leonard, K. (2010, July 27). Executive Vice President, Second City. (A. Dagnes, Interviewer)

Lewis, P. (2006). *Cracking Up: American Humor in a Time of Conflict.* Chicago: University of Chicago Press.

Lewis, J., "Molly Ivins Quotes." Retrieved January 10, 2012, from About. com: http://womenshistory.about.com/od/quotes/a/molly_ivins.htm.

Libertarian Party. "FAQ: What Is a Libertarian?" Retreived on September 2, 2011, from lp.org: http://www.lp.org/faq.

Libit, D. (2009, February 2). "The Lonely Life of Conservative Comics. Retrieved December 29, 2011, from Politico: http://www.politico.com /news/stories/0209/18367_Page2.html.

Lichter, R. (2010). *JAY LENO IS RED, JON STEWART IS BLUE.* Arlington, VA : Center for Media and Public Affairs.

LOC. (n.d.). "Herblock's Presidents: Political Cartoons from the Crash to the Millenium." Retrieved March 31, 2011, from loc.com: http:// www.loc.gov/rr/print/swann/herblock/presidents.html.

Lovley, E. A. (2010, September 30). "Congress Cools on Stephen Colbert." Retrieved December 29, 2011, from Politico: http://www .politico.com/news/stories/0910/42929.html.

Maher, B. (2001, September 17). *Politically Incorrect.* Television show.

Maron M. (2011a, January 31). WTF. Podcast.

Maron, M. (2011b, September 9). Host, WTF. (B. Gladstone, Interviewer)

Maron, M. (2011c, December 13). WTF. (A. Dagnes, Interviewer)

Mattera, J. (2012). *Hollywood Hypocrites.* New York: Threshold.

Matthews, K. (2007). "A MAD Propositin in Postwar America." *The Journal of American Culture*, 212–221.

McCarthy, M. (2010, July 30). Writer. (A. Dagnes, Interviewer)

McGrath, C. (2012, January 4). "How Many Stephen Colberts Are There?" From *New York Times*: http://www.nytimes.com/2012/01/08 /magazine/stephen-colbert.html?pagewanted=all.

McMenamin, E. (2012, January 23). "Rock Me Like a Herman Cain, Stephen Colbert and Herman Cain Host Rally to Highlight Super PACs." Retrieved January 26, 2012, from *Huffington Post*: http://www.huffingtonpost.com/ eileen-mcmenamin/rock-me-like-a-herman-cai_b_1220962.html.

Mencken, H. (1925, June 29). "Homo Neanderthalensis." *The Baltimore Evening Sun.* From Math.utah.edu: http://www.math.utah.edu/~lars/ scopes.pdf.

Milbank, D. (2001, February 1). "Needed: Catchword For Bush Ideology; 'Communitarianism' Finds Favor." *The Washington Post*, A01.

Miller, A. R. (1970). "America's First Political Satirist: Seba Smith of Maine." *Journalism Quarterly*, 499–492.

Miller, D. (2001). *I Rant, Therefore I am.* New York: Broadway.

Miller, D. (2002). "Dennis Miller Rants and Monologues." Retrieved August 3, 2011, from Dennis Miller Rants and Monologues: http://www .igorn.com/dmiller.htm.

Miller, D. (n.d.). *The Rants*. Retrieved December 30, 2011, from Dennis Miller: The Rants: http://webspace.webring.com/people/sp/pacmanonsteroids/miller.html#America_Touchy.

Minear, R. H. (1999). *Dr. Seuss Goes to War*. New York: New Press.

Newport, E. (2010, June 10). Founding Member, The Capitol Steps. (A. Dagnes, Interviewer)

Nilsen, D. (1990). "The Social Functions of Political Humor." *The Journal of Popular Culture*, 35–47.

Noonan, D. (2007, February 19). "The Boomer Files: The Way We Laughed." *Newsweek*, 54.

Oakeshott, M. (1962). *Rationalism in politics and other essays*. Charlottesville, VA: University of Virginia Press.

Obamacare Explained by Trump. (2011, June 29). From Free Republic Online: http://www.freerepublic.com/focus/f-news/2741559/posts.

O'Connor, J. (1986, August 29). "TV WEEKEND; 'SPITTING IMAGE,' POLITICAL CARICATURES." *New York Times*, 26.

Oliphant, P. (2004, Winter). "Why Political Cartoons are Losing Their Influence." *Nieman Reports*, 25–26.

Olsen, A. (2001). "Monster of Monsters and the Emergence of Political Satire in New England." *Historical Journal of Massachusetts*, 1–21.

Olsen, A. (2005). "Political Humor, Deference, and the American Revolution." *Early American Studies*, 364–382.

Onion, The. (2011a, July 20). "Congress Continues Debate Over Whether Or Not Nation Should Be Economically Ruined." from *The Onion*: http://www.theonion.com/articles/congress-continues-debate-over-whether-or-not-nati,20977.

Onion, The. (2011b, May 20). "Government Official Who Makes Perfectly Valid, Well-Reasoned Point Against Israel Forced To Resign." Retrieved July 20, 2011, from *The Onion*: http://www.theonion.com/articles/government-official-who-makes-perfectly-valid-well,20499/.

Parkin, M. (2010). "Taking Late Night Comedy Seriously: How Candidate Appearances on Late Night Television Can Engage Viewers." *Political Research Quarterly 63*(1), 3–15.

Payne, A. (1980). "The Novelist as a Social Force in the 1880s." *Hayes Historical Journal*, 9–17.

Pelley, S. (2011, August 1). "Boehner: I Got 98 percent of What I Wanted." From CBSnews.com: http://www.cbsnews.com/2100–18563_162-20086598.html.

Pew Research Center. (2007, September 20). "The Oprah Factor and Campaign 2008: Do Political Endorsements Matter?" From People-press.org: http://www.people-press.org/2007/09/20/the-oprah-factor-and-campaign-2008.

Pew Research Center. (2012, February 7). "Cable Leads the Pack as Campaign News Source, Twitter, Facebook Play Very Modest Roles." From People-press.org: http://www.people-press.org/2012/02/07/section-1-campaign-interest-and-news-sources.

Pitney, N. (2009, February 18). "NY Post Defends Cartoon, Slams Al Sharpton." Retrieved July 26, 2011, from the Huffington Post: http://www.huffingtonpost.com/2009/02/18/ny-post-cartoon-controver_n_167928.html.

Podhortez, N. (2002, September). "In Praise of the Bush Doctrine." From Freerepublic.com: http://www.freerepublic.com/focus/news/745073/posts.

Posner, M. (2007, October 6). "Not Just a Real Satnd-Up Guy: Mort Sahl's Brand of Satire Revolutionized Comedy." *The Globe and Mail*, R6.

Provenza, P. (2010). *Satiristas! Comedians, Contrarians, Raconteurs & Vulgarians*. New York: HarperCollins.

Pulitzer. (1999). *1999 Pulitzer Prize Citation*. Retrieved March 31, 2011, from http://www.pulitzer.org/citation/1999-Commentary.

Purdie, S. (1993). *Comedy: The Mastery of Discourse*. Toronto: University of Toronto Press.

Ramirez, M. (2011). "On the Debt Ceiling." From Hotair.com: http://hotair.com/archives/2011/07/25/ramirez-on-debt-and-divine-intervention/.

Razowsky, D. (2010, September 2). Writer, Performer. (A. Dagnes, Interviewer)

Rice, N. (2010, September 14). Writer. (A. Dagnes, Interviewer)

Ridge, L. (2003). "The Politics of Satire: A Look at American Satire From the Stamp Act to The Simpsons." *Harvard Political Review*, 37–38.

Riggle, R. (2011, July 21). Actor. (M. Maron, Interviewer)

Right Network, The. (n.d.). "About." Retrieved December 7, 2011, from The Right Network: http://rightnetwork.com/about.

Robst, J. (2007). "Education, College Major, and Job Match: Gender Differences in Reasons for Mismatch." *Education Economics*, 159–175.

Rollins, P., and O'Connor, J. (2005). *Hollywood's White House: The American Presidency in Film and History*. Lexington: University of Kentucky Press.

Roosevelt, F. D. (1937). "Second Inaugural Address." From Bartleby.com, http://www.bartleby.com/124/pres50.html.

Rudnick, R. (2010, July 28). Actress. (A. Dagnes, Interviewer)

Sagal, P. (2010, July 27). Host, *Wait, Wait…Don't Tell Me!* (A. Dagnes, Interviewer)

Sahlins, B. (2011, August 4). Founder, The Second City. (A. Dagnes, Interviewer)

Sayet, E. (2010, July 28). Comedian. (A. Dagnes, Interviewer)

Silverman, A. (2010, June 15). Writer. (A. Dagnes, Interviewer)

Slagle, T. (2010, September 8). Writer. (A. Dagnes, Interviewer)

Smith, C. (2010, September 20). "America is a Joke." *New York*, 30–98.

Smith, C., and Voth, B. (2002). "The Role of Humor in Political Argument: How 'Strategery' and 'Lockboxes' Changed a Political Campaign." *Argumentation and Advocacy*, *39*, 110–129.

Smolla, R. (n.d.). *Speech: First Amendment Center*. Retrieved February 16, 2011, from the First Amendment Center: http://www.firstamendmentcenter.org/speech/overview.aspx.

SNL. (1976). *Saturday Night Live* Transcripts. Retrieved March 14, 2011, from SNL.com: http://snltranscripts.jt.org/76/76ocarter.phtml.

SNL. (1988, October). *Saturday Night Live* Transcripts. Retrieved March 15, 2011, from SNL.com: snltranscripts.org: http://snltranscripts.jt.org/88/88adebate.phtml.

SNL. (1990, April 21). *Saturday Night Live* Transcripts. Retrieved March 15, 2011, from SNL.com: snltranscripts.org: http://snltranscripts.jt.org/89/89rbush.phtml.

Speier, H. (1998, March). "Wit and Politics: An Essay on Laughter and Power." *The American Journal of Sociology, 103*(5), 1352–1401.

Stack, B. (2010, July 31). Writer, Conan. (A. Dagnes, Interviewer)

Staff, C. (2008, December 19). "Young Voters in the 2008 Presidential Election." Retrieved September 26, 2011, from civicyouth.org: http://www.civicyouth.org/PopUps/FactSheets/FS_08_Exit_polls.pdf.

Stein, S. (2009, February 18). "*New York Post* Chimp Cartoon Compares Stimulus Author to Dead Primate." Retrieved October 22, 2009, from the Huffington Post: http://www.huffingtonpost.com/2009/02/18/new-york-post-chimp-carto_n_167841.html.

Stevens, H. (2011, October 29). "Kennedy Center's Mark Twain Prize: Conservative Humorists Need Not Apply. Retrieved December 29, 2011, from *The Washington Times*: http://www.washingtontimes.com/news/2011/oct/29/kennedy-centers-mark-twain-prize-conservative-humo/?page=all.

Stewart, J. (2011, November 10). "Mercy Rule Edition." From *The Daily Show* (television show): http://www.thedailyshow.com/watch/thu-november-10–2011/indecision-2012 – -mercy-rule-edition.

Stewart, J. (2012, January). "Newsletter." Retrieved January 25, 2012, from The Definitely Not Coordinating With Colbert Super PAC: http://www.colbertsuperpac.com.

Strauss, R. (1994, April 3). "Television: From the Halls of Ivy…to a Table at the Ivy." From *Los Angeles Times*: http://articles.latimes.com/1994–04–03/entertainment/ca-41612_1_harvard-lampoon-conan-o-brien-comedy-writing.

Sullivan, J. (1973). "The Case of 'A Late Student': Pictorial Satire in Jacksonian America." *American Antiquarian Society*, 277–286.

Svebak, S. (1996). "The Development of the Sens eof Humor Questionairre." *International Journal of Humor Research*, 341–361.

Taylor, D. F. (2009). "'The Fate of Empires': The American War, Political Parody, and Sheridan's Comedies." *Eighteenth-Century Studies*, 379–395.

Test, G. (2008). "Satire, Spirit and Art." In J. Baumgartner, and J. Morris (eds.), *Laughing Matters: Humor and American Politics in the Media Age*. New York: Routledge.

Thomas, D. (2008, September 23). "Emmy Awards Highlight Hollywood Bias." From *San Diego News Examiner*: http://www.examiner.com/article/emmy-awards-highlight-hollywood-bias.

Thomas, S. J. (1986). "The Tattooed Man Caricatures and the Presidential Campaign of 1884." *Journal of American Culture*, 1–20.

Thomas, S. J. (2004). "Mugwump Cartoonists, the Papacy, and Tammany Hall in America's Guilded Age." *Religion and American Culture: A Journal of Interpretation*, 213–250.

Tingle, J. (2010, November 11). Comedian. (A. Dagnes, Interviewer)

Toles, T. (2011). "Honey! John Boehner is Here!" From Democratic underground.com: http://www.democraticunderground.com/discuss /duboard.php?az=view_all&address=439x889729.

Treiger, L. K. (1989). "Protecting Satire Against Libel Claims: A New Reading of the First Amendment's Opinion Privilege." *The Yale Law Journal*, 1215–1234.

Trudeau, G. (2011, September 16). Cartoonist. (B. Garfield, Interviewer)

Turner, J. (2007). "The Messenger Overwhelming the Message: Ideological Cues and Perceptions of Bias in Television News." *Political Behavior*, 441–464.

Twain, M. (1940). *Mark Twain in Eruption*. New York: Harper.

Uygur, C. (2010, July 30). Writer, Performer. (A. Dagnes, Interviewer)

Vidal, G. (1991). Foreward. In M. E. Rogers (ed.), *The Impossible H.L. Mencken*. New York: Anchor.

Viser, V. J. (2001). "Winning the Peace: American Planning for a Profitable Post-War World." *Journal of American Studies*, 111–126.

Von Drehel, D. (2011, March 25). Author. (B. Gladstone, Interviewer)

Walker, N. (1985). "Humor and Gender Roles: The 'Funny' Feminism of the Post-World War II Suburbs." *American Quarterly*, 98–113.

Weinraub, B. (2004, January 15). "The Joke Is on Liberals, Says Dennis Miller, Host Of His Own Show Again." *The New York Times*, E4.

West, R. S. (1988). *Satire on Stone: The Political Cartoons of Joseph keppler*. Urbana: University of Illinois Press.

Whitfield, S. J. (1985). 'Richard Nixon as Comic Figure." *American Quarterly*, 114–132.

Writers, S. (2006, April 30). "*The Colbert Rapport*." Retrieved December 29, 2011, from *The Washington Post*: http://www.washingtonpost.com /wp-dyn/content/article/2006/04/29/AR2006042900126_pf.html.

Zoglin, R. (2008). Comedy at the Edge: How Stand-Up in the 1970s Chamged America. New York: Bloomsbury.

Index